The Reign of Louis XIV

The Reign of Louis XIV

Editor

Paul Sonnino

Associate Editors

William Roosen
John C. Rule
Charlie R. Steen

Humanities Press International, Inc.
New Jersey ◇ London

First published in 1990 by
Humanities Press International, Inc.
Atlantic Highlands, N.J. 07716 and 3 Henrietta Street,
London WC2E 8LU

©1990 by Paul Sonnino, William Roosen, John C. Rule,
Charlie R. Steen

Reprinted in paperback 1991, 1992

Library of Congress Cataloging-in-Publication Data

The reign of Louis XIV / editor, Paul Sonnino ; associate editors,
William Roosen, John C. Rule, Charlie R. Steen.

p. cm.

Reprint.

Includes index.

ISBN 0-391-03705-6 (Pbk.)

1. France—Civilization—17th-18th centuries. 2. Louis XIV, King
of France, 1638–1715—Influence. I. Sonnino, Paul. II. Title:
Reign of Louis fourteen.

DC128.R45 1991

944'.033—dc20   90–48479

CIP

British Cataloguing in Publication Data

A CIP record for this book is available from the British Library.

Printed in the United States of America

Contents

CONTENTS

Illustrations

Dedicated to

Andrew Lossky

ONE

The Demographic History
of the Reign

WILLIAM ROOSEN

Questions of how priests were to record vital events cannot have been very high on the agenda of early modern French kings. Nevertheless, in 1539 Francis I did issue the Edict of Villers-Cotterets, which included provisions for the recording of births, marriages, and deaths in parish registers throughout the kingdom. Later kings frequently repeated these provisions until, in 1667, the Edict of Saint-Germain successfully established a standard format for recording such events.[1]

The registration of vital events was originally intended for religious and some civil purposes, but after the Second World War Pierre Goubert and Louis Henry each thought of using the parish registers as sources for demographic studies. The method of "family reconstruction" developed by Henry has become the standard tool for using parish registers to answer a variety of questions about population.[2] As a result of the efforts of many scholars, especially those connected with the Institut National d'Etudes Démographiques and the Laboratoire de Démographie Historique, we now have a better picture of the population of early modern France than the early modern French had themselves.[3]

One of the most important characteristics of this population was that it was little affected by events of high culture like the "Renaissance" and the "Enlightenment". Its history was more closely connected with the very old "immobile" material culture that has been the subject recently of important works by historians like Emmanuel Le Roy Ladurie and Fernand Braudel.

The geographic distribution of early modern French population, for instance, was determined primarily by the size and location of parishes that had existed unchanged for centuries. These ecclesiastical divisions apparently had more effect on population density than the natural quality or productivity of the soil. In other words, the distribution of rural populations was determined more by the historic structuring of land as property than by the amount and quality of land available.

The continuing importance of towns that had been founded by the Romans is also striking. Of the twenty-five great Gallo-Roman cities in the area around Paris, all but three were among the 152 localities called towns (*villes*) by the *Statistique générale* of France in 1725.[4] Despite substantial changes in the size of their populations, the relative importance of these towns has continued even into the late twentieth century.

Similar continuity existed in transportation networks. It is not surprising that rivers were used throughout the centuries, but the major land routes originally established by the Romans were still followed in the early modern period. The regional transportation networks and interurban spatial relationships of northern France showed tremendous stability. They often dated from at least the Middle Ages and persisted well into the nineteenth century.

Transportation networks both determined and reflected patterns of migration. Although hard evidence is usually lacking about population movements before the eighteenth century, we know that there was some mobility in early modern France. Most people lived and died within a few kilometers of where they were born, but others moved long distances. Many of the patterns of migration between villages and towns were very long-standing, certainly dating back to the seventeenth century and even before. Migratory movements had their own laws and their own internal logic, in short their own traditions. So-called human factors—like joining a relative—had a considerable role in migratory behavior, perhaps even more influential than economic motives.[5]

Some international movement occurred in the early modern period.[6] Large numbers of poor Frenchmen went to Spain in the sixteenth and early seventeenth centuries, and others left for the colonies. Many Protestants fled the kingdom after the revocation of the Edict of Nantes in 1685. Although their number has often been exaggerated, probably fewer than three hundred thousand Huguenots left. There was also immigration into France. In the sixteenth century, the French exodus to Spain was at least partly balanced by incoming Italians. In 1656, 1694, and 1697 many Swiss Catholics sought to escape their country's religious wars by moving to France. Irishmen and Jacobites settled in France after England's "Glorious" Revolution. Nevertheless, the actual number of French subjects leaving the kingdom and of foreigners entering was never large enough to have a significant demographic impact; the kingdom of France was in effect a closed demographic unit.

Despite changes in the culture of the elites, the life patterns of most ordinary French people scarcely changed in the centuries between the end of the Middle Ages and the end of the old regime. A peasant who lived during the reign of Saint Louis would have recognized many of the tools, animals, food, utensils, and buildings used by his distant descendants in the sixteenth-century France of Henry IV and even the eighteenth-century France of Louis XV. Throughout the centuries people were born, ate, suffered, married, worked, loved, had children, and died essentially as their ancestors had done.[7]

In recent years some reputable scholars have attempted to estimate the population of France at the time of the Roman Empire. The data are so sparse, however, that it is difficult to take such estimates seriously, and it matters little whether the estimates are for today's hexagon, the territory of Louis XIV's France, or some other area. The estimate that France reached a population high in the Middle Ages of about seventeen million seems reasonable, however. The Black Death may have cut the number of inhabitants nearly in half, but the medieval maximum was probably recovered or surpassed with a population of about twenty million in the territory of today's frontiers during the reign of Henry II. From the Wars of Religion to the end of Louis XIV's reign, French population oscillated around that figure before increasing dramatically during the eighteenth century.[8]

This simplified picture can be made much more detailed for the early modern period. Although figures for the late sixteenth and early seventeenth centuries are still based more on impressions than on hard facts, our knowledge of both the overall pattern of change and the actual numbers is much more substantial after about 1670.

There was an overall drop in population during the Wars of Religion, but the traditional picture of recuperation and growth under Henry IV is accurate. The growth continued through Marie de Medici's regency until the late 1620s. Despite a number of problems, especially in the northern and eastern regions, French population held its own until the 1640s, when the effects of the Thirty Years' War, some plagues, the Fronde, and the famine of 1661 brought about another minimum in population size just about the time Louis XIV was beginning his personal reign.

The modest recuperation leading to another, somewhat modest maximum in 1675–1680 is sometimes associated with the name of Colbert; it was especially noticeable in eastern France, while the west tended to be demographically stagnant. The population of the kingdom also increased from the incorporation of Franche-Comté and other territories. In sum, the kingdom's population in the 1680s probably was very close to twenty million inhabitants. Disaster struck again shortly after the start of the War of the League of Augsburg with the great famine of 1693–1694, which was particularly deadly in the northern cereal-producing regions. Vauban's estimate that the kingdom of France sheltered about nineteen million inhabitants in 1698 was probably close to the mark, and if anything a little low.[9]

The population of France and most of the rest of the world increased greatly in the eighteenth century. It is uncertain, however, just when the population explosion began in France. It would seem that the deadly dysentery of 1706, the War of the Spanish Succession, and the incredibly cold "Great Winter" of 1709 must have had effects similar to those of earlier disasters. Yet there are indications that the population of the kingdom may have already begun to grow significantly by the end of the Sun King's reign.[10]

In any case, in the early eighteenth century, French population exhibited a "push" quite comparable to that which had occurred in the sixteenth century. By 1740, perhaps the earliest date at which the population of France can be stated with near certainty, there were 24.6 million people living in the territories that are now part of France. The fantastic growth continued, completely surpassing the figure of twenty million, around which the population had oscillated for so long. By 1789 there were twenty-seven million French subjects.[11]

Impressive as this increase was, it was not as great as among some of France's neighbors in the eighteenth century. Although the basic pattern of population change was virtually identical in early modern France and England, the proportional increase was smaller in France.[12]

Any generalization about the population of early modern France is inherently oversimplified and unsatisfactory. A statement about the whole kingdom inevitably conceals differences between regions or even neighboring villages. Historical demographers are quite aware of this problem. As Pierre Goubert asked rhetorically, did malarial coasts and dry sunny ones have the same demographic characteristics? Were patterns the same in rich and poor territories? The answer, obviously, is no. Goubert is even doubtful that sampling techniques can ever be accurate, since there was such variety in the early modern period.[13]

Innumerable examples of such differences are known. Whereas many parts of the Paris basin never became as populous during the seventeenth century as they had been during the sixteenth century, such levels were often recovered in Brittany as early as 1610, and in Louis XIV's reign they may well have reached as high as fifty percent above the earlier peak. The "Colbertian recovery" in the early years of Louis XIV's personal reign was fairly strong in eastern areas, like Franche-Comté, Burgundy, and Champagne, whereas the western parts, like Normandy, seem to have been almost demographically stagnant. It appears that the spurt of population growth toward the end of the seventeenth and beginning of the eighteenth centuries was much greater in northern France than in other regions. As early as the eighteenth century, people recognized the classic division of France into the parts north and south of a line running from Geneva to Saint-Malo. There were differences in such diverse things as literacy levels, abundance of doors and windows, quality of transportation networks, and demographic behavior. With the exception of Paris, for example, the northern population seems to have abandoned children less often than the south, and women seem to have married younger in the south than in the north.[14]

Agricultural societies like early modern France tend to maintain definite patterns in birthrates and death rates, which result in long-term stability of population size despite short-run fluctuations in fertility and mortality.[15] The natural question is, How does this happen? In the early twentieth century, some scholars thought the answer was that many people never married so that the kingdom was filled with bachelors and spinsters who did not have children. We now know that this idea was wrong.

Today many demographic historians believe the most important factor limiting the number of births in early modern France was late marriage.[16] Late marriage meant that, on the average, six or seven years of conjugal life were avoided; consequently, fewer children were born to the average couple. This idea has been developed and popularized by Jacques Dupâquier. In numerous publications he has explained why he believes that there was a self-regulating demographic mechanism by which the population unconsciously replaced losses rapidly without creating an oversupply of people.[17] The key to the argument, although Dupâquier seldom mentions it, is the idea that the average number of children ultimately born to early modern French women (i.e., their final descendance) was significantly lower than it would have been had they married at an earlier age.

It is certainly correct that early modern French women did marry late—at about twenty-six or twenty-seven years of age. They thus had their children late too—at about age thirty-one, on the average, in the seventeenth century. No one knows when the practice of late marriage became widespread in France. It used to be thought to have started toward the end of the Middle Ages, but suspicion is growing that it may not have developed until the early seventeenth century. Late marriage was not a uniquely French phenomenon, either. In many parts of early modern Europe, the average age of women at their first marriage was twenty-four to twenty-eight.[18]

Why did people marry late? It was certainly not because of a conscious decision to limit the number of children. The most important reason seems to have been that a couple had to have the economic resources necessary to provide for their own subsistence before they married. It usually took a long time for young people to acquire such resources on their own; otherwise they had to wait until the death of parents or other relatives presented them with the necessities.

For late marriage to play an important role in limiting the size of population, most children had to be born within the bonds of wedlock. Literary evidence gives the impression that early modern France was full of bastards. If that were true, the pattern of late marriage would have had little effect on population size, for bastards increase population size just as much as legitimate children. In fact, one of the great surprises several decades ago, when historical demographers first started to reconstruct families, was the discovery that bastards were very rare. In the Beauvaisis near Paris and Crulai in Normandy, for example, only about half of one percent of births were illegitimate.

It is, of course, possible that illegitimate births were simply not recorded or that unwed mothers hid such births by fleeing to the nearest town, where the infants were abandoned; those infants who did not die became foundlings, a group about which we know little for the seventeenth century. Urban areas did have somewhat higher illegitimacy rates, as well as a higher number of foundlings, than rural areas. Nevertheless, the average for the whole kingdom certainly was not more than one in a hundred toward the end of the seventeenth century. Illegitimate births were rare in Louis XIV's France. Although the figures rose during the regency following Louis XIV's death, and even more so later in the eighteenth century, the proportion of illegitimate births in the old regime never approached today's levels.

Some scholars have argued that the low illegitimacy rates show that ordinary people were moral in the sense of not engaging in sexual relations outside of marriage. Even an elementary understanding of human sexual urges suggests how unlikely it is that this behavior resulted simply from a desire to behave morally. Early modern society somehow forced young people to repress or sublimate their sexual urges. Unfortunately, we know so little about the topic that we can only guess how this was done.

One possibility is that couples did in fact have sexual relations before their wedding day. Even considering only those children born within eight months of their parents' marriage (the criterion used in most family reconstruction studies), it still is clear that at the beginning of the eighteenth century only about twenty percent of brides were pregnant, and probably no more than a third were at the end of the old regime—a figure analogous to those of today. It is also interesting to note that there were apparently more prenuptial conceptions in northern France, north of the line from Geneva to Saint-Malo, than in Brittany, Provence, and the Midi, a pattern that still exists today, three centuries later. Even though sexual relations may have been more common just before marriage, that still does not explain the behavior of people in their teens and early twenties.

The striking fact is that although so many French men and women lived through their youthful years, when sexual urges are usually quite strong, without engaging in acts that produced children, they somehow retained or acquired the ability to have children after their late marriages. Since sources are rare and historians are hesitant to deal with a subject that is still largely taboo, we know little about how they did this.

Many undoubtedly masturbated, while others engaged in homosexual acts. Perhaps bestiality was practiced in this essentially agricultural society. Perhaps prostitution was more common than we think. Perhaps the social control of the Catholic church was very strong. Perhaps living in very small communities where everyone knew everyone else's business controlled sexual behavior. Perhaps the sexual urges that appear to be so strong today were weaker in a population that lived close to the borderline of subsistence. At the moment no one knows for sure.

The situation was, however, undoubtedly more complicated than is implied by the simple statement that people married late. There are questions that should be raised about that thesis. First, what was the actual effect of late marriages on the size of populations? Second, is it appropriate to place so much emphasis on just one part of what was obviously a very complex demographic mechanism?

For late marriage to have been the "mainspring of the mechanism of self-regulation",[19] the total number of children of women who married late had to be less than that of women who married young. At first glance, this seems probable. Since early modern French women averaged one child every two years, it would seem that a woman who married at age twenty-seven rather than, say, twenty-three would have had two fewer children. It is not known, however, whether this really happened. The only sure way of knowing how many children a woman ultimately had is to examine completed families (families in which women reach their forty-fifth birthday while still married). Relatively few such families are found in reconstruction studies.[20]

Common sense suggests that later marriage meant fewer children, but common sense may be wrong. Other factors were involved. For example, the fertility of women married as teenagers was lower than that of women married after age twenty.[21] In fact, there was a direct correlation between the woman's age at marriage and the length of time it took her to bear a child: the younger the bride, the longer the average interval between her marriage and the birth of her first child. Louis Henry's work on the southwest quarter of France even suggests that young brides were less fertile throughout their married lives. It also seems that they became permanently sterile at an earlier age than women married at more mature ages. Women who married early also appear to have died younger than those who married later. On the other hand, a young bride was more likely to be widowed, and widows with several children were less likely to remarry than those with few or no children.

The net effect of all these factors may well have been that at least two-thirds of the so-called extra children born to women who married early were counterbalanced by the lower fertility at later ages attributable to this same early marriage. The real number of extra children born because of early marriage may have been so small as to be almost meaningless. If this were the case, late marriage could hardly have had the central role attributed to it by Jacques Dupâquier.

There is another problem with placing so much emphasis on the role of late marriage in regulating population size. The process was very complex. Each demographic factor constantly interacted with and affected all the others, each being both cause and effect at the same time. Crediting or blaming one factor for maintaining the whole is inherently suspect. To paraphrase Mr. Rogers, the star of a children's television program, everything works together because it is one piece. Late marriage undoubtedly played a role in determining the population of Louis XIV's France, but the other factors were important, too. If nothing else, the fact that late marriage continued to be characteristic of rural France in the eighteenth century, when the population explosion was well under way,[22] suggests that late marriage alone was not responsible for the self-regulation of early modern population. What were the other elements?

Fertility was one important regulating factor. One of Louis Henry's original goals was to discover the "natural fertility" of early modern populations. Although most demographers have now abandoned the concept of "natural fertility", the techniques of family reconstruction studies turned out to be very valuable for learning what fertility patterns were really like. The earliest studies seemed to show that there were great differences in fertility rates from place to place and from year to year. Now that more care is taken to correct for underregistration of births, we know that fertility rates were more constant than the rates of most other demographic events. One such constant was that a typical married couple not using any contraceptive method had only about one chance in four of conceiving a child during any given fertility period. This does not mean there were no changes in fertility rates, however. In most parts of France, for example, rates seem to have been higher than usual during the third quarter of the seventeenth century.

Several biological factors affected fertility. One of the most rigid constants in France between 1650 and 1750 was that almost all women had their last child between the ages of thirty-seven and forty-six. As is always true, a woman's fertility diminished as she grew older, and the more children she had, the greater was the possibility of her becoming sterile. It may also have been for biological reasons that a woman was much more likely to become pregnant again if her latest infant was stillborn or died very young.

Social factors were equally important or more so, however. The drop in conceptions during famines has been said to result from women's loss of body fat during such periods. But individuals may have been more concerned about other things than conjugal love during famines; the decreases in fertility may simply have reflected decreased sexual activity.[23]

Today it is known that a woman who is breast-feeding her newborn infant is less likely to conceive again than a woman who is not. This information may not have been known in France before the eighteenth century, but that did not prevent nursing habits from affecting fertility.[24] We know little about the nursing habits of most French women except for wet-nursing, a practice primarily of urban elites, which dates back at least to the sixteenth century. Putting infants out to nurse was so rare, however, that it had only a minimal effect on the fertility of France as a whole.

The subject of intentional birth control is still shrouded in secrecy and mystery, as it has been for centuries.[25] Before the seventeenth century, according to Philippe Ariès, the very idea of limiting births was so tied up with the idea of sexual perversion that it is difficult to tell if its reprobation was concerned more with its hedonistic character or the contraceptive effect. He also argues that knowledge of birth control methods was limited to the milieus of gallantry and prostitutes, and was not a part of legitimate marriages. It was during the reign of Louis XIV, he thinks, that the desire to limit family size appeared—as a feminine rather than a masculine goal. The most famous evidence is Mme. de Sévigné's letter to her daughter in 1672 thanking her for not getting pregnant. Whether ordinary people practiced birth control in the seventeenth century is unknown. In the eighteenth century, however, the idea that married couples might limit births had become acceptable rather than being linked to sexual perversions and quasi-criminal activities.[26] According to Rousseau and many other authors, contraception was widespread everywhere, even in the countryside.

The only methods of contraception available in the early modern period were those rather ineffective ones that had been known and used in some milieus for centuries. For women these included vaginal ablutions or tampons containing some spermicidal substance; for men, coitus interruptus, or the "art of outwitting nature". While these methods were used in towns during the reign of Louis XV and probably as early as the seventeenth century, there is disagreement among demographers as to whether the general population used any of them except early withdrawal by men, a method that is quite obvious and can be spontaneously rediscovered by any couple very easily. The only certain thing is that we still do not know whether or not early modern French people consciously practiced birth control to restrict the number of their descendants.

Abortion is a more obvious way of limiting population than contraception. Although it was a hanging crime in early modern France, it was surely attempted at times. A woman had to be desperate, however, because it was known to be very dangerous. Stories are still current of the atrocious suffering some women having an abortion went through before dying. We do not know what methods were used, although at least some of them involved using an instrument. Abortions were probably not widespread in the general population.

Infanticide is not, strictly speaking, birth control, because it does not prevent births. Thinking purely in cold-blooded demographic terms, however, it is an efficient method of voluntarily limiting population. In the seventeenth century giving birth was less dangerous to the mother's health than was an abortion. Furthermore, the child was carried to full term and thus took up a larger proportion of the mother's fertile period, thereby making her less likely to conceive another.[27] Modern historians do not like to consider the unpleasant possibility that killing an infant was a viable alternative for certain mothers. Nevertheless, if Philippe Ariès was right that tiny children were not really considered human in the early modern period, such an act might not have been so difficult to perform.

Another possibility is that infanticide was not a conscious or deliberate act. It could result from suffocation while a child was sleeping in its parents' bed or from other kinds of neglect and ill treatment to which newborns were exposed in the seventeenth century. Considering how difficult it is even today to discover cases of child abuse, even repeated ones, it seems very likely that fatal abuse of children in the much harsher conditions of seventeenth-century France must have been much more common than any extant sources suggest.

The famous thesis on subsistence crises in early modern France published by Jean Meuvret in 1946 and popularized by Pierre Goubert in 1960 was widely accepted by nondemographic historians.[28] One of the beauties of Meuvret's theory is its simplicity: A meteorological accident (such as extremely cold weather) resulted in poor grain harvests; this led to scarcity and a substantial increase in the prices of wheat and other cereals and all the products made from them, especially bread. Since so many people could no longer afford their basic food, hunger and even famine provoked a great rise in mortality and a decrease in marriages and conceptions. After the crisis passed, the price of grain dropped, mortality diminished, survivors married or remarried, and conceptions increased, although the size of the population was substantially lower than it had been before the crisis began. Population then grew slowly until the next crisis hit. In this way the population of early modern France was kept at levels that the country could support.

Unfortunately, this simple, easily understood description of the role of subsistence crises in maintaining population size has been shown to be inaccurate.[29] There are problems with its fundamental assumption— the key role of the weather. If meteorological accidents arrived too often or were too hard, the population would die off. If, on the other hand, the weather remained too good for too long, the population would increase too much.

Studies have also shown that there was no definite connection between the price of grain and high mortality. At times harvests were good but mortality was high—in 1690–1691, for example. On other occasions poor harvests led to greatly increased grain prices but no large numbers of deaths. How could this happen? One answer is that the price of cereals was not really as important as so many historians have thought. Since prices depended on demand as well as supply, a low grain price did not necessarily signify plentiful production. Nor did high wheat prices necessarily mean hunger; other crops, like fruits and vegetables, might exist, often in dried form, which could be eaten in place of grain products. Most demographic historians now accept the idea that there were subsistence crises in the sense that meteorological accidents led to high grain prices, but no one any longer accepts the "absurd equation" that subsistence crises automatically meant high mortalities.[30]

The least confusing way to examine mortality is to discuss some of the patterns that occurred regularly and then some of the basic causes of death in early modern France—particularly those that have been known for centuries, but that in recent centuries have been called "positive Malthusian checks": war, hunger, and disease.

It is more difficult to measure mortality than other early modern demographic phenomena, because this was very often the least well recorded, especially of the very young.[31] Much of the work on mortality published before 1970 was flawed because it was based on the assumption that most deaths had been recorded. Now researchers attempt to take faulty registration into account. Another problem with mortality is that it exhibited much more variability from place to place and time to time than the other major demographic phenomena. Nevertheless, a number of generalizations seem well enough established to be called certainties.

Even now the most dangerous day in anyone's life is the day of birth. Perhaps three percent of all births in early modern France produced stillborn children. It is impossible to be sure, because a midwife was quite likely to declare that a child was born alive and died immediately after baptism when it was in fact born dead. Only living children could receive the sacrament of baptism, which opened the gates of Paradise to a soul that would otherwise have been excluded.[32]

Each day that a child lived decreased its likelihood of dying. In the same way its second month was less dangerous than the first, the third less dangerous than the second, etc. Although there is no special biological significance to the first birthday, demographers traditionally group infant deaths in the first year together. For early modern France as a whole it appears that one-quarter of all children died before reaching their first birthday. Such high infant death rates were so common in early modern Europe that any rate below two hundred per thousand is grounds for suspicion that infant deaths were underregistered or calculations were done incorrectly.[33] It is likely that the widely held belief that early modern England had a substantially lower mortality rate than France is wrong; the error resulted mainly from not taking into account the underregistration of deaths of young children.

Another quarter of France's population died before the age of twenty. Thus, nearly half of all children born alive disappeared before they were of an age to bear children of their own—a clear example of the importance of mortality in the regulation of population size.

Life expectancy at birth in the seventeenth century was approximately the same for everyone, including both sexes. As people grew older, however, social differences became apparent. Not surprisingly, poor people had higher mortality rates than the wealthy. The oldest people in early modern France lived as long as the oldest people live today. Who these individuals were seems to have been primarily a matter of chance.

There were also seasonal differences in mortality, which changed little from year to year or even century to century. Northern Europe tended to have many deaths in the spring and fewer in the summer. Southern Europe had fewer deaths in the spring but many more in the summer. France seems to have followed an intermediate pattern, with both a spring peak, reflecting adult deaths, and a slightly lower late summer peak, which was deadlier for children under five. The winter respiratory infections appear to have had more effect in the north, while intestinal problems were more influential in the south.

Where a person lived also had an effect on how likely he was to die. It has long been known that there was almost always an excess of deaths over births in European towns from antiquity until the twentieth century. This may have been because the urban environment helped spread disease by mixing people from different areas who did not share immunities. The problem was made worse by the unfavorable urban environment itself, especially in the sixteenth and seventeenth centuries, when some of the previously existing urban amenities, like open spaces, tended to disappear.[34] The high urban mortality rates may also have reflected the "extra" deaths of the "floating" populations which so often arrived in towns in search of safety, work, and food.

Although towns are better known for consuming population, many villages throughout France were equally murderous. The tremendous variation in village mortality rates in old regime France resulted especially from differences in the quality of water. Two villages only a few kilometers apart could have totally different mortality rates if one had a clean water supply while the other drew its water from polluted wells and streams. The time of the year could also make a difference. If a village's water source dried up in summer, for example, and its inhabitants were forced to drink whatever they could find, the death rate could be as high as or higher than that of any of the larger towns.

From what did early modern French people die? The question cannot be answered directly, since very few documents recorded the cause of death and those causes that are mentioned seldom have medical meaning today. The question can be answered, however, if one thinks in terms of what caused additional or excess deaths—those beyond what one would expect as part of daily life in the period. Although there is still much uncertainty, it is probably appropriate to say that most excess deaths resulted from disease, the third of the so-called positive Malthusian checks on population. But even the others, hunger and war, did not necessarily operate in the way one might expect.

War, far from being a negligible factor in mortality, played a substantial role both directly and, more importantly, by bringing famine and sickness in its wake. War's direct effect on France was especially import-ant before the personal reign of Louis XIV, during the Wars of Religion, the Thirty Years' War, and the Fronde. The fighting, exactions, and ravages of troops during the Fronde of the Princes, for example, devas-tated and depopulated the area around Paris. Overall, the areas most affected by the military operations, especially to the south and east of the capital, suffered about one death per hearth. Areas where troops stayed a long time, such as near Turenne's camp at Champlan, had about 1.8 deaths per hearth. Many of these deaths resulted from direct acts of soldiers.[35] The kingdom's territory did not see much fighting during the first part of the Sun King's personal reign, but was again invaded during the wars at the end.

The presence of any army, friendly or not, increased mortality. This was true even if there was no mistreatment of the local population or foraging by the troops. The arrival of soldiers and their inevitable cortege of auxiliaries, merchants, prostitutes, and vagabonds disrupted agricultural life and spread disease. Furthermore, military operations prevented the establishment of the *cordons sanitaires* which limited the spread of disease; operations also created refugees who carried disease with them in their flight. In the eighteenth century most of these factors became less significant. France was involved in fewer wars than it had been under Louis XIV, and the battlefields were usually outside the kingdom.

Hunger existed in early modern France, but the chances of dying from starvation decreased as the years passed, partially as a result of in-creased governmental intervention in the economy. One of the attrac-tions of towns was that even poor inhabitants were less likely to starve than were their brethren outside the walls. Even Lyons, a town with poor sources of food supplies, appears to have gotten through the crisis of 1709 with at least some food available for nearly everyone.[36] The situa-tion undoubtedly was better for most town dwellers during the eigh-teenth century.

People in the countryside were more dependent on their own resour-ces when hunger struck. It is because so many of them left home to look for food elsewhere that it is appropriate to say they did not die directly from starvation. Other factors were often the immediate causes of death. One was violence by other wanderers or people into whose area they fled. Another was disease they picked up along the way. Since the main protection against disease in the early modern period was isolation from other people, the possibility of catching something deadly was increased by the sudden mixing of disease pools when people were on the roads, fleeing hunger.

It should be obvious that disease, the third scourge, was the most important immediate cause of death in early modern France. Both war and famine tended to bring death by increasing the incidence of disease rather than by their own direct effects. Some diseases were endemic. Smallpox caused about twelve to fourteen percent of all deaths in France during any given year, although nearly all of the victims were children less than ten years old. Vaccination against smallpox did not have any demographic effect until the end of the old regime.

Plague still caused much fear, but, for reasons that are still unknown, it struck less and less often (the story of the war of the rats is not a satisfactory explanation, since other creatures besides rats carried fleas which transmitted the disease). Although there was an outbreak of plague at Marseilles in 1720, the disease had virtually disappeared from France in Louis XIV's reign, as it had previously from England and the Low Countries. Although the proportion of deaths due to plague occasionally reached twenty-five to fifty percent in the early seventeenth century, this probably added only an extra five to eight percent to the number which would have occurred anyway. Overall, in comparison to its depredations in earlier centuries, the effect of plague on the France of Louis XIV was minimal. Much attention has been paid to the disappearance of the plague, and many attempts have been made to explain it. Yet such a disappearance was not without precedent; leprosy, a scourge of medieval Europe, had also disappeared on its own with only a few lingering cases to be found in the seventeenth century. In any case, other diseases, like the devastating dysentery that struck Brittany in the later years of Louis XIV's reign, could have a much more devastating short-term effect than more spectacular diseases, like smallpox or plague.[37]

Because of its political, social, and temporal connotations, there are problems with using the phrase "old regime" to describe the main demographic characteristics of Louis XIV's France. It is, nevertheless, appropriate to speak of the demographic old regime, since so many of those characteristics were also found in the centuries both before and after his reign.

The demographic old regime was characterized by high mortality rates, especially infant mortality, which fluctuated significantly from year to year and from region to region. Half the young people died before reaching adulthood. Fertility was also high, with a married couple generally having a child about every two years. Fertility varied somewhat from time to time and from region to region, but not as much as mortality. Most people married rather late, with the mean age for first marriages being about twenty-seven. Each woman had about five or six children, fewer than might be expected in a society that did not practice voluntary birth control, but certainly believable for a society that practiced late marriage and seldom conceived children out of wedlock. French population grew substantially in the sixteenth and eighteenth centuries. During Louis XIV's reign, however, it was relatively stable, oscillating around eighteen to twenty million.

Although we can describe this demographic regime, our understanding of the process whereby it maintained itself is still unsatisfactory. There are fundamental developments for which we do not have satisfactory answers. For example, there were times of high mortality when there was no famine, disease, or war to explain why there were so many deaths. Another problem is presented by the population explosion that began toward the end of Louis XIV's reign. Its origin and pattern were not very different from the earlier population increases, that of the sixteenth century, for example. The difference is that the eighteenth-century population explosion did not stop, but still continues today.

NOTES

1. These notes can give only a glimpse of the many valuable works that deal with the demography of France during the reign of Louis XIV. Their bibliographies, the *Bibliographie internationale de la démographie historique,* and recent issues of *Population* and *Annales de démographie historique* may be consulted for more information. I wish to thank Jacques Dupâquier, Jean-Pierre Bardet, Hervé Le Bras, Jean-Noël Biraben, and the other instructors in *Démographie historique* at the Ecole des Hautes Etudes en Sciences Sociales in Paris, as well as Gerard Cabot, Jacqueline Hecht, Jacques Houdaille, and Daniel Courgeau of the INED, for their invaluable assistance in the preparation of this essay.

2. Etienne Gautier and Louis Henry, *La Population de Crulai, paroisse normande,* INED, Travaux et Documents, XXXIII (Paris, 1958), has become a classic and still serves as the model for parish demographic studies. See also Michel Fleury and Louis Henry, *Nouveau manuel de dépouillement et d'exploitation de l'état civil ancien,* 3rd ed. (Paris, 1985).

3. A valuable overview is Michael W. Flinn, *The European Demographic System: 1500–1820* (Baltimore, 1981).

4. Jacques Dupâquier, *La Population rurale du bassin parisien à l'époque de Louis XIV* (Paris and Lille, 1979), 194 and 198.

5. Jean-Pierre Poussou, "Réflexions sur l'apport démographique des études consacrées aux migrations anciennes," in *Migrations intérieures: méthodes d'observation et d'analyse* (Paris, 1975), 149–50; Daniel Courgeau, *Etude sur la dynamique, l'évolution et les conséquences des migrations: trois siècles de mobilité spatiale en France,* Rapports et documents des science sociales, LI (Paris, 1982).

6. Jean-Pierre Poussou, "Les Mouvements migratoires en France et à partir de la France de la fin du XVe siècle au début du XIXe siècle," *Annales de démographie historique* (1970), 43–4.

7. Emmanuel Le Roy Ladurie, "L'Histoire immobile," in *Le Territoire de l'historien* (Paris, 1978), 2 vols. 2: 16 and 27–9.

8. *Histoire de la France rurale*, II, *L'Age classique: 1340–1789*, ed. Emmanuel Le Roy Ladurie (Paris, 1975), 576.

9. Jacques and Michel Dupâquier, *Histoire de la démographie: la statistique de la population des origines à 1914* (Paris, 1985), 88.

10. Jacques Dupâquier, *La Population française aux XVIIe et XVIIIe siècles*, Que Sais-je? #1786 (Paris, 1979), 34.

11. Louis Henry and Yves Blayo, "La Population de la France de 1740 à 1860," *Population* XXX, special number (Nov. 1975), 71–122.

12. W. A. Wrigley and R. S. Schofield, *The Population History of England, 1541–1871* (London, 1981), 210.

13. Pierre Goubert, "Vingt-cinq ans de démographie historique: bilan et réflexions," in *Hommage à Marcel Reinhard: sur la population française au XVIIIe et au XIXe siècles* (Paris, 1973), 322.

14. Jean Meyer, *Etudes sur les villes en Europe occidentale: milieu du XVIIe siecle à la veille de la Révolution française* (Paris, 1983), 57.

15. Carlo M. Cipolla, *The Economic History of World Population*, 7th ed. (New York, 1978), 87; Jacques Dupâquier, *Pour la démographie historique* (Paris, 1984), 74.

16. This was suggested by Pierre Chaunu in *La Civilisation de l'Europe classique* (Paris, 1966), 204.

17. He first presented it in "De l'animal à l'homme: le mecanisme autorégulateur des populations traditionnelles," *Revue de l'Institut de Sociologie* (1972), 177–211.

18. *Démographie historique*, ed. Maria Luiza Marcilio and Hubert Charbonneau (Paris, 1979), 16–7.

19. Dupâquier, *Population rurale*, 12.

20. Hubert Charbonneau, "Jeunes femmes et vieux maris: la fécondité des mariages précoces," *Population* VI (1980), reprinted in *Population*, ed. Hervé Le Bras (Paris, 1985), 150.

21. Jacques Houdaille, "Reconstruction des familles d'Ivry-sur-Seine, 1601–1686," *Population* XXXVIII (1983), 594.

22. Georges Tapinos, *Eléments de démographie: analyse, déterminants socio-économiques et histoire des populations* (Paris, 1985), 236.

23. *The Great Mortalities*, ed. Hubert Charbonneau and André Larose (Liège, [1979]), 340.

24. Etienne and Francine van de Walle, "Allaitement, stérilité et contraception: les opinions jusqu'au XIXe siècle," *Population* IV–V (1972), reprinted in *Population*, ed. Le Bras, 110.

25. Jean Sutter, "Sur la diffusion des méthodes contraceptives," in *La Prévention des naissances dans la famille: ses origines dans les temps modernes*, INED, Travaux et Documents, XXXV (Paris, 1960), 347.

26. Philippe Ariès, "Interprétation pour une histoire des mentalités," in *Prévention des naissances dans la famille*, 435–36.

27. E. A. Wrigley, *Population and History* (London, 1969), 126.

28. Jean Meuvret, "Les Crises de subsistances et la démographie de la France

d'ancien régime," *Population* IV (1946), 643–50; Pierre Goubert, *Beauvais et le Beauvaisis de 1600 à 1730: contribution à l'histoire sociale de la France au XVIIe siècle* (Paris, 1960), 2 vols.

29. *Great Mortalities*, 333–4.
30. Dupâquier, *Pour la démographie*, 42–5.
31. Jacqueline Hecht, "L'Evaluation de la mortalité aux jeunes âges dans la littérature économique et démographique de l'ancien régime," 35–40, and Jacques Houdaille, "La Mortalité des enfants en Europe avant le XIXe siècle," 85, both in *La Mortalité des enfants dans le monde et dans l'histoire*, ed. Paul-Marie Boulanger and Dominique Tabutin (Liège, 1980).
32. Dupâquier, *Population française*, 63.
33. Goubert, "Vingt-cinq ans de démographie historique," 320–1.
34. Jean-Pierre Bardet, "La Démographie des villes de la modernité (XVIe–XVIIIe siècles): mythes et réalités," *Annales de démographie historique* (1974), 124. See also his *Rouen aux XVIIe et XVIIIe siècles: les mutations d'un espace social* (Paris, 1983), 2 vols.
35. Jean Jacquart, "La Fronde des Princes dans la région parisienne et ses conséquences matérielles," *Revue d'histoire moderne et contemporaine* VII (1960), 265 and 283–4.
36. W. Gregory Monahan, "Year of Sorrows: The Great Winter and Famine of 1709 in Lyon and the Saône Valley," Ph.D. dissertation, West Virginia University (1985), 194.
37. Jean-Noël Biraben, *Les Hommes et la peste en France et dans les pays européens et méditérranéens* (Paris, 1975–76), 2 vols.

TWO

The Economic History of the Reign

THOMAS J. SCHAEPER

In a very broad sense, the economic history of France and much of Europe from the fifteenth through the eighteenth centuries was "immobile", largely because there were many social and technological obstacles to overcome.[1] Throughout these four centuries roughly eighty percent or more of Frenchmen were peasants who devoted most of their efforts to working the land. Agricultural and manufacturing techniques experienced few major alterations during this long span.

Although our available statistics are often scanty and imprecise, it seems that French agriculture during these centuries had reached a ceiling above which it could not pass. Crop yields remained very low by today's standards, with grains averaging only about six seeds for every one planted. Depending on the soil and the climate, from one-quarter to one-half of a peasant's or an estate's fields were left fallow each year. Of course, production would plummet in crisis years, when diseases, drought, or rain ruined most of the harvests. But even in the best years, most Frenchmen just barely scraped out a living. There is thus some justification in saying that the most meaningful way of classifying society during the early modern period is by separating those who got enough to eat from those who did not.

Manufacturing likewise witnessed no fundamental transformations in France from the fifteenth through the eighteenth centuries. There were no factories as we know them today. Only a few dozen coal mining operations, metallurgical enterprises, and artisanal workshops employed over a hundred persons. By far the largest area of manufactures was textiles, especially woolens. Most typically, yarn and cloth were produced in peasant cottages or in small workshops. The average workshop included two or three looms, a master, and a handful of journeymen and apprentices.

Despite the fact that the lives of most Frenchmen changed little from roughly 1400 to 1800, some fluctuations and innovations certainly did occur. The sixteenth century was a period of relative economic growth for most of Europe. The influx of gold and silver from the New World gave a boost to every sector of the economy. Much of this precious metal went initially to Spain, but the Spanish traded the greater part of their treasures to France and other countries in return for manufactured goods and other items. The monetary inflation and the economic upswing continued into the early decades of the seventeenth century.

However little change there was in the life of the average Frenchman, the early modern period was characterized by increasing efforts on the part of the monarchy to regulate his economic activity. These efforts were often patchy, always justified by paternalistic considerations, and sometimes purely rapacious, but by the seventeenth century political economists had given them a kind of theoretical foundation based on the preeminence of the state, hard money, and a static view of the world economy. The goal of these economists was the fostering of a growing, healthy, and industrious population, through the retention of a surplus of precious metals in one's country (bullionism), the protection and encouragement of manufactures, the building up of colonies, the acquisition of a favorable balance of trade, the establishment of privileged trading companies, and the maintenance of a powerful navy and a large merchant marine. All these factors engendered the belief that if one state grew in trade and manufactures, then other states necessarily had to suffer. This system, however, was never a coherent unchanging economic philosophy, much less a consistent government policy. Only in the late eighteenth century was the term "mercantile" applied to it.[2]

Thus, ministers such as Sully and Laffemas under Henry IV and Cardinal Richelieu under Louis XIII initiated a series of economic programs that later writers have included under the term "mercantilism". These ministers derived their ideas from their own experiences and from the books of Englishmen such as Thomas Mun and Frenchmen such as Antoine de Montchrétien. Henry IV and his ministers created special royal workshops like the Gobelins (tapestries) and the Savonnerie (rugs). They granted scores of tax exemptions, monopolies, or subsidies to the makers of fine cloth, glass, soap, and other materials. Henry IV's government also encouraged the regulatory functions of the guilds and established chartered companies for trade with the East Indies and Canada. Likewise, the crown restricted the export of bullion, built more roads, and drained swamps to help agriculture.

Much of this effort evaporated after the assassination of Henry IV in 1610, but Richelieu began to reestablish many of the same programs when he became prime minister in 1624. The cardinal was especially important for encouraging colonization in the West Indies and for building up the navy and merchant marine. After his death in 1642 and that of Louis XIII in 1643, many of these programs were again neglected. During the regency of Anne of Austria and the minority of Louis XIV in the 1640s and 1650s, the new prime minister, Cardinal Mazarin, was too occupied with fighting internal and external enemies to give much attention to the economy. Despite this fact, Mazarin's finance minister, Nicolas Fouquet, kept alive several mercantilist policies. His most notable contribution came in 1651, when he helped French merchant shipping by placing a special tax on all foreign trading vessels entering French ports. It is easy to see, therefore, that the economic policies of Louis XIV's reign grew from a well-established tradition.

Nevertheless, the coming to personal power of Louis XIV in 1661 and the emergence of Jean-Baptiste Colbert as his chief economic minister do mark important thresholds in the history of French mercantilism. These two men brought consistency, thoroughness, and longevity to their actions, thereby giving firmer roots to the scattered economic policies of their predecessors. Louis XIV himself did not give a great amount of personal attention to the details of trade, manufactures, and agriculture. It would be wrong, however, to assert that the king was heedless of the needs of his people. In his *Mémoires*, which cover the early years of his personal reign, he repeatedly bemoans the hardships that his people had suffered from the Fronde, from the poor harvests of 1661–1662, and from the *taille*, a land tax that was especially hard on peasants through-out most of the country. He frequently stresses that the glory of the king is the glory of the people. Thus a state could not be powerful unless the nation was prosperous. Louis XIV was also keenly aware that a king who did not work for the benefit of his people would be judged harshly by God and posterity.[3]

French mercantilism was not mere fiscalism. The state did not regulate the economy just for the sake of collecting taxes—though certainly the government did regard these revenues as important. Many of the crown's economic and social policies were promulgated with the best of intentions. Of course, one must admit that some of the government's actions hurt various segments of the economy. On his deathbed Louis XIV himself admitted that he had gone to war too often. But even here it is not clear that royal decisions were totally bad for the economy. As will become evident below, many areas of trade and manufactures prospered throughout even the bleakest moments of war.

Colbert was the principal economic minister from 1661 to 1683.[4] Because he, more than any other French minister, applied all of the various mercantilist elements listed above, several authors have defined French mercantilism as "Colbertism". Colbert came from a recently ennobled family that owed most of its wealth and influence to its cloth trading business in Rheims and its financial dealings in Paris. During the 1650s Colbert worked for Mazarin. When the latter was close to death early in 1661, he told the young king that he was leaving Colbert to the government. The cardinal believed that this legacy would compensate for any of his own failings during the regency.

Colbert was a tireless worker, and his dour personality earned him such nicknames as *le Nord* (the North) and *l'écrevisse* (the crawfish). He did not always get along well with the king. For instance, Colbert opposed Louis XIV's grandiose building schemes at Versailles. After the Dutch War began in 1672, it quickly dissipated the financial surplus that Colbert had accumulated in the 1660s. Thereafter the minister had to scramble more than ever before to enable the government to meet its expenses. This caused occasional friction with the monarch. Up to the very end, however, Louis XIV firmly upheld Colbert's efforts to strengthen the economy. The king continued to support Colbert's successors, and they in turn followed the general outline that Colbert had laid down. Because of this basic continuity, there is no need to divide the economic history of the reign into "Colbert" and "post-Colbert".[5]

In 1661, Louis XIV and Colbert had to confront not only poor harvests at home and increasing commercial competition from the Dutch and the English, but also a general economic problem facing most of Europe. Although people in the seventeenth century did not realize it, they were living in the midst of a long economic downturn. This slump began sometime between 1620 and 1650, and ended sometime between 1720 and 1750. Not every country was equally affected; indeed, this was the "Golden Century" for the Dutch. It was formerly thought that the fundamental cause of this economic malaise was a sharp drop in gold and silver supplies from Spanish America. It is now clear, however, that these shipments remained fairly steady throughout the seventeenth century.[6] Furthermore, around 1700, newly found Brazilian gold began to filter into Europe. The reasons for the seventeenth-century sluggishness thus lay elsewhere. They included crop failures, increased frequency and severity of epidemics, wars, and internal political upheavals. Rather than use the word "crisis" for the economic picture of this period, it is better to speak of stagnation, stabilization, or hesitation.[7] At any rate, we cannot blame Louis XIV if his reign transpired during a long period when economic growth had slowed down.

Although agriculture was certainly the largest sector of the economy, Colbert and his successors gave less attention to it than to other areas. This was partly because they did not want to tamper with a system that, as often as not, seemed to work well enough on its own, and partly because of their general ignorance of ways to improve farming.

As far as overall food production is concerned, it clearly, in the aggregate, did not do as well under Louis XIV as it had in the sixteenth century. A lack of adequate statistics and the extreme degree of regional variations make it difficult to be more precise. On the average, harvests in the "long" seventeenth century (i. e. 1620/50–1720/50) may have been about ten percent lower than they had been earlier. Probably the major cause of this decline was meteorological. We now know that Europe experienced a "little ice age" from about 1560 to 1840. In the seventeenth and early eighteenth centuries in particular, the winters were slightly colder, and the springs and summers cooler and wetter.

Scholars have used various methods to measure agricultural output. Several researchers have discovered that agricultural prices and rents (paid by tenant farmers to estate owners) were mostly lower in the seventeenth century. The conclusion therefore would seem to be that agriculture was in a depressed state. However, one must be very cautious when relying on the price history of the old regime.[8] Of course, the dramatically higher prices for grains in 1693–1694 and 1709–1710 did reflect the disastrous harvests of those years. But evaluating those years when prices moved only slightly up or down is much more difficult. Lower prices for wheat, barley, and oats in the 1670s and 1680s, for example, did not necessarily mean less money for peasants and estate owners. More often it could mean that production was up and that urban and rural poor were able to purchase food more cheaply.

A more fruitful approach to the study of total output is the study of *dîmes*, or tithes. This ecclesiastical tax was usually collected in kind, just after the harvest. It was chiefly a tax on grains and wines. From one area to another it could vary from about four to twelve percent of total production, the average for the country being nine or ten percent. If production declined, then so did tithes, though not necessarily to the same degree. Numerous regional studies of tithes have produced this aggregate picture: periods of decline, 1580–1600, 1630–1660, and 1690–1720; periods of increase, 1600–1630, 1660–1690, and 1720–1770. Of course, there were many local exceptions to this general pattern.[9] One conclusion that can be drawn from these studies is that Louis XIV's reign was merely part of a longer pattern of slight ups and downs.

Though not fundamental, some changes did occur in agriculture during the reign. For example, wine production increased in the Midi and the southwest; this growth caused a corresponding cutback in grain output. Colbert sponsored the draining of several swamps, and he encouraged horse breeding. Eager to preserve as much wood as possible for the royal navy, he also began to exclude peasants from the royal forests (where they would collect wood, hunt animals, and pick berries). The seigneurial reaction that historians speak of for the eighteenth century was already evident under Louis XIV. Whether they were nobles, clergy, or bourgeois, estate owners were encroaching on common grounds, chasing peasants from woods, seizing the lands of debtors, and collecting all-but-forgotten dues. Of course, this process did not occur on every estate; and in the places where it did occur, the results were not uniformly deleterious for the peasants. The more effective exploitation of large estates could lead to modest gains in production and employment.[10]

Periodic crop failures dotted the entire old regime, the three worst ones of Louis XIV's reign occurring in 1661–1662, 1693–1694, and 1709–1710. In each of these instances most of the kingdom experienced horrible grain shortages, and thousands of people starved to death. These famines, plus the more frequent outbreaks of epidemics, Louis XIV's wars, and the general economic slowdown, had led most scholars to believe that the French population decreased from about twenty million in 1661 to about eighteen million in 1715. Demographic experts now estimate, however, that the population probably numbered 21.5 million at the death of Louis XIV. The fact that no decline occurred indicates several things. It shows that the grain crises were not as deadly as was thought earlier. It also demonstrates that agriculture could not have been in so bad a shape as many authorities have stated, since people obviously were being fed. Furthermore, it helps to confirm that the government could be humanitarian and at least moderately effective in controlling the internal grain trade, importing grain from abroad, and distributing grain to the poor.[11]

Colbert and his successors devoted considerably more attention to manufactures. As noted earlier, there were few large operations during the old regime. The Van Robais woolens-manufacturing company in Abbeville was probably the largest employer in the country. Colbert helped to establish it in 1665, and by 1700, it had about two thousand workers. But this large firm clearly was an exception. We have very few statistics about the production of glass, mirrors, tapestries, iron, paper, and other nontextile products. The few figures that we do have give a mixed picture. Colbert and his successors granted regional or national monopolies as well as other privileges to hundreds of manufacturers of items such as those listed above, and the production of most of these goods seems to have increased during the reign.[12] Despite the dislocations caused by wars, shipbuilding remained steady, and sugar refining grew. One of our best indications of the relative health of both textile and other manufactures is the fact that in 1713, at the conclusion of the War of the Spanish Succession, many English manufacturers vociferously opposed any lowering of tariffs on French goods; they feared that England would be inundated with French paper, hardware, glass, wines, brandies, silks, linens, and laces.[13]

In addition to the granting of various privileges to manufacturers, Colbert aided them in many other ways. His tariffs of 1664 and 1667 brought more uniformity to French customs duties and placed higher duties on most foreign manufactures. These as well as the later tariffs of the reign were specifically designed to encourage the import of raw materials and the export of French manufactures. After hearing reports about some defects in French products, especially textiles, Colbert commissioned investigations and met with businessmen in order to solve the problems and to protect the good reputation of French workmanship. Furthermore, he encouraged guilds in their responsibility for guaranteeing high quality, and he issued detailed regulations that stated precisely what the proper standards were for each type of product. In the 1660s he began to appoint inspectors of manufactures to examine woolens, linens, and silks throughout the country. In order to facilitate the movement of goods within France, he endeavored to eliminate the archaic and cumbersome system of tolls and internal customs duties that existed throughout the country. In this he failed, because of the opposition of several cities and provinces that feared the loss of special local or regional privileges. Finally, one should note that Colbert did not regulate merely to regulate. If he believed that a company or an entire sector of the economy did not need government intervention, then he let events take care of themselves as much as possible. His successors worked to complete and refine the guidelines that he set down.

As noted above, textiles were the largest area of manufactures, and to them the government gave a correspondingly large amount of care. But even here it is difficult to gauge the results. We have few good statistics from before the 1690s, and our figures even for the latter part of the reign must be used with tender caution. Our best sources are guild records, the scattered reports of inspectors of manufactures, and the royal surveys of 1692, 1703, and 1708. But the calculations that we can make from these materials can serve only as minimum figures. No one can measure the volume of fraud, the amount of rural production that simply escaped being inspected and counted, and the quantity of cloth that was made and used at home and thus never reached a market. Therefore one should use the statistics available to judge trends rather than to gauge total production.

Until the last fifteen years or so, most historians believed that Colbert's modest achievements in building up industries were almost completely destroyed late in the reign. The causes included the king's wars, the exodus of thousands of Huguenots, and the strangulating effects of mercantilism. Recent studies have shown that this picture is false. Although some businesses suffered in the wars, others profited. It is true that about two hundred thousand Huguenots fled to other countries after 1685, taking their skills and much of their money with them. But we now know that their departure was not nearly as harmful to the French economy as was formerly thought.[14] Also, their loss was largely compensated for by the arrival in France in the late seventeenth and early eighteenth centuries of over one hundred thousand Irish and English political and religious refugees.

Most of the available data indicate steady or growing textile output during the reign. Colbert aided Languedocian woolens to regain the primacy in the Levant trade that they had been losing to English and Dutch textiles. In 1669 he granted the city of Marseilles free port status, which eliminated most of the duties collected on goods entering and leaving the city. Most Languedocian cloths going to the eastern Mediterranean passed through that port, and Colbert's favor (reaffirmed by the crown in 1703) thus gave a significant boost to the export of French manufactures. In order to ensure the high quality of these woolens, Colbert established royal inspectors in Languedoc and Marseilles to detect any flaws that the guilds might have missed. We lack reliable figures for Colbert's period, but we do know that production continued to grow through most of the eighteenth century.[15] One scholar has estimated that woolens production for the entire country amounted to 860,500 pieces, with a value of 46.9 million *livres,* in 1700 and 1,121,000 pieces, valued at 70 million *livres,* in 1715.[16] Other studies also have shown that the period 1680–1715 was one of general growth for woolens production in Amiens, Alençon, Paris, Montpellier, Beauvais, Rouen, Caen, Toulouse, Orléans, Rheims, and perhaps other areas as well. In the *généralité* of Rouen, for instance, the total number of woolens looms grew from 1,210 in 1692 to 1,536 in 1715 (a rise of twenty-seven percent), and the number of pieces produced annually rose from thirty-three thousand to forty thousand (up twenty-one percent).[17] New, lighter types of woolens and linens were finding markets in the Levant, in Spain and its colonies, and in the French West Indies. Many manufacturers remained busy making uniforms for the army and navy.

French manufactures were not uniformly prosperous throughout Louis XIV's reign. Nor were mercantilist policies always wise. Some protective tariffs, monopolies, and subsidies obstructed technological change and coddled inefficient industries. In the long run, for example, the government's efforts from the 1680s to the 1750s to prohibit the import of and the manufacture in France of calicos (printed cottons) was a failure. Frenchmen continued to smuggle the goods into the country, and therefore all that the government achieved was a delay in the development of the French cotton industry. On behalf of the crown, however, one should acknowledge that it had wide support from the merchants and artisans, who feared competition from the new kinds of cloth.

Near the end of Louis XIV's reign, the man who was in the best position to evaluate French manufactures was Controller-General Nicolas Desmaretz. Soon after he assumed this post in 1708 and again in 1713 at the end of the War of the Spanish Succession, he wrote letters in which he expressed great pleasure with the flourishing state of French textiles and other products.[18] Desmaretz might have been too optimistic, but his testimony does help to demonstrate that government policies did not destroy French industries.

Closely related to manufactures was foreign trade. Although the great majority of all French manufactures remained within the country, the export of a substantial part of them was essential. Only by exporting manufactures, wines, and a few other types of goods could France obtain the raw materials and naval stores that it needed and still maintain a favorable balance of trade. The chief instrument that Colbert and other ministers used in stimulating foreign trade and in building up French colonies was the chartered trading company. As noted earlier, a few such enterprises had existed under Henry IV and Louis XIII. But it was Colbert who made the biggest strides in this direction. His two most famous companies were the West India Company and the East India Company; the former lasted from 1664 to 1674, and the latter, with changes and interruptions, from 1664 to the end of the old regime. Other companies included the Levant Company, the Guinea Company, the Sénégal Company, the Company of Saint-Domingue, and the Company of the North. Each of them possessed various monopolies, subsidies, and tax exemptions. And the government itself was a major investor in most of them.

Except for a few brief episodes, none of these companies ever proved very successful. The same was true for the companies founded before and after Louis XIV's reign. Most of them disappeared after a few years, ceasing to operate or simply transferring their privileges to private traders. Most scholars who have studied these companies during Louis XIV's reign have concluded that their failures constitute evidence of commercial lethargy. The companies failed, so the story goes, because of the heavy-handedness of the government and because of a lack of entrepreneurial spirit among French merchants. But such analyses have missed one crucial point. Although it is true that the companies themselves did not do well, the French colonial empire and trade in general in the Atlantic and Pacific did grow during and after the reign. Colbert and his successors understood that government capital and other kinds of support were needed to increase French trade within Europe and to establish it with far-off lands. Thus, chartered companies played an essential role in the initial stages of this process. Once an area of trade was well established or a trading company had outlived its usefulness, the government itself often disbanded the company or stripped it of its more important privileges. A dramatic example of this occurred in 1674, when Colbert abolished the West India Company. Though it is true that the crown allowed some companies to linger on, the fact is that by the end of Louis XIV's reign such bodies were a highly visible but nonetheless secondary element in French external trade. In recent years, historians increasingly have come to realize this and have begun to focus their attention instead on private merchants in the large port cities.[19]

We can get a good idea of the developments in French foreign trade by considering the general relationship of France with its colonies and with other parts of the globe at the beginning and at the end of Louis XIV's reign. This was the situation in 1661: France had only the most tenuous of connections with its colonies in North America and the Caribbean; it had only a very small presence in Africa, India, and East Asia, which remained the domains of English, Dutch, and Portuguese traders; Marseilles was gradually losing its dominant place in the Levant trade to the English and the Dutch; and French commerce with the Baltic was carried on almost exclusively in Dutch ships. In 1715 the picture was as follows: despite the loss of the Hudson Bay territory, Newfoundland, and Acadia to England in 1713, the population of French Canada had grown to about fifteen thousand, and the colony was administered by a royal intendant and a royal governor; French explorers had charted and established settlements along the Mississippi Valley and in Louisiana; the Antilles, especially Saint-Domingue and Martinique, had become France's most important colonies, providing increasing amounts of sugar to the *métropole;* trading companies and private shippers were engaged in the slave trade along both the eastern and western coasts of Africa. France had established itself as one of the major Western powers in South and East Asia; Marseilles had firmly regained its preeminence in the Levant trade. The only area in which no significant change occurred was the Baltic; by 1715 French merchants had made only modest progress in bypassing Dutch middlemen and carriers. One should not exaggerate the changes that had transpired in the overall posture of external trade during the reign. French North America never came close to the English colonies in population or wealth, and trade with Africa and Asia likewise did not equal that of Albion. Nevertheless, remarkable new directions had been taken, and their significance would become clearer in subsequent years.

A major reason for this increase in French foreign trade was the growth of the French navy and merchant marine. In a famous *mémoire* of 1669, Colbert complained to the king that the Dutch dominated European trade. He asserted that this "nation of shopkeepers" (as Louis XIV disparagingly referred to them) possessed between fifteen thousand and sixteen thousand merchant ships, whereas the English had three thousand to four thousand, and the French only five hundred to six hundred.[20] Clearly, as Colbert reminded the king, such a situation was damaging to French prestige and disastrous for French trade. Colbert's figures were inaccurate, but they did reflect the relative vitality of the Dutch and the weakness of the French. Therefore Colbert initiated a program to correct the imbalance. He renovated or enlarged several old naval and commercial harbors, and he built new naval ports and arsenals. He and his successors continued Fouquet's tax on foreign merchant vessels in French ports. Likewise, they increased the size of the navy, which was important not only to fight wars but to protect trade. Colbert's navy was number one in the world by the 1680s. Formerly, scholars thought that the navy deteriorated badly after the loss to an English fleet at La Hogue in 1692, but we now know that the French fleet was at least equal to England's until about 1713. This means that the navy (aided by privateers) was able to play a strong role in protecting trade even in the final wars of the reign. Statistics also reveal the growth of the merchant marine. The number of large trading vesels (one hundred tons or more) increased from 329 in 1664 to 648 in 1704. The overall tonnage of the entire merchant fleet grew more modestly: from approximately one hundred thirty thousand tons in 1661 to between one hundred forty thousand and one hundred fifty thousand tons late in the reign. This was no spectacular rise, but it was a rise nonetheless.[21]

Evidence from individual ports also indicates that war caused alterations in trading patterns, but little if any drop in overall activity. From 1680 to 1715 Saint-Malo experienced one of its most prosperous periods ever. Wars forced Malouin shippers to forego many of their normal pursuits, but merchants and shipowners more than compensated for these losses through lucrative expeditions to the *Mer du Sud* (the coast of Peru and Chile) and through privateering.[22] During Louis XIV's final two wars, enemy ships captured perhaps as many as five thousand French merchant vessels (in many cases this involved the recapture of ships that had been ransomed). But French privateers did even more damage to English and Dutch commerce. During the War of the Spanish Succession, they captured more than 6,600 enemy vessels, which were valued at over 120 million *livres*. Privateering thus became a profitable business for thousands of shippers and investors in all of the larger Atlantic ports and to a lesser extent in the Mediterranean.[23] Similarly, the trade of Bordeaux continued at an even pace throughout the latter part of the reign. The city's wine exports remained steady, and its Caribbean trade was growing long before the "takeoff" of the 1720s.[24]

The total level of French seaborne trade seems to have increased only moderately throughout the reign. But more important was the fact that a higher percentage of this trade gradually extended beyond European waters to America, Africa, and Asia. These longer voyages necessitated bigger investments and more complex business arrangements. They also engendered a new dynamism among many merchants.[25] This fresh entrepreneurial spirit would contribute to the impressive growth of long-distance trade throughout most of the eighteenth century.

When we look at the reign of Louis XIV we must be careful not to give the government all of the blame or all of the credit for the economic failures or successes. Just as the crown's absolutism was far less powerful in practice than in theory, so also its economic policies had less influence on the daily lives of Frenchmen than most accounts on the subject indicate. For instance, despite all of the tariffs, inspectors, and police officials that were established or appointed, the plain truth is that smuggling goods in and out of the country was ridiculously easy. Throughout the old regime perhaps as many items entered France illegally as entered legally.

Critics of Colbertism have accused the government of placing manufacturers and traders in a virtual straitjacket. As proof of this they have cited such things as the government's lengthy textile regulations, Colbert's campaign to force all artisans to join guilds, and Colbert's "army" of inspectors. But we must remember three factors that mercantilism's detractors tend to forget. First, virtually every government economic program had significant popular support, at least from certain sectors of trade and industry. Colbert and his successors rarely made an important economic decision without consulting with the business community, either directly or through their subordinates. In order to get expert advice from merchants and manufacturers, Colbert created a council of commerce in 1664. This council ceased to function in the 1670s, but the crown formed another one, with the same name but a different organization, in 1700. Second, the records demonstrate that many of the government's policies did have a salubrious impact on the economy. Third, not even the Sun King's bureaucracy was big enough to have the kind of effect—positive or negative—that twentieth-century governments customarily have. For example, Colbert's inspectors of manufactures never numbered more than about fifty throughout the old regime. This small number of men clearly could not make regular visits to the forty thousand or so towns and villages where textiles were produced and sold.[26] Furthermore, the percentage of its annual expenditures that the government devoted directly to regulating or encouraging trade and industry was extremely small. In 1683 the figure was about 323,000 *livres* out of a total of over 115 million *livres*.[27] It is clear therefore that the crown's economic role was that of a supporting actor rather than that of main character. More often than not, the best information on the economy of Louis XIV's reign comes from looking at the economy itself rather than at government policies.

If we consider the years after 1715, we can see both continuities and changes. In general the economic picture for most of Europe in the eighteenth century was brighter. Beginning sometime in or shortly after the 1720s, several factors came together to produce this shift. The climate improved slightly (becoming warmer and drier), and the bubonic plague's visits became rarer and less severe. Population grew faster than it had since the thirteenth century; by 1789 France had about twenty-seven million inhabitants.

Another aspect of this growth was increased agricultural production. There was no agricultural revolution in France in the eighteenth century, but the more clement weather tended to boost production. In addition, peasants and estate owners began to apply their traditional methods more efficiently. Only in a few areas of the country, however, did peasants plant maize, potatoes, and other new crops from America prior to the Revolution. In some parts of northern France farmers borrowed new techniques from England and Holland, but this had only a marginal impact until the nineteenth century. Tithes did increase after 1720, but all that they demonstrate is that production in the eighteenth century succeeded in attaining the levels achieved during the first two-thirds of the sixteenth century.[28]

There is also evidence of a more negative nature concerning agriculture in the eighteenth century. Prices for grains generally rose at a modest rate, and certainly landlords and peasant landowners benefited from this trend. But most peasants did not produce enough food for their families. These persons, plus all of the artisans, the shopkeepers, and the poor who lived in cities, were hurt by the rising food costs.[29]

Population was growing faster than food production. And wages were not keeping up with inflation. Those who were low on the social ladder had to spend an ever greater portion of their income on food. Thus the gap between the rich and the poor grew. It is quite possible that poor Frenchmen actually were better fed under Louis XIV than in the more "prosperous" eighteenth century.[30]

In general, royal ministers continued to follow the mercantilist policies of Louis XIV's reign. In the 1750s and thereafter a few ministers and their assistants began to relax parts of the system and to introduce more free trade elements. Again, however, we must recall that mercantilism itself had never been a dogmatic, inflexible monolith. Most French manufacturers and merchants supported the traditional mercantilist programs and resisted bold changes. For instance, merchants opposed the opening up of French colonies to foreign traders. Thus, contrary to what one might expect, it was usually the business community that was retrograde and the government that was "on the wave of the future".[31]

Manufacturing and trade statistics indicate steady growth for the eighteenth century, though, as noted above, not every Frenchman shared in this bounty. France lost virtually all of its North American holdings and most of its territory in India as a result of the Seven Years' War. This was a blow to national prestige, but by this time Frenchmen had increased their direct trade with Asia, Africa, the West Indies, and other countries in Europe enough to offset these losses. The most spectacular area of growth came in the major Atlantic ports. The leaders were Nantes, number one in the slave trade, and Bordeaux, number one in the West Indian. The latter city's population grew from approximately forty-five thousand in 1700 to over one hundred ten thousand by 1789. The increase in oceanic trade generated a rise in the export of manufactures. One should remember, however, that the groundwork for this economic expansion was laid during the reign of Louis XIV.

NOTES

1. See Emmanuel Le Roy Ladurie, "L'Histoire immobile," *Annales E. S. C.* XXIX (1974), 673–92; Hubert Méthivier, *L'Ancien régime en France: XVIe–XVIIe–XVIIIe siècles* (Paris, 1981), 26–7.
2. The best general introductions to French mercantilism remain the books of Charles Woolsey Cole: *French Mercantilist Doctrine before Colbert* (New York, 1931); *Colbert and a Century of French Mercantilism* (New York, 1939), 2 vols.; and *French Mercantilism: 1683–1700* (New York, 1943). See also the various works cited in Thomas J. Schaeper, *The French Council of Commerce: 1700–1715: A Study of Mercantilism after Colbert* (Columbus, 1983), xiv–vi. Other recent discussions incude Salim Rashid, "Economists, Economic Historians and Mercantilism," *Scandinavian Economic History Review* XXVIII

(1980), 1–14; Carl G. Uhr, "Eli F. Heckscher (1879–1952) and His Treatise on Mercantilism Revisited," *Economy and History* XXIII (1980), 3–39; and Robert K. Schaeffer, "The Entelechies of Mercantilism," *Scandinavian Economic History Review* XXIX (1981), 81–96.

3. *Louis XIV: Mémoires for the Instruction of the Dauphin*, ed. Paul Sonnino (New York, 1970), passim.

4. Although in fact Colbert became the chief economic minister in 1661, he acquired the power before he got the official titles that designated his functions. In 1661 he was an intendant of finances. In 1664 he became superintendant of buildings, but only in 1665 did he become controller-general of finances. Not until 1669 did he acquire the office of secretary of state for the navy. On Colbert see the works cited in note 2 above. Daniel Dessert presents an overly bitter yet interesting portrait of Colbert in "Le Lobby Colbert: un royaume ou une affaire de famille?" *Annales E. S. C.* XXX (1975), 303–36. Two recent, lengthy biographies are uneven and must be used with caution. They are Inès Murat, *Colbert* (Paris, 1980), English edition (Charlottesville, 1984), and Jean Meyer, *Colbert* (Paris, 1981).

5. From 1663 to 1789 the secretary of state for the navy usually controlled all foreign trade, whereas the controller-general of finances administered internal trade. Of course, the distinctions between these two areas often were fuzzy, and this caused intraministerial debate and compromise. The division between the two types of commerce was especially blurred in the 1690s, when Louis Phélypeaux de Pontchartrain (like Colbert) was both controller-general and naval minister. Some historians have attacked Colbert's immediate successors for being unimaginative and inflexible. I strongly disagree with this argument. Please see my *French Economy in the Second Half of the Reign of Louis XIV* (Montreal, 1980).

6. See the works of Michel Morineau cited in Pierre Deyon, Jean Jacquart, Michel Morineau, and Jean-Pierre Poussou, *Les Hésitations de la croissance: 1580–1740*, vol. II of *Histoire économique et sociale du monde*, ed. Pierre Léon (Paris, 1978), 584, 590, 594.

7. Among the many discussions of seventeenth-century French and European economic developments, see *Crisis in Europe, 1560–1660*, ed. Trevor Aston (Boston, 1965); Pierre Goubert in *Histoire économique et sociale de la France, 1660–1789*, ed. Fernand Braudel and Ernest Labrousse (Paris, 1970), vol. 2, and especially pp. 161–2, 329-65; Méthivier, 126–7, 284–7, and passim; Schaeper, *French Economy*, 87–8, ns. 170–1; Peter J. Earle, "The Economics of Stability: The Views of Daniel Defoe," in *Trade, Government and Economy in Pre-Industrial England*, ed. D. C. Coleman and A. H. John (London, 1976), 279. *France in Crisis: 1625–1675*, ed. P. J. Coveney (London, 1977), 1–30; Jan de Vries, *The Economy of Europe in an Age of Crisis: 1600–1750* (New York, 1976); *The General Crisis of the Seventeenth Century*, ed. Geoffrey Parker and Lesley M. Smith (Boston, 1978); Andrew Lossky, "The General European Crisis of the 1680s," *European Studies Review* X (1980), 177–98.

8. Various objections to the use of prices have been raised by the following, among others: Jean Meyer, *La Noblesse bretonne au XVIIIe siècle* (Paris, 1972), 174–8; Michel Morineau, "Budgets de l'état et gestion des finances royale en France au dix-huitième siècle," *Revue historique* CCLXIV (1980), 334 n. 123; Paul Butel, *Les Negociants bordelais, l'Europe et les îles au XVIIIe siècle* (Paris, 1974), 107; Robert Forster, "Achievements of the Annales School," *Journal of*

Economic History XXXVIII (1978), 66–7; Immanuel Wallerstein, *The Modern World System*, II: *Mercantilism and the Consolidation of the European World Economy, 1600–1750* (New York, 1980), 275–6.

9. Emmanuel Le Roy Ladurie and Joseph Goy, *Tithe and Agrarian History from the Fourteenth to the Nineteenth Centuries: An Essay in Comparative History*, trans. Susan Burke (New York, 1982), especially pp. 120–53. For another approach to measuring production, see Emmanuel Le Roy Ladurie and Jean-Pierre Legrand, "Les Dates des vendanges annuelles de 1484 à 1977," *Annales E. S. C.* XXXVI (1981), 436–9. Some historians have criticized the use of tithes for gauging harvests. See Michel Morineau, "History and Tithes," *Journal of European Economic History* X (1981), 437–80; Deyon et al., 349–50.

10. Pierre Goubert, in *Histoire économique et sociale*, II, 117, 138; Wallerstein, 14–5; Deyon et al., 368–428, 473; Nancy N. Barker, "Philippe d'Orléans, *Frère Unique du Roi*: Founder of the Family Fortune," *French Historical Studies* XIII (1983), 145–71.

11. See Jacques Dupâquier, *La Population rurale du bassin parisien à l'époque de Louis XIV* (Paris, 1979); Schaeper, *French Economy*, 16–23.

12. See Pierre Leon, in *Histoire économique et sociale*, II, 217–66; Braudel, *The Wheels of Commerce*, trans. Sian Reynolds (New York, 1982), 297–350; Schaeper, *French Economy*, 25–32; Tihomir J. Markovitch, "La Croissance industrielle sous l'ancien régime," *Annales E. S. C.* XXXI (1976), 644–55.

13. Archives Nationales (AN), G^7 1699, fols. 36, 80, 126; Thomas J. Schaeper, "French and English Trade after the Treaty of Utrecht: The Missions of Anisson and Fénellon in London, 1713–1714," *British Journal for Eighteenth-Century Studies* IX (1986), 1–18.

14. Warren C. Scoville, *The Persecution of Huguenots and French Economic Development, 1680–1720* (Berkeley, 1960).

15. Michel Morineau and Charles Carrière, "Draps du Languedoc et commerce du Levant au XVIIIe siècle," *Revue d'histoire économique et sociale* XLVI (1968), 108–21.

16. Tihomir J. Markovitch, *Les Industries lainières de Colbert à la Révolution* (Geneva, 1976), 489.

17. Ibid., 22 and passim; Pierre Deyon, "Variations de la production textile aux XVIe et XVIIe siècles: sources et premiers resultats," *Annales E. S. C.* XVIII (1963), 939–55.

18. AN, F^{12} 125ᵃ, fols. 55–8, Desmaretz to inspectors of manufactures, September 11, 1708; AN, G^7, 1699, fols. 79–80, Desmaretz to Anisson, April 13, 1713.

19. See Pierre H. Boulle, "French Mercantilism, Commercial Companies and Colonial Profitability," in *Companies and Trade*, ed. Leonard Blusse and Femme Gaastra (The Hague, 1981), 97–117.

20. Discussed in Cole, II, 343.

21. By Jean Meyer see "Louis XIV et les puissances maritimes," *Dix-septième siècle* CXXIII (1979), 155–72; "The Second Hundred Years' War," in *Britain and France: Ten Centuries*, ed. Douglas Johnson, François Crouzet, and François Bedarida (Chatham, 1980), 139–63; "Survey of Research Trends in French Maritime History (Seventeenth and Eighteenth Centuries)," unpublished paper (c. 1981).

22. Schaeper, *French Economy*, 36–9; Jean Meyer, *L'Armement nantais dans la deuxième moitié du XVIIIe siècle* (Paris, 1969), 60–4.

23. See the works cited in Schaeper, *French Economy*, 50–2. See also J. S. Bromley, "The North Sea in Wartime: 1688–1713," *Bijdragen en Mededelingen Betreffende de Geschiedenis der Nederlanden* XCII (1980), 270–99; and Bromley, "La Mer du Nord: d'une guerre à l'autre: 1688–1697/1702–1713," *Amis du vieux Dunkerque* XVI (1983), 133–68.
24. Christian Huetz de Lamps, *Géographie du commerce de Bordeaux à la fin du règne de Louis XIV* (Paris, 1974); Jonathan Howe Webster, "The Merchants of Bordeaux in Trade to the French West Indies, 1664–1717," Ph. D. dissertation, University of Minnesota (1972).
25. Meyer, "Survey," 3–4; Jean Pierre Poussou, *Bordeaux et le sud-ouest au XVIIIe siècle* (Paris, 1983), 238–9; for others see Schaeper, *French Economy*, 59–60.
26. Schaeper, *The French Council of Commerce*, ch. 6; Pierre Deyon and Philippe Guigent, "The Royal Manufactures and Economic and Technological Progress in France before the Industrial Revolution," *Journal of European Economic History* IX (1980), 611–32.
27. Meyer, *Colbert*, 210–2.
28 Robert Forster, "Obstacles to Agricultural Growth in Eighteenth-Century France," *American Historical Review* LXXV (1970), 1600–15; Michel Morineau, *Les Faux-semblants d'un démarrage économique: agriculture et démographie en France au XVIIIe siècle* (Paris, 1971); Stephen L. Kaplan, *The Famine Plot Persuasion in Eighteenth Century France*, Transactions of the American Philosophical Society, LXXII, pt. 3 (Philadelphia, 1982); Laurence Evans, "Gulliver Bound: Civil Logistics and the Destiny of France," *Historical Reflections/Réflexions historiques* X (1983), 19–44; Schaeper, *French Economy*, 8–16.
29. Peasant families that had to buy additional food for themselves paid for it with money earned through their work in the fields of other persons and from the sale of yarn or cloth that they made.
30. On the growing economic and social disparities of the eighteenth century, see, among others, Maurice Garden, *Lyon et les Lyonnais au XVIIIe siècle* (Paris, 1970), 275, 294–9, 318–9; Olwen Hufton, "Social Conflict and the Grain Supply in Eighteenth Century France," *Journal of Interdisciplinary History* XIV (1983), 303–32; Poussou, *Bordeaux et le sud-ouest*, 296, 320–39.
31. For Illustrations of the widespread public support for continued government intervention in the economy, see Janis Spurlock, "What Price Economic Prosperity? Public Attitudes to Physiocracy in the Reign of Louis XVI," *British Journal for Eighteenth-Century Studies* IX (1986), 183–96, and Patrice Higonnet, *Sister Republics: The Origins of French and American Republicanism* (Cambridge, 1988), chs. 2 and 4.

THREE

The Popular History of the Reign

MARY ELIZABETH PERRY

Bands of vagabonds roamed the streets and byways of early modern France. Homeless men and women drifted together, terrorizing peasants with threats of arson, and overwhelming urban dwellers with demands for alms. As part of the floating population that had grown out of the dislocations resulting from the Hundred Years' War and the Black Death, their numbers grew unevenly during Europe's transition from a feudal to a modern economy.[1] Ever more visible in growing cities, their presence concerned local authorities, who saw them as agents of disease, disorder, and crime.

Rootless vagrants who congregated in urban areas such as Paris developed a cultural identity in opposition to respectable merchants, artisans, clerics, and officials. They lived more lustily and acted less piously than respectable citizens. Sometimes, it is true, they worked for their bread, but usually they sought other forms of survival. Many dabbled in crime, and most saw the humor of hoodwinking the pious and well-fed. They spoke to one another in a vernacular filled with crude invective, understandable only to themselves. Homeless children learned their argot from experienced vagrants who initiated them into gangs of this distinctive subculture.[2]

In the sixteenth century Rabelais wrote of these people in *The Heroic Deeds of Gargantua and Pantagruel*. Entering Paris to study, Pantagruel met Panurge, "a notable cheater and cony-catcher," who became his good friend.[3] "He was a very gallant and proper man of his person," Pantagruel assured us, "only that he was a little lecherous, and naturally subject to a kind of disease, which at that time they called lack of money". To handle this problem Panurge had many tricks, "of which the most honorable and most ordinary was in manner of thieving, secret purloining, and filching, for he was a wicked, lewd rogue, a cozener, drinker, roysterer, rover, and a very dissolute and debauched fellow".

No clear boundary separated the poor from this subculture of rootless vagrants so colorfully described by Rabelais. As the most mobile sector of French population, the poor floated in and out of respectability. For them as well as for vagrants, survival was the highest goal, superseding the values of sobriety, piety, thrift, and work, which the better-off could cultivate. The cruel tricks of rogues such as Panurge sometimes delighted the poor, who saw this humor as a means to undercut the privileges of the well-fed and officious. The poor adopted into their popular vernacular many argot expressions, and they shared with vagrants the same daily realities of hunger, cold, and violence. Both paupers and vagrants gathered crumbs and bits of stale bread and sometimes purchased the right to dunk these in a common soup kettle.[4]

Begging supported many of these people. Traditionally, all good Christians were expected to give shelter and food to the poor. A multitude of small hospices had taken root in France by the sixteenth century, but the demand for charity overwhelmed their resources and challenged local authorities to find more effective policies. In 1545 a single Bureau des Pauvres had been established in Paris to replace scattered charitable shelters. At the same time, a *cour des miracles* developed in the city where false beggars gathered. Beggars who limped by day and suppurated in hideous rags came here at night to throw off their crutches and unwind putrid bandages, which they had colored with egg yolk and the blood of slaughtered animals.[5] They warmed themselves over communal fires in their courtyard and celebrated the day's take from the hands of the hoodwinked devout.

Prostitution supported many others who drifted between poverty and deviance. Continuing a medieval tradition, most cities in sixteenth-century France legalized prostitution, although Charles IX had prohibited houses of prostitution in Paris in 1560. Rather than attempting to banish all prostitutes, authorities tried to enforce regulations on them that would protect public health, preserve a religious and moral order, distinguish them by dress from respectable women, and provide for a profitable urban monopoly.[6] The question of who should share in this profitable commerce divided prostitutes and their pimps from officials and rentiers.

Distinguished from respectable citizens, rootless vagrants nevertheless shared a mentality common to most citizens of early modern France. Deviance both delighted and horrified people at this time. Carnival and other religious festivals provided license to indulge in such deviations as men's dressing in womens' clothes, choirboys' ruling as bishops, and masqueraded persons' throwing eggs. Through such forms of deviance, of course, people could use laughter to dispel fears, and ridicule to reinforce mores.[7] Public executions, with their bloody use of the body and celebration of confession, offered rituals that appealed to both the delight and the horror of spectators. Rumors of werewolves filled people with a thrill of fear. In 1598 the discovery of three individuals in Anjou who were said to change themselves into wolves created a sensation. More than mere popular superstition, in 1603 the belief in werewolves led the *parlement* of Bordeaux to sentence a teenage werewolf to life imprisonment in a monastery.[8]

Witchcraft, another form of deviance, also concerned both officials and common people in the sixteenth century. Growing out of a "magical milieu" in popular culture, witchcraft assumed that supernatural forces could work outside the official church.[9] Some people, it was believed, made a pact with the devil and received special powers to work evil, such as causing a child to fall ill or a horse to die, a milch-cow to dry up or hail to ruin a harvest. Others could use their powers benevolently to heal the sick or to find lost property or hidden treasure. Some folk practitioners prepared amulets and potions believed to restore one's virginity and heal another's impotence. Many people paid fortune-tellers for advice as well as prophecies. Pantagruel, for example, took his friend, Panurge, to the sybil of Panzoust for advice about marriage. Described as "an old hag", the sybil made a fire with a spindle, yarn windles, walnut shells, heather, and dry laurel, and covered her head with her apron as she examined the shape in which the laurel bough burned. Giving a "most hideous and horridly dreadful shout", she frightened away the two young men before they could hear her advice.[10]

During the sixteenth century, witchcraft accusations increased remarkably in France, and authorities treated them very seriously as cases of heresy. In response to intensified fears in the latter half of the century, witch hunts focused on deviant females as scapegoats, whose prosecution and punishment could relieve social tensions.[11] Exhorted perhaps by Jean Bodin's *De la Démonomanie des sorciers* and other official warnings about the dangers posed by witches, Henri IV issued a commission to the president and counselor of the *parlement* of Bordeaux to investigate reports of witchcraft in French Navarre. Within four months nearly one hundred people had been convicted and burned there as witches.

In Paris the marginally respectable people of the kingdom became more visible and audible. It is true that crime also stalked village residents, and records show that some prostitutes traveled the roads of rural France.[12] Nevertheless, Paris attracted many of the *gens sans aveu*, and it was here that the underside of the kingdom of France appeared most nakedly. Hawking patent medicines, cutting purses, begging, filching, soliciting, and cursing, rootless vagrants somehow survived.

Those who did not survive undoubtedly ended up in the Cemetery of Holy Innocents, where an open pit provided mass burial for some two thousand poor each year.[13] Paris, as Rabelais' Pantagruel noted, "was a good town to live in, but not to die."[14]

Ten thousand beggars were estimated in the city of Paris by 1610. Overwhelmed by their numbers, Louis XIII's government attempted to distinguish deserving paupers from the notorious false beggars. The crown decreed in 1612 that all paupers who wanted to receive charity go to the asylums created for them. Thirteen years later Louis XIII called for

> vagabonds, even all apprentice barbers and tailors, and all others [without employment] and all debauched girls and women to find work within 24 hours, and if not, to leave this town and faubourgs of Paris, under summary penalty for men of being put on the chain and sent to the galleys, and for girls and women, of being whipped, shaved and banished in perpetuity.[15]

However, these attempts to control begging proved ineffective, and beggars continued to swarm through the towns and countryside of early modern France. The Company of the Holy Sacrament began to study the problem of disorder among paupers in 1631.[16] The brothers attacked mendicity in the provinces, arguing that begging in Paris could never be controlled until the poor throughout the kingdom could be confined to their native regions. Despite their efforts, more than forty thousand beggars were estimated in Paris by the middle of the seventeenth century.[17]

Healers and midwives walked a very thin line between respectability and deviance. Many had flourishing businesses, even though they faced the possibility of witchcraft and debauchery accusations. Between 1560 and 1640 more than one thousand cases of witchcraft reached the *parlement* of Paris alone. Physicians described folk healers as charlatans who did more harm than good. They sarcastically referred to *sages-femmes*, the French term for midwives, as "wise women" steeped in superstition. Yet the medical practices of physicians appeared very similar to those of unlicensed healers, and most people found the latter more affordable. Cardinal Richelieu, who could have afforded almost any medical treatment, followed the instructions of a female healer who ordered him on his deathbed to drink a concoction of horse dung in white wine.[18]

Charlatans, false beggars, and other forms of Parisian lowlife both repelled and fascinated all levels of seventeenth-century French society. In 1653, for example, the courtyard of miracles of this city provided a scene for the *Ballet royal de la nuit*, composed for Louis XIV. To the music of Lully and the verses of Benserade, dancers appeared before the king on a stage that represented the courtyard of miracles, where, the directions indicated, "in the evening return all sorts of the poor and maimed who come out healthy and merry".[19] Such interest in the false beggars of Paris reflected a fascination with the grotesque that Rabelais had earlier explored, and it also demonstrated the underside of a baroque obsession with suffering. Focusing on tricks of false beggars, perhaps, lessened the guilt that the wealthy might otherwise feel for the plight of the poor. Converting these charlatans into a *corps de ballet* served to neutralize their symbolic power as rebels and misfits whose very existence belied the monarchy's ability to provide order. Louis XIV, who later excelled in the political use of royal spectacles as diversions for his courtiers, received here an invaluable lesson in the significance of transporting the bogus cripple from his own haunts in Paris to the stage of a royal ballet.

In 1656 under the direction of Mazarin, the royal government established the General Hospital, a very large charitable foundation that would enclose paupers in the Salpêtrière and the Bicêtre as well as the Hôtel-Dieu of Paris. The twenty-six directors for this institution included twelve members of the Company of the Holy Sacrament, the group that had been working to establish institutions to enclose the poor well before Louis XIV became king. This confraternity of *dévots*, whom Louis would later identify as political rivals, conducted an energetic campaign against begging as an affront to public morals. Assisting in the foundation of a network of charitable institutions in France, the company insisted on a regimen of work discipline and religious observation for the poor.

By founding the General Hospital of Paris as a royal institution, the government of Louis XIV effectively curbed a movement of religious lay people who seemed to be gaining political power. In a sense, this royal policy co-opted the seventeenth-century concern about the poor and brought under royal tutelage the charity that Saint Vincent de Paul and others had promoted. In royal hospitals, the Sisters of Charity would act as wardens in service to the kingdom rather than as independent agents for establishing justice on earth. The crown did not have to outlaw the Company of the Holy Sacrament; it simply adopted the company's major project of establishing institutions for the poor and then watched it die out in the 1660s.

The General Hospital of Paris was supported in its functions by a special police for enforcing the laws against mendicity. The "archers of the poor", as this police became called, rounded up beggars and the "idle poor" so as to confine them in the hospital. During its first year, the hospital sheltered some six thousand people, even though the archers of the poor met considerable resistance from those who did not want to be confined there. In 1659, in fact, the effort to round up beggars led to eight armed riots. Ten years later complaints attributed the numbers of beggars still on the streets of Paris to similar resistance.[20] Servants, artisans, soldiers, and others intervened to prevent the archers from arresting beggars.

"In order to remedy the usual disorders in Paris," Louis wrote in 1667, "I decided to reestablish its police".[21] More than simply reviving an ancient city watch, he created the office of Lieutenant-General of the Police and appointed Nicolas de La Reynie to this position. The new lieutenant-general, he stipulated, would be assisted by forty-eight commissioners of the Châtelet and twenty police inspectors, each of whom purchased his office. The king charged this police force with maintaining supplies of food and other necessities for the people of Paris, with cleaning and lighting the streets, and with preventing and extinguishing fires. He directed the police to execute all royal orders; administer the prisons; and regulate printers, peddlers, nurses, hospitals, and fairs. He also instructed this force to supervise tax farmers, guilds, and the police court, and to maintain surveillance over trade and manufacturing, brokers, lotteries, the stock exchange, hotels and rented rooms, making certain that foreigners did not engage in injurious or illicit practices.

To carry out all these responsibilities, La Reynie was given command over a little army of some one hundred and fifty men, the *guet,* which would patrol the gates and ramparts, as well as the *garde* of about one thousand armed men, to be deployed in groups of twelve throughout the city. In addition, he directed the corps of process servers and sergeant mace bearers, who were concerned mainly with collecting and reselling confiscated property. Finally, he could count on a regiment of French guards and two companies of Swiss guards when necessary to restore order.[22]

Additional support for the police came from less-visible but ever-present informers. La Reynie developed a network of *mouches* among former felons, drunks, prostitutes, gamblers, and thieves. By paying them for information, he diverted for his own purposes some of those people who were believed to be most responsible for the disorder of Paris. He owed much of his success to the large numbers of informers who enabled him to keep much of Paris under surveillance and demonstrated on a local scale the love for work and gathering information that his king described in the *Mémoires* he wrote for his son the dauphin as:

keeping an eye on the whole earth, of constantly learning the news of all the provinces and of all the nations, the secret of all the courts, the dispositions and weaknesses of all the foreign princes and of all their ministers, of being informed of an infinite number of things that we are presumed to ignore, of seeing around us what is hidden from us with the greatest care, of discovering the most remote ideas and the most hidden interests of our courtiers coming to us through conflicting interests, and I don't know, finally, what other pleasures we would not abandon for this one, for the sake of curiosity alone.[23]

La Reynie moved energetically to establish order in Paris. He cleared out many *cours des miracles*, personally directing a police bombardment of their walls. At one place the inhabitants responded with a hail of broken bottles, rocks, and cooking pots. He shouted to them that he would give them one last chance to leave; the last twelve men to leave would be made into examples, the first six to be sent to the galleys for twenty years, and the last six to be hanged immediately. Most of the rioters, however, escaped to participate in still more *cours des miracles*.

The Lieutenant-General of Police combated nocturnal disorder in Paris by lighting the streets and patrolling the city with both cavalry and foot guards. By the time he left office in 1697, he had installed more than 6,500 lanterns, making Paris, as his supporters said, a true "city of lights". His lanterns represented the king's wish to protect his subjects from nighttime assaults, even though the wind frequently blew out the candles in the lanterns, and soot from the candles often dulled the available light.[24]

Correspondence between Louis XIV and La Reynie revealed a special concern about developing a *police féminine* to control the disorderly conduct of women. Relying especially on the forty-eight police commissioners to keep careful watch on all unsavory people in their districts, the king and his Lieutenant-General of Police made the misconduct of women the responsibility of their husbands or fathers. In 1683, for example, the police began to issue reprimands to the husbands of women who entered Parisian churches immodestly dressed. During the following year, Louis XIV directed La Reynie to draw up a list of all known women who sold their daughters into prostitution.[25] La Reynie sent a list of thirty women to Louis, who then ordered them all arrested and confined.

An ordinance in 1684 attempted to control prostitution in Paris by providing that prostitutes be punished with imprisonment. It also distinguished between two categories of prostitutes: the incorrigibles who had venereal disease or were so hardened that they did not want to repent, and the women who repented and wanted to reform. For the latter, the ordinance called for spiritual instruction and rehabilitation in the Salpêtrière. There, under the supervision of nuns, prostitutes began each day with Mass, spent a quarter-hour in prayer in both morning and afternoon, and followed a very strict discipline of work and personal conduct. Authorities did not believe that syphilitic prostitutes could be reformed, and the Salpêtrière did not provide medical care for syphilitic women until doctors petitioned for one small room to be used to treat these women.[26] They kept only mild cases here, however, and sent most women with venereal disease to the Bicêtre, which usually had three or four hundred patients at a time for a program that could treat only one hundred.

Illicit prostitution replaced witchcraft as the form of deviance most commonly prosecuted against women during the reign of Louis XIV. After 1672, witchcraft trials virtually disappeared from the Kingdom of France.[27] Although officials no longer viewed witches as real threats, popular belief persisted in the ability of certain women and men to use supernatural powers for both good and evil results. Midwives continued to be seen as white witches in popular culture, but officials saw them as people empowered to baptize a child as either Protestant or Catholic, a most serious question following the revocation of the Edict of Nantes.[28] Louis XIV set a royal example of how to neutralize the power of midwives: he called a male obstetrician to attend Mlle. de La Vallière's childbed.

Disease, crime, and disorder directly affected Louis' concerns about his army and navy. To protect his military men from disease that could sometimes be more devastating than enemy fire, the monarch ordered that ears and noses be cut off all camp followers found to have venereal disease.[29] Peace as well as prostitutes posed problems for these men, who could become unemployed vagabonds when Louis released them from armed service. Louis wrote in his *Mémoires* that he tried to retain as many officers as possible, even in peacetime, because "some depended on their position for their living, and struck me with pity."[30] As a practical person, he also recognized that simply releasing his fighting men at the end of a war could promote all sorts of disorders.

The king had good reason to recognize a potential for disorder among the men in his army and navy. In this period, service in the army offered a refuge for sons rebelling against fathers, young men impatient with customary social controls, those unwilling to work at available civilian jobs, and men threatened with lawsuits or facing heavy debts. Authorities sometimes encouraged delinquents to enlist in the army or navy, offering enlistment as an alternative to judicial punishment.[31] Despite Colbert's efforts to find a better system for recruiting naval personnel, Louis' navy continued to rely on impressed sailors and convict labor for the galleys. Colbert, in fact, urged police and judicial authorities to support the king's navy by arresting and impressing without trial scores of people variously described as gypsies, vagabonds, sturdy beggars, discharged soldiers, counterfeiters, salt smugglers, malefactors, and thieves.[32] An ordinance of September 19, 1676, commuted the death penalty for desertion from the army to a life sentence of rowing on the galleys. In 1684 a royal decree provided that army deserters be punished by cutting off the ears and nose, branding each cheek with a fleur-de-lis, as well as the life sentence on the galleys, although the next year a galley officer urged that noses no longer be cut off because "after a little work the difficulty of breathing notably diminished their strength, so that they have to be relieved."[33]

The convict labor that served on the galleys created another form of camp follower, especially with the expansion of the navy under Louis XIV. Until 1688, the wives of men condemned to the galleys followed their husbands, who were taken in chains to the naval station at Marseilles. Authorities complained, however, that there the convicts' wives became "a public charge, the greater part of them having nothing on which to live." They warned that "there are also some who lead a scandalous life, and others who manage to contribute to escapes".[34] As in many cases, this attempt to deal with disorder seemed, ironically, to result in more disorder.

The king himself appeared to recognize the association between poverty and disorder. Frequently expressing the wish that poverty could be eradicated from France, he believed that the body politic based on God's natural order should provide a fair share of blessings and advantages.[35] Human ignorance or knavery that disrupted this order required a response. Government-inspired propaganda in broadsheets and cartoons ridiculed and shamed profiteers during his reign, and his government also supported a program to sell cheap bread directly to the poor.[36] None of his governmental programs could prevent the terrible famines of the 1690s or "the great winter" of 1708–1709, when more than twenty thousand were said to have died of hunger in Paris.[37] Louis was blamed for bringing on all these problems so that, as Fénelon wrote, "all of France is now no more than one great hospital, desolated and unprovided".[38]

A police report of 1709, however, warned that the paupers and vagrants who gathered in Paris could not be discounted as innocent victims of poverty:

> The slime of Paris, despite its blackness and infection, contains nothing as infamous as the race of men called crooks, cheats, Greeks, Egyptians, astrologers, fortune tellers, English. All this pack of rabble gets up in the morning not knowing where or what they will eat, where they will warm themselves or sleep. They live only on swin-

dles, thefts, rapine and wrong-doing. . . . One must add the whores, public or hidden, all devoured by evil and vice; they live with thieves whom they support most of the time with the fruit of their debauchery, and who blackmail them, a slang term, that is, who force them to give them money, when these creatures refuse to do so.[39]

Crime did not die with Louis XIV in 1715, and some of those who worked with his police as thief takers proved to be as dangerous to public order as the lowlife described in the police report. Louis-Dominique Cartouche, for example, went from working as thief taker and army recruiter to leading a criminal gang. His group of more than two hundred men terrorized Paris and nearby highways from 1717 to 1721. Yet it was not simply their robberies that concerned authorities; Cartouche and his men became popular heroes, adored by the poor for their dashing exploits that defied the law. If they were not quite Robin Hoods who robbed the rich to give to the poor, they were nonetheless praised as honorable and benevolent men who never let another go in need. Crime appeared too attractive in these men. Cartouche became praised, in the words of Nicolas Ragot de Grandval, as:

Valiant in fighting, skillful in retreats,
Firm in misfortune, sober in the taverns,
Loyal to his peers, calm, moderate,
And above all the declared enemy of traitors. . . .
Everyone admired his appearance;
His gentleness, his way of speaking, his air, his quiet bearing,
In short, everyone took him for a man of honor.[40]

Even as crime continued after the death of Louis XIV, so did disorder and poverty. Witch hunts ended during the seventeenth century, perhaps replaced by hospitals and archers of the poor who defused popular fears of deviants by bringing them under institutional control. If witches and werewolves received less official attention in the eighteenth century, midwives and folk healers received much more as "charlatans" and practitioners of the "baneful secrets" of contraceptives and abortifacients.[41] The Galley Corps formally ended in 1748, and galleys became much less significant in the French navy; yet the army continued to attract the rebellious and the lawless, and the navy had to maintain impressment.

Authorities sent thousands of women and children to the Salpêtrière in the eighteenth century. Abandoned infants went first to the Couche in Paris and then to the Salpêtrière or the Pitié after they were weaned.[42] Their numbers greatly increased following the death of Louis XIV, especially because provinces began sending their foundlings to Paris. Both legitimate and illegitimate children, they reveal the terrible vulnerability of parents in times of dearth and the tragic position of unmarried servant women.[43] Some of the small percentage of foundlings who survived became apprentices or servant girls, but many escaped from the options that officials offered them and found their way to the courtyard of miracles that persisted in eighteenth-century Paris.

Louis' attempts to deal with disorder did not eradicate the thief, the prostitute, or the smuggler. In fact, as highway travel increased, highway robbery became a common capital crime. Tax farmers, attempting to collect duties and taxes more effectively, found themselves confronting not individual smugglers, but whole villages in which women baked loaves of salt disguised with a thin crust of dough, and children buried salt in the little carts of rabbit food they gathered. Prostitution continued to be tolerated, a livelihood for "daughters of the poor", of concern mainly for officials who feared that it spread disease.[44]

The reign of Louis XIV neither created nor ended the problems of poverty, deviance, and crime. The policies of this monarch help us to recognize their political significance, however. To combat the disorder of these people, the king established a much stronger police system, which helped to expand the power of secular government. Rather than creating a police state, Louis and La Reynie simply demonstrated how a police system can work to expand both the bureaucracy and the authority of secular government. The king cannot take credit for creating the system of confining the poor in large institutions during the seventeenth century, but he was able to ensure that his government would be identified as a significant source of charity and the most vital agency for controlling the poor. If his archers of the poor ran into popular resistance, they also reinforced the association between poverty and disorder. Louis' policies, in short, recognized the significance of false beggars and vagrants, witches and healers; not merely deviants, these groups symbolized a justification for establishing and maintaining order.

Louis XIV by his policies also contributed to a developing secularization. He clearly recognized the primacy of God and wanted to use the French church as an ally. In his concept of society, God's order was the ideal, which human error disrupted. However, the king's efforts to correct human error and to control its disorderly consequences contributed to the growing awareness of the responsibilities and powers of secular government. It is no accident, for example, that witch hunts died out during Louis' reign; his police system demonstrated that deviant women really had no power at all, as it subjected them to surveillance and confined them in institutions. Where was the strength of the supernatural against archers and informers and Sisters of Charity, who maintained regulations in the Salpêtrière? What delicious incongruity that the skepticism of the "Enlightenment" may have owed as much to the wards of the Salpêtrière as it did to the erudition of Montesquieu.

"We must consider the good of our subjects far more than our own, " Louis XIV in his *Mémoires* had urged his son. "They are almost a part of ourselves, since we are the head of a body and they are its members."[45] In addition to sharing a corporeal relationship with his subjects, however, the king challenged them. He challenged the right of the "slime of Paris" to take over physical space in his capital city and to establish their strongholds in the *cours des miracles*. He challenged the power of deviant women to control mental process in the consciousness of his subjects who so easily believed in their good and evil miracles. He challenged the audacity of deserters, the pettiness of thieves, the dishonesty of smugglers, all who dared to demean his grandeur, honor, and glory. He challenged the idle poor, whose very presence could belie his ability to restore God's order.

The relationship of this monarch with his least respectable subjects suggests that the modern world did not result merely from economic changes and the writings of learned men. The experience of living with Louis' policies on poverty, deviance, and crime contributed significantly to a transition from feudalism and an introduction to the "Enlightenment". This is not to argue that history proceeds only through deviance, nor that "the slime of Paris" presents the entire picture of the old regime as it changed into modern France. Perhaps, however, this view from the underside can reveal a few more pieces of the jigsaw puzzle that eventually will provide a complete picture of Louis XIV's France.[46]

NOTES

1. For more discussion of these dislocations, see Chantal Dupille, *Histoire de la Cour des Miracles* (Paris, 1971); and Fernand Braudel, *The Mediterranean and the Mediterranean World in the Time of Philip II* (New York, 1972), especially "Poverty and Banditry" in Volume II.
2. Jeffry Kaplow, *The Names of Kings: The Parisian Laboring Poor in the Eighteenth Century* (New York, 1972), 150.
3. François Rabelais, *The Heroic Deeds of Gargantua and Pantagruel* (Sydney and London, 1951). For the cited passages, see p. 202.
4. Kaplow, 73. Olwen Hufton, *The Poor of Eighteenth-Century France: 1750–1789* (Oxford, 1974), especially pp. 5 and 70.
5. Natalie Zemon Davis, *Society and Culture in Early Modern France* (Stanford, 1975), 25; Dupille, 35–40.
6. Jacques Rossiaud, "Prostitution, jeunesse et société dans les villes du sud-est au XVe siècle," *Annales E. S. C.* XXXI (1976), 291–2. English version in *Deviants and the Abandoned in French Society*, ed. Robert Forster and Orest Ranum (Baltimore and London, 1978), 1–46. See also William W. Sanger, *The History of Prostitution: Its extent, Causes, and Effects Throughout the World* (New York, 1859), 119.

7. For more on the carnivalesque, see Mikhail Bakhtin, *Rabelais and His World* (Cambridge, 1968), 4–12; Peter Burke, *Popular Culture in Early Modern Europe* (New York, 1978), 178–204; Davis, 97–123; and Robert Muchembled, "Witchcraft, Popular Culture, and Christianity in the Sixteenth Century with Emphasis upon Flanders and Artois," in *Ritual, Religion, and the Sacred,* ed. Robert Forster and Orest Ranum (Baltimore, 1982), 213–36.

8. E. William Monter, *Witchcraft in France and Switzerland: The Borderlands during the Reformation* (Ithaca, 1976), 145–6.

9. Muchembled, 214. See also Monter, 167; Robert Mandrou, *Magistrats et sorciers en France au XVIIe siècle* (Paris, 1968).

10. Rabelais, 328–9.

11. Muchembled, 221–9; H. R. Trevor-Roper, *The European Witch-Craze of the Sixteenth and Seventeenth Centuries and Other Essays* (New York, 1967). See especially p. 112. See also E. William Monter, "The Pedestal and the Stake: Courtly Love and Witchcraft," in *Becoming Visible: Women in European History,* ed. Renate Bridenthal and Claudia Koonz (Boston, 1977), 128–35.

12. For rural crime, see Nicole and Yves Castan et al., "Crimes et criminalité en France sous l'ancien régime," *Cahiers des annales* XXXIII (1971), especially pp. 289–90.

13. Kaplow, 6.

14. Rabelais, 169.

15. Quoted in Emanuel Chill, "Religion and Mendicity in Seventeenth-Century France," *International Review of Social History* VII (1962), 402. See also Dupille, 160–3.

16. Chill, 406.

17. Ibid., 413.

18. Howard W. Haggard, *Devils, Drugs, and Doctors: The Story of the Science of Healing From Medicine Men to Doctors* (New York and London, 1929), 328.

19. Quoted in Dupille, 148.

20. Chill, 417.

21. Louis XIV, *Mémoires for the Instruction of the Dauphin,* ed. Paul Sonnino (New York, 1970), 222.

22. Kaplow, 22–3.

23. Louis XIV, *Mémoires,* 30.

24. Dupille, 186–8; Kaplow, 18.

25. Philip E. Riley, "Women and Police in Louis XIV's Paris," *Eighteenth Century Life* IV (1977), 37–42.

26. Sanger, 135–6.

27. Monter, *Witchcraft,* 84.

28. Mireille Laget, "Childbirth in Seventeenth- and Eighteenth-Century France: Obstetrical Practices and Collective Attitudes," in *Medicine and Society in France,* ed. Robert Forster and Orest Ranum (Baltimore, 1980), 144.

29. Alexander Parent-Duchatelet, *De la prostitution dans la ville de Paris, considerée sous le rapport de l'hygiène publique, de la morale et de l'administration* (Paris, 1837), 2 vols. See especially I, 587–605.

30. Louis XIV, *Mémoires,* 108.

31. André Corvisier, *Armies and Societies in Europe: 1494–1789* (Bloomington, 1979), 132–3.

32. Eugene Asher, *The Resistance to the Maritime Classes: The Survival of Feudalism in the France of Colbert* (Berkeley and Los Angeles, 1960). University of California Publications in History, LXVI. See especially p. 23. See also

Geoffrey W. Symcox, *The Crisis of French Sea Power: 1688–1697: From the Guerre d'Escadre to the Guerre de Course* (The Hague, 1974), 17; and Paul Bamford, *Fighting Ships and Prisons: The Mediterranean Galleys of France in the Age of Louis XIV* (Minneapolis, 1973), 181.

33. Quoted in Bamford, 178.
34. Quoted in Bamford, 195.
35. Andrew Lossky, "'Maxims of State' in Louis XIV's Foreign Policy in the 1680s," in *William III and Louis XIV: Essays 1680–1720 by and for Mark A. Thomson,* ed. Ragnhild Hatton and J. R. Bromley (Liverpool, 1968), 9.
36. Ragnhild Hatton, *Louis XIV and His World* (New York, 1972), 114.
37. Pierre Goubert, *Louis XIV and Twenty Million Frenchmen* (New York, 1970), 219–20 and 258–9; Dupille, 195.
38. Quoted in Goubert, 220.
39. Quoted in Kaplow, 29.
40. Kaplow, 140.
41. Alison Klairmont Lingo, "Empirics and Charlatans in Early Modern France: The Genesis of the Classification of the 'Other' in Medical Practice," *Journal of Social History* XIX (1986), 583–604; Jean-Pierre Goubert, "The Art of Healing: Learned Medicine and Popular Medicine in the France of 1790," in *Medicine and Society in France,* ed. Robert Forster and Orest Ranum (Baltimore, 1980), 1–23.
42. Claude Delasselle, "Abandoned Children in Eighteenth-Century Paris," in *Deviants and the Abandoned in French Society,* ed. Robert Forster and Orest Ranum (Baltimore, 1978), 48.
43. Ibid., 78. See also Cissie Fairchilds, *Domestic Enemies and Their Masters in Old Regime France* (Baltimore, 1984); and Hufton, 318–51.
44. The phrase quoted is in Hufton, 317; see also p. 290 and chs. 9–11.
45. Louis XIV, *Mémoires,* 68.
46. The metaphor of the jigsaw puzzle is shamelessly borrowed from Andrew Lossky's "'Maxims of State,'" 7.

FOUR

The Social History
of the Reign

CHARLIE R. STEEN

In 1600 French social structure seemed to have escaped unchanged from the turbulence of the last half of the sixteenth century. On the surface, France retained an orderly set of social hierarchies that had their origin in the customs and traditions of the past.[1] Traditionally, social structure had been revealed through estates, with churchmen, nobles, and wealthy townsmen enjoying social dominance in one form or another. From its inception, French society divided its members into these categories, which were theoretically in accord with function as well as condition.[2] Few writers considered an examination of traditional social practices necessary, and those who did tended to draw analogies between society and nature. The tree of commonwealth served nicely as a justification of social and political distinctions. The teachings of the Christian churches reinforced the belief that each person had a place in a divinely inspired, hierarchically arranged order. Spiritual comfort in anticipating the next world was more common than any questioning of inequities in this world. After all, why should citizens of the Christian commonwealth concern themselves with worldly problems that were rooted in original sin and that would be destroyed in a terrifying last judgment? Thus, in 1600 the conditions of the past dominated French society, allowing the orders of the feudal world to govern the practices of the day. Theoretically, churchmen remained preeminent because of their place as the first estate. It was, however, the nobility that dominated society in practical terms. The nobles maintained possession of their dominant place by insisting on the unquestioning continuation of a disciplined, deferential society with the vast majority of the people occupying a position visibly subordinate to their own. At every social level individual status was determined by the position of the group into which one had been born, and only the most extraordinary efforts or abilities could overcome that original determination of place. The ideal was a hierarchically arranged order in which every individual belonged to a group that carried out its functions in harmonious relation to all the others. With luck and good discipline, the bulk of the people at the bottom would never question the validity of the structure, and indeed they rarely did, thus allowing the nobles to dominate society.

The crown never questioned the social structure either, with Henry IV and his successors seeking only to manipulate it. The attitudes and practices of the past governed society, confirming a structure that perpetuated provincialism. In each order or estate, only those who occupied positions at the very top of the hierarchy could be considered French; all others defined themselves in local terms. The key to status remained grounded in a combination of birth and property. Noble status improved with age, especially if it was associated with a seigneurial fief, or *fief de dignité*. Incumbents of such fiefs occupied the finest places in the social order and held the titles of duke, marquis, count, viscount, or some variation. That select group, never numbering more than a few hundred, occupied a social place just below that of the Children of France and the Princes of the Blood and set itself off from the rest of the French. It led the *noblesse d'épée*, the nobility of the sword, maintaining a strict hierarchy within the second estate and establishing the standards of living nobly that gave them a distinctive style of life. That large group of provincial nobles who ranked just below the great and powerful families were only slightly less proud. Their origins were also with the sword, but their fiefs and fortunes limited their activity. The leading families of the provincial nobility gained in prestige and status during the old regime because they did not associate themselves with the court or with the excesses of living nobly. They became a model for advocates of the virtuous noble, or the noble savages in *culottes*. At the very bottom of the sword's hierarchy rested the *hoberaux*, the crowd of country squires who, although at the head of the rustic social system, had such limited means that their influence was restricted to the manor and village and excluded them from most provincial affairs.

Entry into the ranks of even the provincial *noblesse d'épée* was theoretically impossible. However, in practice new blood had traditionally entered through royal service or usurpation. At the meeting of the Estates-General at Blois in 1576, the nobles showed enormous hostility toward new faces in their midst, and they denounced the practices that allowed social mobility. In particular, the nobles sought an end to the practice of validating claims to noble status by those whose families had lived nobly for three generations. Moreover, to prevent further gate crashing, the nobles demanded royal enforcement of exclusionary sumptuary laws and of edicts that granted the nobility powerful privileges and jurisdictions, thus setting the true gentleman off from the mere pretender.[3]

The nobles gathered at Blois were especially eager to segregate themselves from a growing number of commoners, or *roturiers*, who used wealth to advance their social status. This early indication of hostility to social change brought on by the practices of the sixteenth century became an enduring feature of French society until the Revolution. Brushing aside accusations of social climbing, the wealthy members of the *bourgeoisie* wished to cast off their leading roles in the third estate and to achieve real place and status by intruding into the privileged world of the nobility. In this quest, the *bourgeoisie* had a friend in the crown, which favored the ambitious commoners for financial and political reasons. As unlanded wealth grew, numbers of the *bourgeoisie* began to live nobly. Some of that group managed to convert wealth into noble status through direct purchase of patents from the crown. Others arrived in the second estate through service to the crown. Consummating a long-standing practice of ennobling royal servants, Henry IV created the *noblesse de robe*, the nobility of the robe, granting noble status to certain officeholders in exchange for payment of the *paulette*, a yearly fee. Although this simply codified a regular practice, the nobility of the sword felt insupportably outraged, for the position of the robe had been secured by money or work, hardly the marks of a true gentleman. However, the fact that many nobles of the sword served the crown and sat on the *parlements*, or great law courts, confused the issue and made separating members of the robe and sword a difficult task. Nevertheless, throughout the seventeenth century, the nobility of the sword regarded the robe as usurpers, and flagrant purchasers of titles were subject to particular ostracism. Nobles of the sword abhorred such vile and base transactions, although they did not hesitate to demand that crown revenues support their self-imposed duty to live surrounded by pomp and luxury. The newly ennobled nobles of the robe, for their part, did not rush to emulate the swashbuckling behavior of the sword, but they lost no time in securing their social position, setting themselves off from their recently shed *roturier* status and, wherever possible, confirming their new dignity through the purchase of seigneurial lands.[4]

The desperate quest for noble status revealed one of the great problems of the old regime's social structure. Although not all of the rewards and pleasures of life necessarily belonged to the nobility, the commoners revered noble status at every turn and vilified their own place and efforts. Only a few could escape the ranks of the third estate, but all seemed in agreement that to be a commoner was in itself disreputable.

In both country and city, the populace honored the status of the nobility and condemned their own corporate groups to a decidedly secondary position. Those groups established separate hierarchies within the third estate, with distinct, if limited, privileges and prerogatives. Wide variations based on property, wealth, and profession regulated the social status of the commoner. In the cities, distinctions among the inhabitants were as rigid as any inspired by the nobility. Social leadership rested in the hands of the economically successful group, the *bourgeoisie*, and an elaborate hierarchy stretched out below them, imposing a complicated series of distinctions on urban residents. Within the cities, the *bourgeoisie* often enjoyed monopolies and privileges that resembled those of the nobility, and they tended to be quick to display their wealth, living within their means but above their station and wanting nothing so much as social promotion.[5]

In the countryside, manorial rules governing labor and, where they existed, seigneurial obligations defined the quality of life and made change difficult.[6] In villages, separate hierarchies created a complete social system in which families maneuvered through land purchases and marriages to improve their status. Outside of propertied or wealthy families the variations were wide. A few serfs and mortmain laborers remained, and there were growing numbers of *métayers*, or sharecroppers. However, all rural groups remained in a position of dependence. The presence of common lands, the quality of the collective organizations of the peasant communities, and the nature of manorial or feudal obligations intruded into village life, making it vulnerable. Social definitions thus depended on the conditions of land tenure, the level of personal dependency, and the organization of village life. Collective behavior was a stark necessity, but it could be either beneficial or harmful.

The position at the very bottom of the social hierarchy was occupied by outcasts and vagabonds. They lived in frightful poverty, an unpleasant but often prominent fringe in both rural and urban life. The bulk of the population lived dangerously close to the social and material level of the beggars at the doors of the old regime, for crop failures or a particularly expensive war could destroy the very modest place they held in life.

Between the death of Henry IV in 1610 and Louis XIV's assumption of personal rule in 1661, the social structure changed little. The behavior of the nobility during that period was outrageous, for they indulged in a series of civil wars and revolts designed to enhance their own power and weaken that of the crown. In this they failed miserably, not because they were defeated on the field of battle, but because they were triumphant, and in their victory revealed a poverty of policy that greatly enhanced general sympathy for the crown. In the aftermath of the Fronde, the nobility retained only social authority, having themselves undermined any claim to political preeminence. However, in his efforts to restore order in France, Cardinal Mazarin had allowed them to retain a powerful position in all social matters.[7]

The society that Louis XIV inherited from Mazarin, therefore, was both submissive and obedient to the dictates of the past. The concept of estates and functions, the great value placed on hereditary transfer of social status, and all the other traditional trappings of French society remained unchallenged. However, Louis XIV took advantage of the political disgrace of the nobility to place strict limits on their activities. He had no intention of changing the social structure of his realm, but he wished to manipulate it, applying the principles of divine right monarchy and absolutism to social as well as political affairs. Since he exalted order in every part of life, Louis retained and refined the social structure of the past. The king believed in natural hierarchy, and in all but a few instances, he exhibited an intense spirit of orthodoxy in social matters. Thus the sword continued to enjoy social prestige even after Louis limited its political power in the early years of his personal rule. Like the sword, the robe had to accept the loss of political initiative and find consolation in social distinction. Only the church illustrated the adjustments that Louis would allow in social structure. In 1661 all social groups could mingle freely within the institutions of the Gallican church, and Bishop Bossuet exemplified the social mobility it offered. However, Louis' own interest in the church, combined with his sensitivity to the nobility's relentless quest for sinecures and places, helped to reduce the social freedom it offered by making it increasingly aristocratic in its leadership.

Those who found advancement as well as those who simply maintained their place had to join the king in respecting due order and hierarchy. Only when the change benefited the crown was it considered the least bit desirable, and Louis was extremely conservative in this regard. For most of his subjects life changed only in a material way during his reign, and then usually for the worse. If anything, the king allowed the divisions and distinctions between and within the various hierarchies to become more pronounced. He appropriated the leaders of each hierarchy for his own use, bringing them to live or work at court, where they enjoyed a brilliant life-style. All others lived as best they could, which depended greatly on circumstances beyond their control.[8]

Louis never regarded the wide disparity between the privileged and the unprivileged as other than a natural feature of life. The mass of the people, perhaps twenty million in all, rarely expressed opinions on the subject except during the episodes of provincial rebellion that accompanied the taxes and misery of Louis' early wars. Only the revolt of 1675 in Brittany expressed social complaints, but it never shed its provincial character. As the reign continued, provincial outbursts ceased, leaving calm if not prosperity in the countryside, a suitable rural accompaniment to Louis' special social creation, the orderly, lovely Versailles, where grandeur and *règlement* mingled freely.

Nor was the structure of society a general issue, for discussion of human affairs rarely went beyond debate over the value of humanity itself. Writers from Pascal to Montesquieu contributed to the discussion. Early in the reign of Louis XIV, the works of Pascal set a tone that was compatible with the view held at court.[9] Writing in the shadow of the Fronde, Pascal expressed displeasure with all human initiative, and thus with society itself. Strongly repudiating the rationalists, he dismissed all human initiative as a product of pride, the fatal human flaw. In these views, Pascal was close to the attitudes of the king, who advocated divine right monarchy for many of the same reasons that led Pascal to espouse religion. Without strict authority, the world was a miserable place, and human nature, and thus society, was corrupt and had to be restrained by the imposition of order based on the state, tradition, and religion. It was Louis' particular genius to be able to express these ideas with grandeur, which gave his absolutistic regime and his indifference to social problems an aura of glory.

A host of other writers and theoreticians added their weight to that dismal view of humanity. Racine, the chief author of the brief classical moment sponsored by the king, disliked disorder or any unrestrained, unmeasured action.[10] To him, authority was necessary to prevent humans from being governed by passions, which kept them from acting from lofty or disinterested motives. These were also the opinions of the Jansenists, whose grim view of mankind left little room for questioning the sorry lot of society. Even La Fontaine, who avoided such rigorous religious views, blamed the ills of society on human failings rather than inequities or injustices within the social system. All members of society shared notoriety, exhibiting the characteristics of lions, wolves, foxes, and other less-admirable species. Disgust with humanity also affected the debate between the ancients and the moderns. The advocates of antiquity, led by Boileau, regarded their own world as pitiful. Society manifested human depravity, and modern corruption and idolatry had smothered the concerns for humanity and truth that had been so clear in the classical period.[11]

In an intellectual and literary atmosphere of such pessimism about humanity, it should hardly be surprising that the nature of society did not become a debatable issue until quite late in the reign. Initially, there was general acceptance of all Louis XIV's views and plans. Mme. de Sévigné's letters revealed acquiescence on the part of the nobility. Good form, precise manners, and rigid attention to place and function were the hallmarks of the privileged, who felt that obedience and acceptance of discipline were sufficient for the unprivileged. Should anyone harbor doubts about the validity of social inequality in a Christian world, Bishop Bossuet stood ready to affirm the need for authority as an antidote to human nature. After all, excessive freedom, disregard for one's station, and failure to be properly submissive encouraged people to judge matters for themselves, which to Bossuet was a horrid thing. Bossuet acknowledged that social behavior was natural to humans, but he despised the results. To the bishop, and supportive legists such as Domat, passions had destroyed good society and rendered all human associations suspect. Authority was the only thing that could make society work as God had intended.[12] Louis was in basic harmony with attitudes that denigrated human endeavor, but he believed that action by the monarch, acting in God-like fashion, could raise people and France itself to the highest possible level. For society, there was to be good order consonant with each person's place and function. However, a separate order was to exist for those at court, which he considered to be the natural center for French life. Thus it was at the huge court, which surrounded him even before the construction of Versailles, where social life was most carefully orchestrated and where the greatest changes took place. The king's social labors were concentrated in the first part of his reign, the period extending to 1685, during which time he contrived a new court society while building an appropriate palace in which to house it. Even before the palace was complete, he used the gardens and some of the building for elaborate *fêtes* that showed clearly his desire for strict regulation of the nobility in a culturally splendid environment. A number of figures showed their genius at Versailles, but Louis' name belongs with those of Molière, Lully, Le Vau, Le Nôtre, Le Brun, and Mansart, for he too was an artistic giant.[13] His sumptuous *fêtes* allowed him to create a *tableau vivant* that drew the court nobility into a grand but rigid order in which the king occupied the spotlight. The memory of the turbulent years of the Fronde left Louis with a dislike for active, powerful nobles, whose disorders had created a Hobbesean society in which unrestrained predators fed upon the body politic. Taking advantage of their general loss of prestige in the aftermath of the Fronde, the king selected some nobles for favor and others for disdain. Those whom he favored received honors and place as long as they agreed to abide by his new regulations for behavior. They were already among the highest-ranking nobles of the sword, but they had never before enjoyed such preferment or received such attention to their pleasures. Moreover, society at large subscribed to Louis' new order, and the prestige of the court nobility was immense. In exchange, the nobility abandoned political power and exercised only social authority.

The court was a clear symbol of the king's triumph over the nobility and of his social attitudes. In his mind, people were essentially base, but in a regulated environment a few could adorn the realm. Some nobles rejected the concept, or were rejected by Louis, and took refuge in the salons, in provincial life, or in exile abroad, but most were attracted to court life. The strict hierarchies, the exacting etiquette, the exquisitely arranged rituals, and the endless ceremonies centering on the king established a new standard of behavior. Symbolic meaning governed every act, gesture, garment, or word, setting members of the greatest families of the realm against each other. The system was formalistic and static, governed by refinements of etiquette that imposed a life of endless attention to detail and horrifying boredom on its participants. Louis manipulated the nobility with exquisite understatement, constantly rearranging the nobles around him, turning them into decorations, mere mannequins around his throne.

The only other noticeable social movement was within the ranks of the *bourgeoisie*. For a few, places in the administrative wing at Versailles offered opportunities for service that signaled social as well as political advance. Others continued the tradition of social climbing. La Mothe–Le Vayer's treatise early in the reign condemned the *bourgeoisie*'s habit of gathering vast wealth and then immediately living nobly.[14] This was not, of course, an easy transformation. Some were allowed to advance through an advantageous marriage or the purchase of an office, but the number of those who did so was small. However, there were times during the reign when money and service did attract the attention of the king in such a way as to facilitate ennoblement. Such favor lent considerable legitimacy to a person's advancement. Although *anoblis* might have to suffer the indignity of buying a dispensation from a subsequent royal revocation of their recent patents of nobility, they clung with pride to their new status and honored the king who had made it possible. Yet no one ever admired the desperate flight of the *bourgeoisie* in their endless quest for titles and status.

Molière was the best witness to the hopes of the *bourgeoisie* and the delight they took in their king. Some of his characters announced Louis' changes; others offered a firm commitment to continuity and tradition. Molière meant to honor only the king, not the social system itself, for in it honor and integrity were in short supply, while falseness, pretense, preciosity, and social climbing abounded. Molière was a mild critic, mocking the *bourgeoisie's* propensity for social climbing and chiding the nobility, albeit very gently, for becoming busybodies or even villains. The social climbing habits of the *bourgeoisie* were not invented by Louis XIV, but the witless, arrogant noble of the *Impromptu à Versailles* was definitely of royal manufacture. In both cases, Molière's comments were benign. He was thus a perfect playwright for the king, meting out rewards and punishments for his characters in harmony with the rules of the game. When Louis so wished, the *bourgeoisie* could occupy places of honor, but if he did not, then Molière's morality plays about maintaining proper place and station served their purpose.[15] However, the generation of writers who succeeded Molière were less well disposed to the king. After 1685, his calm, orderly, and ceremonious world gradually became the subject of increasing criticism, including unfriendly comments about the social policies of the reign. The orderly facade remained, but admiration became increasingly labored. At court, the *fêtes* ceased to be a novelty, and their repetitive splendor became part of the daily life of Versailles. They became permanent, controlled more by etiquette than by purpose. Life became a grand procession, with the appropriate rules to cover every detail. The court nobility was forced into an intricate pattern of deferential relationships that confined them by regulating their behavior and imposed enormous financial burdens on them. Nevertheless, these nobles reveled in their social prestige and heaped contempt on those who stayed away. Like Louis himself, the nobles ceased to venture far from Versailles, where they lived in splendid isolation.

In this isolation, the nobles tended to become increasingly exclusive. The sword families became ever more conscious of breeding and the rituals of etiquette that set them off from the nobility of the robe and especially from those members of the *haute-bourgeoisie* who were allowed to buy their way into the second estate. By 1694, the Académie Française's official *Dictionary* noted that not all nobles were true gentlemen. True nobility required proper breeding, but style of life remained important, especially as the noble became identified with the court. Remote from the world beyond the gardens of Versailles, the nobles nonetheless approached life with enormous self-confidence and almost total incapacity. Saint-Simon's lengthy review of the habits and practices of the court nobility showed how deeply involved the nobles were in court ritual and how far removed they were from everyday life.[16]

Isolation invited criticism, which started modestly. In his *Charactères*, La Bruyère considered the social cost of the court and of the king's wars.

For some peasants, life had become brutish and squalid, not far from that of the animals. In contrast, the nobles lived refined, elegant, and empty lives. However, even this criticism sought restoration of the noble to a proper place rather than questioning the social structure. Indeed, despite the painful times in the final twenty years of Louis XIV's reign, social matters never became a dangerous political topic.[17]

Silence did not mean that all people rejoiced at the king's policies. Beyond the gates of Versailles, some critics began to chafe at the restraints imposed by absolutism. Some, like the playwrights Le Sage and Dancourt, criticized society, finding it to be governed by unpleasant nobles and predatory tax farmers.[18] Others, led by Fénelon, cared less for social problems than they did for what they perceived to be imbalance in the political order of the realm.[19] Bitterly denouncing Louis' concept of kingship and his quest for glory, Fénelon sought a restoration of aristocratic influence in political and social order. He had vast faith in aristocrats who had not been tainted by the court, and his criticism was radical only within the context of life at Versailles. A selective critic, he dreamed of a Christian commonwealth in which people would be treated fairly and justly in exchange for obedience. Fénelon clearly regretted the effect of the king's absolutism upon the people. While Fénelon did not consider humanity as particularly admirable, misery did not need to be quite as pervasive as it had become. In retaliation, Louis forced Fénelon from the court, but the king could not weaken the influence of his conservative critic. In his social creation, Louis XIV showed a definite detachment from and disdain for reality. The glittering world of Versailles represented the pinnacle of status, but the hierarchies of wealth and power did not correspond with that of the court. Late in the reign, the organization of the capitation tax revealed some of the discrepancies. According to the assessment of his tax gatherers, nobles, ranked according to their resources, were to be distributed in nineteen of the twenty-two categories. The *hobereaux* were placed in the same category as the prosperous peasant proprietors. Although economic classifications are limited as guides to social distinctions, it was clear that the group most favored by the king would have lost significance in many areas of life had it not been for the royal protection of their privileges.[20]

However, this artificial social stratification became the model for the remainder of the old regime. Obsessed with their status and place within society, the nobility thrived in the contrived atmosphere of court, relishing the infinite variations of place and degree within their own ranks. While Louis XIV lived, nobles had to limit their activity to social maneuvering, but on his death they extended their claims for precedence once again into public life. Their resurgence after 1715 resulted in the nobility's capturing all the lucrative positions of both church and crown. More powerful than ever before, the nobility attempted to preclude further entry into their ranks, bringing an end to ennoblements and creating a caste mentality within their ranks, one made possible by the acceptance of robe members by the sword during the eighteenth century. Much of their life continued to be centered in Versailles, but the court had lost its leadership. Lacking the close management of a powerful king, court society became aimless. Versailles ceased to have any admirable quality. Honesty and integrity were entirely out of fashion, and Montesquieu's Persian travelers noted the prevalence of hypocrisy in high circles. Like Fénelon, Montesquieu disqualified nobles from important places in his political scheme if they had resided at court.[21] Indeed, Versailles and the indifference of its residents toward the world outside served to excite social as well as political criticism for the duration of the old regime, thereby helping to sponsor the refined but cutting remarks of Voltaire and the far less friendly views of Rousseau.

The criticism associated with eighteenth-century thought reflected the frustration felt by the *bourgeoisie* after the king's death. He had favored them in an irregular and sometimes humiliating manner, raising some to the coveted status of *anobli*. Others found social advance through service to the crown, for Louis' regime needed dedicated servants and rewarded them for labor and loyalty. Still others increased their wealth and status through enterprises sponsored by the crown or through financial transactions arising from the long years of war. After Louis died, only the financiers continued to prosper, and political and social promotion became exceedingly difficult as the nobles seized control. The gulf between the *bourgeoisie* and the nobility had never been greater.[22]

Similar but far more painful problems affected the unprivileged in society. Whether in the city, the countryside, or the church, people without privilege lost ground after 1715. Rapid urban growth was accompanied by widespread misery, and the horrifying economic conditions of the urban poor adequately described their social position. In the countryside, the lot of the peasantry continued to vary from place to place, but for most the period continued to be unstable.[23]

The greatest difference between society before and after Louis XIV was not in the varying positions of the social groups. After all, he had simply made the system that he inherited more stable. What was different was the increasing level of criticism of the system and the sudden desire to offer alternatives to it. For Pascal and Bossuet, the nature of humanity and religion were proper subjects to investigate in a traditional framework, but for Voltaire, Rousseau, and Montesquieu, man, society, and civilization had to be examined, and without the same circumspection. Even so, the society of the past, as refurbished by Louis XIV, constituted the social order until 1789. Voltaire captured the spirit of his time, for he saw clearly the deleterious effect of traditions that favored the nobles and the crown. However, he also lauded Louis XIV for being a model monarch, one whose triumphs in battle, politics, and culture elevated him to the status of Augustus. The court may have been unfair and iniquitous, but it was the envy of Europe, for it had made the realm splendid even if society suffered.[24]

NOTES

1. Within the vast number of secondary sources on the social history of Louis XIV's reign, the following continue to have great significance. Marc Bloch, *French Rural History: An Essay on Its Basic Characteristics* (Berkeley, 1966); Franklin Ford, *Robe and Sword: The Regrouping of the French Aristocracy after Louis XIV* (Cambridge, 1953); Pierre Goubert, *L'Ancien régime, I: La Société* (Paris, 1969) and *Louis XIV et vingt millions de Français* (Paris, 1966), English edition, *Louis XIV and Twenty Million Frenchmen* (New York, 1970); *State and Society in Seventeenth Century France*, ed. Raymond F. Kierstead (New York, 1975); Emmanuel Le Roy Ladurie, *The Mind and Method of the Historian* (Chicago, 1981); Robert Mandrou, *Louis XIV en son temps* (Paris, 1973). Peuples et Civilizations, X; Roland Mousnier, *Les Institutions de la France sous la monarchie absolue: 1598–1789* (Paris, 1974–80), 2 vols., English edition, *The Institutions of France under the Absolute Monarchy: 1598–1789* (Chicago, 1979–84), 2 vols.; Philippe Sagnac, *La Formation de la société française moderne* (Paris, 1945–6), 2 vols.; Alexis de Tocqueville, *L'Ancien régime et la Révolution française* (Paris, 1856).
2. Charles Loyseau, *Traité des offices* (1606) and *Traité des ordres et simples dignitéz* (1610) provide a treasure of social facts.
3. *Ordonnance rendue sur les plaintes et doléances des Etats-Généraux assembles a Blois en novembre 1576, relativement à la police générale du royaume . . . mai 1579*, in *Recueil général des anciennes lois françaises*, ed. François-André Isambert (Paris, 1822–33), 380–463. The general attitude of the nobles toward social and political affairs can be seen in Bernard de Girard, Sieur du Haillan, *Recueil d'advis et conseils sur les affaires d'éstat* (1578).
4. Mousnier, II, 27–83; and Goubert, *Ancien régime*, I, 161–83.
5. Goubert, *Ancien régime*, I, 192–208.
6. Ibid., 77–116.
7. Mousnier, II, 611–30. The self-mocking *Maximes* of La Rochefoucauld reveal the feelings of the failed Frondeur, which amounted to general disgust with human nature.
8. Louis XIV, *Mémoires for the Instruction of the Dauphin*, ed. Paul Sonnino (New York, 1970).
9. Blaise Pascal, *Pensées de M. Pascal sur la religion et sur quelques autres sujets* (Paris, 1669). Paul Benichou, *Morales du grand siècle* (Paris, 1938), offers an important survey of the major authors of the later seventeenth century.
10. Racine presented a somber view of human endeavor and society, for people

were helpless before their passions. Jean Racine, *Théâtre complet* (Paris, 1960).

11. Jean de La Fontaine, *Fables* (Paris, 1962); and Nicholas Boileau-Despréaux, *Oeuvres complètes* (Paris, 1966), 4 vols.

12. Marie de Sévigné, *Lettres* (Paris, 1953–57), 3 vols.; Bénigne Bossuet, *Oeuvres complètes* (Paris, 1881), 8 vols.; and Jean Domat, *Le Droit public* (1697), a work that reiterated the concept that society was a natural body of related and mutually dependent parts, each of which had to know its place and fulfill its functions.

13. Primi Visconti, *Mémoires* (Paris, 1909) and *Briefe der Herzogin Elizabeth Charlotte von Orléans*, ed. Wilhelm Ludwig Holland (Stuttgart, 1867–81), 6 vols. Bibliothek des Litterarischen Vereins in Stuttgart, vols. LXXXVIII, CVII, CXXII, CXXXII, CXLIV, CLVII. English selection, *A Woman's Life in the Court of the Sun King: Letters of Liselotte von der Pfalz*, ed. Elborg Forster (Baltimore, 1984).

14. François de La Mothe–Le Vayer, *De l'Instruction de Monseigneur le Dauphin* (1640). See the articles on the *bourgeoisie* in Kierstead, 200–64.

15. J. B. Molière, *Oeuvres complètes* (Paris, 1965), 4 vols.

16. Louis de Saint-Simon, *Mémoires* (Paris, 1879–1930), 43 vols.

17. Jean de La Bruyère, *Les Charactères* (Paris, 1963). See also the oblique views in Charles Perrault, *Les Contes de fées* (1700).

18. René-Alain Lesage, *Turcaret* (1709), and the Sieur D'Ancourt, *Agioteur* (1709), offered bitter satire about life in the last years of Louis XIV, so much so that both plays were closed after only a few performances. Fictional travel literature also became increasingly satiric—e.g., Baron de Lahontan, *Nouveau Voyage, Dialogue avec un sauvage americain* (1703), in which disorder is preferred to the falseness of the existing social hierarchy.

19. François de La Mothe-Fénelon, *Oeuvres complètes*, (Paris, 1851–2), 10 vols., and particularly the *Lettre à Louis XIV*, *Télémaque*, and *Examen de conscience sur les devoirs de la royauté*.

20. Ford, 22–34.

21. Charles de Montesquieu, *Lettres persanes* (Amsterdam, 1721), 2 vols.

22. Sagnac, II.

23. For a work that traces the position of the peasantry throughout the period and that shows the net effect on them of Louis XIV's regime, see Emmanuel Le Roy Ladurie, *Les Paysans de Languedoc* (Paris, 1966).

24. F. de Voltaire, *Siècle de Louis XIV* (Berlin, 1751).

FIVE

The Legal History of the Reign

DUANE ANDERSON

As a land that had in prehistoric times been subject to the tribal customs of the Celts, Gaul must initially have presented a variety of usages about which we can say relatively little. On the other hand, the conquering Romans quickly imposed a legal system whose prescriptions are clear and whose influences can hardly be overestimated. The Roman system, particularly in its late imperial form, was characterized by a number of distinct features: (1) considerable respect for the rights of property, at least in civil cases, and great latitude by the possessor to bequeath it as he or she might please; (2) wide powers for the *paterfamilias* (father), extending to his children (except for married daughters) way beyond the age of maturity; (3) an obtrusive and pervasive governmental power justified by the motto *"Salus populi suprema lex est"* (the welfare of the people is the supreme law), and implemented by the principle *"Quod principi placuit legis habet vigorem"* (what the prince pleases has the force of law); (4) inquisitorial judges, guided by arithmetical rules of evidence, restricting the role of juries and lawyers in civil cases, eliminating it entirely in criminal ones. Nor was this system egalitarian. Citizens belonging to the class of *honestiores* were not subject to interrogation under torture or to the most brutal punishments, such as crucifixion. To this were grafted various privileges and exemptions that the emperors periodically granted to the Christian church, the entire system being enshrined in the famous code of Justinian. By contrast, the laws of the Germanic Franks who invaded the empire and gave Gaul its new name harked back to those of the early Celts and Romans in the following manner: (1) less concern about individual rights of property, more reliance on fixed rules of inheritance, often primogenital or preferential to male heirs; (2) greater possibility for children to break away from the group and seek their own destiny; (3) an extremely disinterested social authority, whose concern was at most to authorize the modalities of private vengeance, with the king as the depositary rather than as a

73

creator of the laws; (4) judges who were less interested in the facts of the case than in the reputation of the litigants, with doubtful cases being settled in trials by combat or by ordeal. This system was not egalitarian either. Penalties, usually pecuniary, varied according to the status and nationality of the parties. The Roman system was seductive, however, and the Frankish rulers tried to imitate it insofar as this was feasible.[1]

The royal court, with its pale imitation of imperial Roman organization, was gradually swamped by far weightier competition than the oral customs of a primitive people. The kings of France, and especially the Capetians, were obliged to make room for the power of their feudal vassals, each enjoying the right of high or low justice, each setting up administrative-judicial officials—chancellors, *prévôts*, *baillis*, and *sénéchaux*, as well as *procureurs* (prosecutors)—over his own domains. It was within the framework of this legal structure, as well as that of the church, that the monarchy began little by little to reserve certain *cas royaux* (royal cases) to itself. It was also within the nomenclature of this new structure that the kings titled their chief legal magistrates "chancellor" and appointed subordinate *prévôts*, *baillis*, and *sénéchaux*, as well as *procureurs*, to supervise royal interests on the local level. But it was in the spirit of local custom, whether Germanic in the north or more Romanized in the south, that these officials rendered their decisions. We have only to examine the customs of Beauvais in force at the time of Louis IX to observe the reliance on character witnesses, on verbal consultation to determine usages, and on judicial combat. As the monarchy gained in power, however, so did its judicial prestige. The king's council became more active as a high court, and by 1302, Philip IV established a distinct *parlement* in Paris, a judicial court staffed both by peers and by paid professional *gens de robe* (people of the robe), divided up in three chambers, serviced by a *procureur général*, and soon joined by a *chambre des comptes* (chamber of accounts). The *parlement* represented a powerful force for moral suasion, and it immediately began to formulate such neo-Roman claims as "*Le roi est empereur en son royaume*" (the king is emperor in his kingdom), purely theoretical speculations that scarcely altered the feudal structure of the state. What did gradually change was procedure. For champions, there emerged lawyers, at least in civil cases. For oral consultation, there emerged written proceedings, kept secret in criminal cases. For the certainly of God's judgment through ordeal or combat, there emerged the certainty of the *question préliminaire* (torture— if there was enough suspicion in a heinous crime—to obtain a confession) or *préalable* (to discover accomplices), along with a variety of brutal forms of execution. Specialization extended to the provinces with the creation of *lieutenants* (judges) and other legal officers. But the new institutions, for all their royalist character, were themselves subject to the impact of the feudal system. It was not long before personal alliances, intermarriage, and family succession began to penetrate the courts themselves. It was not long before each civil legal procedure came to be burdened with *épices* (fees). It was not long before the *parlement*, when presented with a new royal measure that the judges did not approve and particularly during the Hundred Years' War, would "remonstrate" against registration. The Kings had to fall back upon the principle of *justice retenue* (jurisdictional primacy), whether by evoking cases to their own council, setting up special commissions, or holding a *lit de justice* (personally attending *parlement*) in order to enforce registration, and even so, many registrations were qualified and subverted at the first opportunity. The temporary defection of much of the *parlement* to the English permitted Charles VII, Louis XI, and Charles VIII to inaugurate another notable maneuver of the French monarchy in the face of entrenched interests—namely, to dilute but not to eliminate them altogether. Between 1451 and 1499 the *parlement* in Paris was joined by five provincial *parlements*, the marshals of France got to set up *prévôtés des maréchaux* (rural police courts), and the *parlements* reverted to a more submissive tone, championing royal authority, in fact, by encouraging a novel procedure, the *appel comme d'abus* (appeal to royal courts) against ecclesiastical or papal pretensions. But to the average subject, and even to the exasperated kings, the principal characteristic of this legal system was its cumbersomeness. Most people simply tried to stay out of its way.[2]

They had not seen anything yet! The great sixteenth-century crises—increase in population, inflation, religious schism—could not help affecting the legal system of France. At first, as during the reign of Louis XII, the transformation was benign. But this was also a time when the kings, not satisfied at leaving well enough alone, kept committing themselves to an ambitious foreign policy. Francis I, in order to finance his wars, engaged in the widespread creation and sale of judicial offices, to the intense chagrin of the established magistrates, who were no less infuriated by his concordat with the pope to the detriment of the Gallican church. This king's highly elaborate *lits de justice* were only temporarily effective in intimidating the *parlement* of Paris, which, along with the other high courts, again resumed their delaying tactics. Nevertheless, the process of bureaucratization continued in 1539, with Francis issuing his famous Edict of Villers-Cotterets. In its concern for eliminating delays in both civil and criminal procedure, this edict consecrated the inquisitorial character of the latter. The edict deprived the accused of any counsel and expected the defendant, in his bewildered condition, to come up immediately with any challenges against his judges or his accusers. Likewise, under the impact of inflation, the royal courts found themselves handling many cases that were no longer under the purview of the seigneural ones. Yet it was primarily in response to the financial needs of the monarchy that its own judicial system grew entirely out of proportion to the increase in population. In 1551, ostensibly in order to relieve the *parlements'* appellate burdens, Henry II began instituting an intermediate level of courts, the *présidiaux*, in most *baillages* and *sénéchaussées*. Such innovations, pursued in the midst of civil and religious wars, produced violent complaints and high-minded programs for reform. This was a time when, at royal instigation, most of the different customs were written down and published. Charles IX and his chancellor, Michel de L'Hôpital, prompted by the Estates-General of 1560 at Orléans, also issued a great ordinance, promising the reduction of the number of judicial officials to the time of Louis XII, an end to inbreeding in the courts, and a curbing of royal evocations. The trend was in precisely the opposite direction. One observer estimated that there were twenty thousand *gens de robe* and over three hundred thousand persons employed at dispensing justice. An assembly of notables held at Moulins in 1566 obtained another idealistic ordinance, additionally promising a reduction in *épices*. Instead, the *parlements* of France soon sprouted *chambres mi-parties* (mixed chambers), made up of Catholic and Huguenot judges. Henry III, buffeted by the Estates-General of 1576 at Blois, apologized in the next pretentious ordinance that venality "to our great regret has been tolerated due to the extreme necessity of our affairs". France was in no mood for excuses. She was looking for scapegoats, and her magistrates, with nary a scruple about the evidence, joined enthusiastically in the great witch hunts that swept the continent. And the *parlement* of Paris, reverting to its behavior during the Hundred Years' War, abandoned its legitimate Huguenot king in favor of the Catholic League. Henry IV, the legitimate king, succeeded only in restoring a semblance of order. Becoming a Catholic himself, he was obliged in 1598 by the Edict of Nantes to grant toleration to his former Huguenot allies. Then, of his own free will in 1604 he instituted the *paulette*, a tax through the payment of which the venal judicial officials could pass their offices on to their heirs. The sixteenth century, with all its upheavals, had therefore seen the emergence of a new aristocracy in France, a fledgling nobility of the robe.[3]

If the aspirations of a society are at all reflected in the proclivities of its legal system, then the mood in France during the minority of Louis XIII was overwhelmingly conservative and authoritarian. As the great crises of the sixteenth century receded, moreover, they gradually revealed the foundations of a more settled structure. Correspondingly, in the areas subject to the written law, the husband became more and more the master of his wife and children, his testamentary power unchallenged. In those areas covered by customary law, the paterfamilial authority was extended as much as possible. And this, even if done with the connivance of the courts, was by no means orchestrated by the central government. Likewise, there was a general acceptance of the social order, of class privileges, and repugnance for the lawbreaker. Where there were outbreaks of popular violence, and these were frequent, they were directed against the innovator, the criminal, the sorcerer. Where there were outbreaks of aristocratic violence, and these too were frequent, they represented an inveterate habit that was hard to set aside. In both instances the *parlements*, following their own standards of evidence and procedure, attempted to stem the tide of lawlessness, and that of Paris displayed considerable skepticism toward accusations of sorcery. Another indication of the mood of France, and particularly of its notables, emerged at the Estates-General of 1614. Each of the orders, notwithstanding some hostility between the old nobility and the emerging nobility of the robe, wanted an elimination of venality, simplification of legal procedures, and objected to extraordinary tribunals. A deputy to this assembly as well as to the assembly of notables of 1617 shared these ideals. When he became prime minister of Louis XIII, the now Cardinal Richelieu tried to put them into effect, collaborating in this regard with his political rival, Keeper of the Seals Michel de Marillac. They quickly discovered, however, that political necessity prevented them from suppressing the *paulette*, and reason of state, as in the tribunal that tried Chalais, required them to circumvent normal legal channels. Still, Richelieu felt obliged to respond to the pleadings of the Estates-General and of still another assembly of notables, that of 1626. He gave his full support to Marillac's pet project, the Code of 1629, longest in the history of the French monarchy and perhaps the most platitudinous. Aside from a cautious effort to curb the *parlements*' right of remonstrance and a disturbing promise to send out "masters of requests" (i.e., intendants) to inspect the functioning of the courts, it limited itself to pious prohibitions of well-known abuses. The most revealing thing about the code was the issues on which it remained silent: inbreeding, venality, the use of special commissions. Still the *parlements* resisted it, derisively dubbing it the Code Michaud, and Richelieu, faced with the ruinous expenses of foreign wars and the need to suppress domestic rebellion, did not press for its implementation. Whatever its underlying tendencies, therefore, the France of Louis XIII has left us memories of extraordinary tribunals, the devils of Loudon, and the brutal suppression of peasant uprisings. Nor should these underlying tendencies make us forget the endemic private conflicts that never reached the courts.[4]

It was precisely the same conservative, if not authoritarian, bent that dominated France throughout the minority of Louis XIV, with its regency of Anne of Austria and its prime ministry of Cardinal Mazarin. This period witnessed one of the strangest revolts in the history of the monarchy, a revolt incited by the *parlement* of Paris in defense of God-only-knows what past utopia and in disregard of extremely compelling present predicaments. At first the *parlement*, led by its moderate first president, Molé, merely complained against the heavy-handed fiscal measures with which the new regime sought to satisfy its financial needs, but even as it was doing its best to conclude one phase of the war with the Peace of Westphalia, the *parlement's* criticism, with all its chambers united, shifted to the entire system of tax farms, intendants, and extraordinary justice that Richelieu had so regretfully instituted. There was even an overtone of concern for individual rights, the judges at one point demanding an end to *all* arbitrary imprisonment. When the regency government sought to suppress the movement by arresting the most obstreperous judges, the *parlement* found itself succored, whether it wanted to or not, by the *bourgeois* of Paris and by a collection of mischievous nobles who immediately garnered for the revolt the derisive name of the Fronde (slingshot). Thoroughly embarrassed by their bedfellows, the magistrates rushed to extract what concessions they could from the regent and make their peace, but it was not easy for two hundred legal pedants to match the agility of Cardinal Mazarin, the Duke d'Orléans, the Prince de Condé, the about-to-be Cardinal de Retz, and the diplomacy of Spain. When Mazarin, in temporary alliance with Retz, effected the arrest of Condé, the *parlement* did little more than to complain feebly. It was the same in the provinces, and most notably in Bordeaux, where the local *parlement*, already at odds with the royal governor, found itself trapped between the party of Condé and the popular violence of the Ormée. When, moreover, the Frondeur party and the Duke d'Orléans combined with Condé to drive out Mazarin, the *parlement's* royalism emerged in full force. This is not to suggest that the magistrates were inept revolutionaries. The contemporary English revolution produced no fewer leaders who were swept along by events. Indeed, the English example had an undeniably chastening effect upon the French and helped to reconcile them to the return of Cardinal Mazarin. Still, the *parlements* did not capitulate entirely. The judges preserved their ownership of office, they continued to obstruct financial expedients, and they persisted in railing against royal evocations. It was under these very circumstances that the frustrated young king is supposed to have reminded the *parlement* of Paris, "L'état, c'est moi!", and that he appointed a new and highly diplomatic first president, Lamoignon. On the other hand, the intendants and the new financial system also remained in place, and the final coming of peace with Spain in 1659 put the monarchy in an extremely enviable situation. By the time Cardinal Mazarin died, on March 9, 1661, the only question was whether Louis XIV had the character or the will to press his advantage.[5]

At first it seemed as if he did. He announced his resolve to rule without a prime minister. He had no doubt about his right to impose his own notions of morality, or of politics. Like his predecessors, he considered himself the ultimate depositary, formulator, and interpreter of all law. Whenever the delicacy of any case warranted, he had no compunction about suppressing it, evoking it to his council, or setting up a special court to try it. He had only a limited fund of patience for religious dissenters, beginning very quickly to apply pressure upon both Huguenots and Jansenists. His was the golden age of the *lettre de cachet*, among other things a graceful arrest warrant that did not stoop to explanations. In collusion with the self-effacing Colbert, one of the first legal spectacles of the king's personal reign, in September of 1661, was the arrest of the overmighty superintendant of finances, Nicolas Fouquet, and the setting up of an extraordinary tribunal, a Chamber of Justice, to try him and his accomplices. The chamber had all the appearances of a drumhead court. It was opened by Chancellor Séguier, presided over by Lamoignon, and included other members—Colbert's uncle Pussort, for example—who could hardly have been sympathetic to the principal defendant. Fouquet was questioned in the usual inquisitorial manner, and yet, as Louis quickly discovered, even the pretense of justice entailed prolonged procedures. The judges eventually accorded Fouquet two lawyers, allowed him to produce his defenses, and got so bogged down in their legal technicalities that the chancellor had to be recalled to restore order. After three years, in December of 1664, one of the two reporting judges recommended banishment, and his recommendation carried the day. All the furious king could do was to "commute" the sentence to life imprisonment, Fouquet spending the remainder of his life in the high security fortress of Pinerolo.[6]

This frustrating matter over, Colbert, as Intendant and later Controller-General of the Finances, dedicated himself to a more positive and vaster project that he had inspired upon Louis, a thoroughgoing reform, simplification, possibly even unification of the apparatus of justice. All of the abuses of the previous century, compounded by those of the previous reign, were crying out for correction. Colbert, not surprisingly, approached them first and foremost from an economic perspective. The legal system, he complained in a *mémoire* that criticized the granting to judges of dispensations of age for their children, was now employing over seventy thousand men and kept over two million subjects immobilized. He recommended in a subsequent *mémoire* entirely suppressing the *paulette*. The king entered enthusiastically into these ideas. He expressed his intention to issue a single body of ordinances on jurisprudence, to reduce the number of judges, and even to render justice free to all subjects. To coordinate this ambitious program, Colbert recommended in a third *mémoire* the establishment of a hush-hush council of justice. Even as he wrote, however, he seemed to be trimming his sails. He showed himself willing, out of purported compassion, to extend the *paulette* for another four years, still convinced that by strictly regulating the price of offices, he could in seven or eight years bring their number down to mid-sixteenth century proportions. He also was prepared to cooperate with docile judges for his own purposes. In August of 1665, Louis detached a number of members from the *parlement* of Paris to hold a Grands Jours tribunal in the unruly Auvergne, which resulted in five exemplary executions. Meanwhile, the high-level plans went forward. On September 25, with the chancellor presiding, the council of justice met for the first time. There was much talk about the plenitude of the king's power; yet as the discussion proceeded, it bacame clear that there was no intention to abrogate local customs or corporate privileges. Moreover, shortly after the first session, the news arrived in France that Philip IV of Spain had died. It was an apparently unrelated event, but it suddenly placed the reform of justice in an entirely different perspective. Louis XIV simply did not attach the same importance to achieving long-term institutional gains against a helpless judiciary as he did to achieving instant military glory against a helpless Spanish monarchy. Possibly he felt he could do both when, on December 22, he held a *lit de justice* for the purpose of issuing three edicts. One of them was on the price of offices. It announced the continuation of the *paulette*, but for only three years, and set the price of judicial offices at a rate slightly higher than the one previously suggested by Colbert. It also regulated the ages of admission, categorically excluding the possibility of dispensations. The judicial officials had much to complain about, but they were still very much alive and kicking. The lower price of offices constituted one more motive for keeping them in the family and could always be subverted under the table.[7]

The king, however, continued to relish the role of a new Justinian. The following year was spent by a conciliar committee scouring all the previous codes and formulating the great Civil Ordinance of 1667. It was thorough and was the first code issued by the kings of France that dealt exclusively with civil procedures and sought to apply them uniformly throughout the kingdom. The ordinance went methodically from *ajour-nements* (summonses), through *contestations en cause* (trials), to *requêtes civiles* (motions for retrial). In every instance the motive of the committee was to shorten the duration of litigation by reducing its steps, combining them here, reducing them there, discouraging them everywhere. Title XI:2 required an exchange of documents between parties. Title XIV:4 prevented some postponements. Title XXXV:35 required an advance deposit of 450 *livres* for a *requête civile*. In the process, of course, the occasions for judges and other officials to collect *épices* were curtailed, and a number of articles subjected offending judges to civil prosecution. Thus, when, early in 1667, the committee for the first time invited Lamoignon and other judges to confer with it, the inevitable complaints were heard in the name of judicial responsibility. This was largely, however, a reaction to the unfamiliar. The judges, after a little balking, learned how to live with the new procedure and even turned it to their advantage.[8]

This reform hardly meant that Louis XIV had the slightest intention of abandoning his personal interventions. Under his system, the ob-streperous Huguenot Roux de Marcilly, who had attempted from abroad to arouse the Protestant powers against the French threat, found himself kidnapped on Swiss territory and imprisoned in the Paris Bastille. Only his superhuman courage in emasculating himself beyond the possibility of surviving under torture prevented his being subjected to the question prior to being broken on the wheel. His execution was followed by the furtive arrest of the mysterious Eustache Dauger, on whom even less could be pinned and who went on to become the man in the "iron" mask. But the king could not do everything himself, and he did his best to engender respect for the existing legal hierarchy. In August of 1669, he issued a major edict regarding waters and forests, as well as a supplementary edict placing substantial fines on all unsuccess-ful appeals, even to his own council, but his greatest contribution to the prestige of the judiciary was this: that he was the first king of France who accepted the entrenched venality of offices and who integrated it into his conception of the natural order. As he wrote about this time in his *Mémoires* for his son the dauphin:

> As long as their authority seemed opposed to mine, whatever their good intentions, it produced some very bad effects for the state and obstructed all my greatest and most useful undertakings. It was just for this utility to prevail and to reduce all things to their natural and legitimate order, even if it had been necessary, although I have

avoided it, to deprive these bodies of part of what they had been given, just as the painter has no hesitation about softening what is most striking and most beautiful in his own work when he finds that it is bigger than it should be and clearly out of proportion with the rest.

This attitude was also very much in tune with the prevailing norms of French society. The recommendations, the special courtesies accorded to prestigious litigants, the assiduous court paid to the judges, the occasional majestic interventions of Louis himself, all these features were generally accepted as merits of the social order rather than as deficiencies of the legal system. And it must be remembered that for the two million subjects who were immobilized by it, there were eighteen million who independently resolved their differences in manners of their own choosing.[9]

The same committee that fashioned the Civil Ordinance of 1667 also produced the Criminal Ordinance of 1670. It too built upon traditional principles, and it too aimed at speeding up the process. The code placed every possible weapon in the hands of the judge in his quest for the truth and left the accused more isolated and intimidated than ever. The intention of Titles XI:12 and XIV:1, requiring judges personally to interrogate suspects within twenty-four hours, was to get the case moving, not any concern for civil rights. As one may observe in the same last article, proceedings were secret, the accused was required under oath to testify against himself, and he was held incommunicado. He was not allowed a lawyer, except for special crimes, such as fraud. As always, if there was enough suspicion of a capital crime, the use of torture was permitted. However, the Ordinance of 1670 innovated in this matter. Henceforth, if a hardy person resisted the torments and refused to confess, he could still be condemned, albeit to a lesser penalty than death. This provision, it should be noted, was not an alternative to torture; it merely lessened the reward for resisting it. When some leading judges were again brought into the discussion and Lamoignon came feebly to the defense of some elemental civil rights, Pussort retorted that slippery attorneys would not obstruct justice and that self-incrimination was good for the soul.[10]

Whatever facilitations of procedure these reforms may have initiated, this movement was almost immediately reversed by the financial necessities of the Dutch War, to which Colbert had to give priority. The regression began early in 1672. Amid a long list of blatantly fiscal edicts, there was one that established the heredity of ushers, sergeants, and archers. Thus the heredity of office took on a new life in the reign of Louis XIV. The trend resumed early in 1673. Amid another outpouring of fiscal expedients, reinforced by a precautionary edict prohibiting remonstrances *prior* to registration, we find the creation of a variety of petty legal offices. So much for the reduction of the bureaucracy! Then, on the not-implausible pretext that the procedures required by the new ordinances were being evaded, the government began to sell stamped paper forms that were obligatory for legal transactions. So much for the rendering of justice gratuitously! There were still, in the course of that year, some faint echoes of the old reformist zeal. Colbert, without even the assistance of a committee, issued a Commercial Ordinance, em-bodying his desire to impose order and discipline upon the business community. In the best of times, such a code might have regulated a booming industry. In the difficult years of the Dutch War the paperwork merely reinforced existing monopolies. By the end of the year, the king completely reinstated the sale of dispensations for age and parentage, "considering the prodigious expenses that we are obliged to maintain in the present war". As it escalated, Colbert's financial expedients became more obtrusive to the judges themselves. In 1674 they were hit by an *augmentation de gages*, in effect a forced loan, of five hundred thousand *livres*. How did they react to these impositions? Unfortunately for them, Louis was no longer eight years old, and the only aristocratic Frondeur on the horizon, the Chevalier de Rohan, was quickly apprehended, tried by a special commission, and executed. All that the magistrates could do was to mutter privately, and in case of trouble, drag their feet. When in 1675 popular revolts broke out in Guyenne and Brittany, the *parle-ments* of Bordeaux and Rennes, though they did not actually support the uprising, were sufficiently compromised to be punished with exile. But as the judges muttered, they also collected their interest payments, purchased their dispensations, and contracted marriage alliances with the older nobility. Any thoughts of further revolutions were completely drowned out by Te Deums for military victories, or by the public shock over Mme. de Brinvilliers, the most brazen poisoner of the age, who was tried and executed by the usual methods. In any event, before he had to press his subjects any further, Louis XIV managed to bring the war to an apparently successful conclusion by 1678.[11]

It was far from the land of Colbert's dreams, but between 1679 and 1685 the king's ministers controlled a political machine that rendered France as submissive as it had ever been. Nowhere did this machine function more smoothly than throughout the legal system. In each high tribunal, there was at least one key official—Achille de Harlay, the *procureur général* in the *parlement* of Paris being the prime example—who could be relied upon to keep his colleagues in line. For their part, the rank and file magistrates were grateful for Louis' carrots and fearful of his stick. The principles of civil law, regulated by the Ordinance of 1667, were hallowed in the law schools, while the proclivities of the criminal law, reinforced by the Ordinance of 1670, went virtually unchallenged. True, there was less and less credulity when it came to accusations of witchcraft, but on the other hand, there was a perennial poisoning panic, which was susceptible to similar criteria of evidence and punishable by the same torments. Following upon the Brinvilliers case was the notorious "affair of the poisons". An anonymous note found in a confessional disclosed a plot against the king and his son. An investigation led in 1679 to a number of arrests, including of the woman La Voisin, and the creation of a special court, all of course in official silence. The suspects, variously tortured, confesed to intrigues, poisonings, and a traffic in potions involving major figures at the court. La Voisin was, with suspicious haste, burned at the stake. After her death, however, three witnesses came forward who implicated none other than Louis' mistress, Mme. de Montespan, not a very suitable candidate for the *question préliminaire*. Colbert thereupon forwarded the evidence to an expert on criminal justice, who suddenly displayed an extraordinary skepticism for the testimony of "scoundrels". It was, however, considered credible enough so that thirty-six persons were consigned to the flames before the *chambre ardente* finished its job. The king was equally well served in his disputes with the papacy. A carefully selected special assembly of the clergy exalted royal authority by issuing the Four Gallican Articles of 1682. When transmitted to the obsequious Harlay for registration, his only objection was that such obvious truths did not require the imprimatur of either the clergy or the *parlement*. He was overruled. Finally, all of France, save for the victims themselves, applauded the intensified persecution of the Huguenots. The role of the *parlements* was to register and enforce a succession of edicts interfering with the family life, the movements, and the property of the Huguenots. This was done enthusiastically. As for the *dragonnades*, the quartering of troops upon the Huguenots in order to bring about their conversions, this was directed by the intendants. Colbert did not live to see the perverse triumph of the machine he had helped to create. It was a smoothly functioning relationship between former antagonists that led to the revocation of the Edict of Nantes in 1685, with its bizarre concluding paragraph. After depriving them of every means of doing so, the revocation left to all Huguenots the perfect right to go on practicing their religion.[12]

In the short run, the revocation made the conservative society of France feel all the more cohesive, permitting it to disregard such unfavorable portents as economic sluggishness and diplomatic isolation. But in the longer run, Louis' trial-and-error vacillations were riding roughshod over the most enduring principles of French law. For the first time in its development, state authority was trampling over paternal authority. By letters or edicts, parents who refused to convert were separated from their children, property of the obdurate or of those who emigrated was sequestered or transferred to more docile members of the family, cadavers of the stubborn were subjected to criminal prosecution. Even though the king, in most cases, professed to be satisfied with pro forma conversions, he nevertheless ended up by interfering more than ever before in the private lives of his subjects. The inner disposition of two girls in Dieppe, of a petty noble in the Boulonnais, or of a doctor in Orléans was now competing with the Monmouth rebellion, the Spanish succession, and the League of Augsburg for his attention. His criminal justice system, which could hardly keep the habitual manifestations of violence under control, now found itself assuming the functions of an inquisition, constantly responding to the complaints of enthusiastic missionaries against their wavering flocks. An entire class of previously law-abiding "new converts" now became objects of suspicion. Others, who refused to conform in any way, were unable to contract legal marriages, and this jeopardized the inheritances of their children. Frustrated by the continuing resistance, Louis in 1688 resolved to banish all obdurate Huguenots from his kingdom and to confiscate their property. This intention was transmitted to the *procureur général* and provides another example of how the high magistracy had learned to beg for scraps. "Since," he wrote apologetically, "the officers are obliged to find a basis for their decisions, I don't think they can consider it a crime for a man to leave the kingdom when he is obliged to do it." The solution? Revoke the ambiguous concluding paragraph. That way simply being a Huguenot would become a crime, and the judges could sequester property with unimpeachable legal logic. And even this display of groveling went for naught amid the adulation of so many indiscriminating sycophants.[13]

The cheering let up a bit after the king embarked an economically declining France into a financially ruinous war against the bulk of Europe. But whatever murmur of discontent began to rise from the masses, it found no support in the disciplined political machine that a new set of ministers, such as Controller-General Pontchartrain, were now directing. It was, rather, Louis who was suddenly gripped by remorse for what he now considered past excesses and who withdrew, out of both conviction and necessity, into an ever more traditional view of society. Pontchartrain, following this lead, actually apologized and castigated himself as he was forced to inaugurate a round of fiscal expedients—creations of offices, *augmentations de gages*, and currency manipulations—that made those of the Fronde pale by comparison. Harlay, now first president of the *parlement* of Paris, would gently chide, suggest a few tactful emendations, and guide the edicts through to registration. From the king's malaise the magistrates regained a modicum of power, although their sensitivities were by no means his prime concern. In 1693, during a critical famine, he restored to his faithful *parlements* much of their traditional role in the regulation of trade and the maintenance of public order. Later that year, on the other hand, in attempting to mend fences with the Holy See, he promised a new pope not to enforce the Four Gallican Articles. The same Harlay who eleven years before had found the articles too axiomatic to legislate was now informed that they had been regrettable "innovations". Still, as the war went on, it was not the magistracy that allied itself with the chorus of discontent, but the high aristocracy. In 1695 the most extreme financial measure of the war, the capitation tax, was registered with patriotic zeal. Later that year, the sensitivities of the legal officials were again sacrificed, this in the most systematic "reform" measure of the later reign, the Ordinance on Ecclesiastical Jurisdiction. Here the chastened and impecunious Louis sought to redress the grievances of the higher clergy. Article 10 prevented judges from licensing preachers, Article 30 ordered the courts to support the clergy in maintaining doctrine, and most significantly, Article 37 discouraged *appels comme d'abus* by slapping a fine on unsuccessful litigants. It is difficult to escape the conclusion that the perquisites of office, the social stability, and the absence of alternatives all combined to make it easier for the magistrates to sympathize with the predicaments of the king.[14]

The chasm between increasing popular cynicism and a largely self-propelled legal system widened during the last fifteen years of the reign. In this period, neither the people nor the government found itself in any position to confront the judiciary. The now Chancellor Pontchartrain made it clear that if the *parlements* would just observe the venerable ordinances, he would support the magistracy to the hilt. Not that he had much choice in the matter, given the financial expedients that the *parlements* proved willing to register throughout the War of the Spanish Succession. Yet he seemed to believe in what he was doing. He was the most accommodating of all the chancellors in explaining the logic of conciliar decisions, and to an overscrupulous *procureur général* who suggested that judges not participate in cases where their sons represented one of the litigants, Pontchartrain enunciated the amazing principle: "It cannot be presumed that a father will believe blindly everything that a son advances . . . besides, this would exclude from the bar all children of judges who aspire to become magistrates". It might have been enough to make poor Cardinal Richelieu roll over in his grave! By these kinds of concessions Louis XIV managed to finance his wars, but what, exactly, he had wrought upon himself became evident shortly before he died. After a lifetime of trying, the one last thing that he wanted to accomplish in his reign was to get rid of the Jansenists. The measure of his frustration was that, in spite of his previous battles, he was prepared to place himself entirely in the hands of the papacy in order to do it. The result was the bull *Unigenitus*, the greatest step since the Council of Trent toward the doctrine of papal infallibility. From the point of view of the magistrates, its most objectionable feature was the condemnation of the proposition that "even the fear of an unjust excommunication must not prevent us from doing our duty", but the king had obviously concluded that the most pervasive threat to royal authority came from below. Without even resorting to a *lit de justice*, he ordered the *parlement* of Paris to register the bull. Nevertheless, it was the magistrates who got the last word. They registered the bull with so many qualifications as to make it a source of contention and a powerful weapon of parlementary resistance during the subsequent reign. The institution had survived the man![15]

And the society too had survived the king! Still very conservative in its habits, it nevertheless experienced after his death a wave of reaction against the paternalistic tyranny he had come to symbolize. There was new sympathy for the rights of youth, of passion, of irreverence. The eighteenth century being a period of renewed growth, there also emerged new interest groups that did not fit conveniently into a static ideal. Yet the legal system that had emerged from the previous reign took little note of these developments. It displayed no interest in unifying the laws, no inclination to limit paternal authority, no repugnance against the use of torture. The high magistrates were by now fully integrated, indeed leading members of the aristocracy, and what they did display was an uncanny ability to take advantage of the political situation in order to recapture what they had always considered to be their proper role. Their opportunity came with the minority of Louis XV, when Philippe d'Orléans, in order to have himself declared sole regent, restored the *parlements* to their full right of remonstrance. They quickly made use of it in two particular directions. One was in criticizing the government's fiscal policies, where they presented themselves as defenders of the oppressed masses. The other was in opposing the implementation of the bull *Unigenitus*, where they presented themselves as bulwarks of royal authority. In their manner of exercising their right of remonstrance, the magistrates unveiled a spirit of innovation fully in keeping with the inventiveness of their age. They developed the technique of making repeated remonstrances on the same issue. They would go on strike. They proved extremely skillful in mobilizing public opinion. But in the substance of their criticism, they demonstrated that their ideas had not changed very considerably since the days of the Fronde. The judges were quick to object, but they were still unwilling to lead. They could always furnish reasons why any given measure was inconsistent with the traditions of the monarchy, but they would never propose the solution to any problem. They spoke oracularly and confused agitation for adulation. They insisted, in other words, that the monarchy respond to eighteenth-century problems by using mythical pre–seventeenth-century methods.[16]

For all the imperfections of the system bequeathed by Louis XIV, the great jurists, even the reformers, of the eighteenth century considered it superior to anything that had gone before. Montesquieu believed that the privileges of the nobility were essential to a monarchy, that the sale of offices was not improper in it, and that "the trouble, the expenses, and the delays, even the dangers of justice are the price that each citizen pays for his liberty". What he wanted, in keeping with his newfangled principle of separation of powers, was to keep the king's council out of judicial proceedings; in keeping with his reformist spirit, a closer relation between crime and punishment, and in keeping with his humanitarianism, the elimination of torture. But still, he felt that "to reduce all particular customs to a general one would be an inconsiderate thing" and that "French law does not hesitate to intimidate witnesess; on the contrary, reason requires it". This self-satisfied sense of progress, however, was periodically jolted by some of the notorious cases of the midcentury, Calas, Sirven, La Barre, which clearly demonstrated that the magistrates were not keeping up with the "philosophical spirit". Indeed, the most radical rejection of practically every principle upon which the French legal system was based did not come from Voltaire or even from Rousseau, but from Cesare Beccaria in Italy. He it was who hurled a challenge to everything from paternal authority to victimless crimes and, of course, to the death penalty, and he had no greater detractors than among the leading French jurists.[17]

By the second half of the eighteenth century, therefore, the entrenched judges of France found themselves living in a world that had largely passed them by. The magistrates had a fair warning when, in 1770, the disgusted Louis XV swept away their *parlements* with a wave of his hand and instituted a judicial revolution that would have daunted Colbert. Instead, when Louis XVI graciously restored the old order, the magistrates again overestimated their own importance and reverted to their classic obstructionism. A few, like Malesherbes, dabbled in the new

ideas, but for the most part, the secession came from a younger generation of lawyers, who did find Beccaria more palatable than Justinian.
The government itself contributed by avoiding the use of *lettres de cachet*,
by relenting on the persecution of the Huguenots, and by attempting to
eliminate torture. When the Bastille fell on July 14, 1789, the liberators
found only seven prisoners there: two madmen, one reprobate, and four
forgery suspects awaiting trial. But there were countless memories of a
legal system that had resisted change until it was too late and that made
the guillotine seem like an improvement.[18]

NOTES

1. Cicero, *De Legibus* III:iii:8, *Corpus Iuris Civilis, Institutiones* I:ii:6, and *Digesta*
   I:iv:1; Vincenzo Arangio-Ruiz, *Storia del diritto romano* (Naples, 1966); *Lex
   Salica*, ed. Karl Eckhardt, in *Monumenta Germaniae Historica: Legum Sectio I*
   (Hanover, 1902–), IV:2; Ferdinand Lot, *Les Invasions germaniques; la
   pénétration mutuelle du monde barbare et du monde romain* (Paris, 1935).
2. Pierre de Fontaines, *Le Conseil de Pierre de Fontaines* (Paris, 1846); Philippe de
   Beaumanoir, *Coutumes de Beauvais*, ed. Amedée Salmon (Paris, 1899–1900), 2
   vols., Collection de textes pour servir à l'étude et à l'enseignement de
   l'histoire, XXIV, XXX; Louis IX, *Etablissements*, in *Recueil général des anciennes
   lois françaises*, ed. François-André Isambert (Paris, 1822–33), II, 361–643; Jean
   Boutillier, *La Somme rurale* (Bruges, 1479); Ernest Perrot, *Les Cas royaux:
   origine et développement de la théorie au XIIIe et XIVe siècles* (Paris, 1910); Eduard
   Maugis, *Histoire du Parlement de Paris depuis l'avènement des rois Valois à la mort
   d'Henri IV* (Paris, 1913–6), I, chs. 1–6; Françoise Autrand, *La Naissance d'un
   grand corps d'état: les gens du Parlement de Paris: 1345–1454* (Paris, 1981);
   Jean-Baptiste Dubédat, *Histoire du Parlement de Toulouse* (Paris, 1885), I, chs.
   1–3; Charles-Bon-François Boscheron des Portes, *Histoire du Parlement de
   Bordeaux depuis sa création jusqu'à sa suppression; 1451–1790* (Bordeaux, 1877),
   I, ch. 1; Amable Floquet, *Histoire du Parlement de Normandie* (Rouen, 1840–2),
   I, 313–55; Gustave Dupont-Ferrier, *Les Officiers royaux des baillages et
   sénéchaussées et les institutions monarchiques locales en France à la fin du Moyen
   Age* (Paris, 1903); Robert Génestal, *Les Origines de l'appel comme d'abus* (Paris,
   1951); Sarah Hanley, *The Lit de Justice of the Kings of France: Constitutional
   Ideology in Legend, Ritual, and Discourse* (Princeton, 1983), ch. 1.
3. Maugis, I, chs. 7–9; Dubédat, I, chs. 4–30; Boscheron des Portes, I, chs. 2–9;
   Floquet, I, 356–535, II–III, IV, 1–269; Jonathan Dewald, *The Formation of a
   Provincial Nobility: The Magistrates of the Parlement of Rouen: 1499–1610* (Princeton, 1980); Hanley, chs. 2–3; *Concordat avec le pape Léon X* and *Ordonnance sur
   le fait de la justice . . . août 1539*, in *Recueil général des anciennes lois françaises*,
   XII, 75–98, 600–40; Albéric Allard, *Histoire de la justice criminelle au seizième
   siècle* (Ghent, Paris, Leipzig, 1868); John H. Langbein, *Prosecuting Crime in
   the Renaissance: England, Germany, France* (Cambridge, 1974); Frederic Saulnier, *Le Parlement de Bretagne: 1554–1790* (Rennes, 1909), I, xix, ch. 9; Ernest
   Laurain, "Essai sur les présidiaux," *Nouvelle revue historique de droit français et
   étranger* XX (1896), 74–6. The various *Coustumes* began coming out in the
   year 1558, under the editorship of Christofle de Thou et al. See also François
   Olivier-Martin, *Histoire de la coûtume de la prévôte et vicomté de Paris* (Paris,

1922–30), 2 vols. *Ordonnance générale rendue sur les plaintes, doléances, et remontrances des Etats assemblées à Orléans . . . janvier 1560, Ordonnance sur la reforme de la justice . . . fevrier 1566, Ordonnance rendue sur les plaintes et doléances des Etats-Généraux assemblées à Blois en novembre 1576, relativement à la police générale du royaume . . . mai 1579,* in *Recueil général des anciennes lois françaises,* XIV, 63–98, 189–212, 380–463. Noël du Fail, *Oeuvres facétieuses,* ed. J. Assézat (Paris, 1875), I, 224. Compare Pierre Ayrault, *De l'Ordre et instruction judiciaire . . .* (Paris, 1576) with Jean Bodin, *De la Démononamie des sorciers* (Paris, 1580). Robert Mandrou, *Magistrats et sorciers en France au XVII siècle* (Paris, 1968), chs. 1–2; Jean Imbert, *Enchiridion, ou bref recueil du droit éscript gardé et observé en abregé en France* (Paris, 1603); Roland Mousnier, *La Vénalité des offices sous Henri IV et Louis XIII* (Rouen, 1946).

4. Pierre Timbal, "L'Esprit du droit privé au XVIIe siècle," *Dix-septième siècle* LVIII–LIX (1963), 30–9; Mandrou, chs. 4–6; Alfred Soman, "Les Procès de sorcellerie au Parlement de Paris," *Annales E.S.C.* XXXII (1977), 790–814; Dubédat, II, chs. 1–9; Boscheron des Portes, I, chs. 10–12; Floquet, IV, 270–687, V, 1–122; Saulnier, I, xxi–ii; J. Michael Hayden, *France and the Estates-General of 1614* (Cambridge, 1974); Jules Caillet, *De l'Administration en France sous le ministère du Cardinal de Richelieu* (Paris, 1857); Gabriel Hanotaux and Auguste de La Force, *Histoire du Cardinal de Richelieu* (Paris, 1896–1947), 6 vols.; *Ordonnance sur les plaintes des Etats assemblées à Paris en 1614 et de l'Assemblée des Notables réunis à Rouen et à Paris en 1617 et 1626 . . . janvier 1629,* in *Recueil général des anciennes lois françaises,* XVI, 223–343; Mousnier, bks. 2–3.

5. There is no better way to get a sense of the Fronde than to read the *mémoires* of the principal participants, such as Retz, Joly, Montpensier, Motteville, La Rochefoucauld, Lenet, Molé, and Talon. See also Pierre-Adolphe Chéruel, *Histoire de France pendant la minorité de Louis XIV* (Paris, 1879-80), 4 vols; Ernst Kossmann, *La Fronde* (Leiden, 1954), Pierre-Georges Lorris, *La Fronde* (Paris, 1961); Julian Dent, "An Aspect of the Crisis of the Seventeenth Century: The Collapse of the Financial Administration of the French Monarchy," *Economic History Review* XX (1967), 241–56; Philip A. Knachel, *England and the Fronde* (Ithaca, 1967); Lloyd A. Moote, *The Revolt of the Judges: The Parlement of Paris and the Fronde: 1643–1652* (Princeton, 1971); Dubédat, II, 232–77; Boscheron des Portes, II, 1–195; Floquet, V, 123–545; Sal A. Westrich, *The Ormée of Bordeaux: A Revolution during the Fronde* (Baltimore, 1982); Helmut Kötting, *Die Ormée (1651–1653): Gestaltende Kräfte und Personenverdindungen der bordeläiser Fronde* (Münster, 1983), Schriftenreihe der Vereinigung zur Erforschung der neueren Geschichte, XIV; Albert N. Hamscher, *The Parlement of Paris after the Fronde: 1653–1673* (Pittsburgh, 1976); William Beik, *Absolutism and Society in Seventeenth Century France: State Power and Provincial Aristocracy in Languedoc* (Cambridge, 1985).

6. Frantz Funck-Brentano, *Les Lettres de cachet à Paris: étude suivie d'une liste des prisonniers de la Bastille: 1659–1789* (Paris, 1903); Albert N. Hamscher, *The Conseil Privé and the Parlements in the Age of Louis XIV: A Study in French Absolutism* (Philadelphia, 1987). Transactions of the American Philosophical Society, LXVII, pt. 2. Pierre Clément, *La Police sous Louis XIV* (Paris 1866), ch. 1; Jules Lair, *Nicolas Foucquet* (Paris, 1890), II, pts. 5–7; Philippe Sagnac, *La Formation de la société française moderne* (Paris, 1945-6), I, bk. 1.

7. *Mémoire au roi . . . 22 octobre 1664, Avis sur l'annuel, Mémoire sur la reformation*

de la justice . . . *15 mai 1665,* published in *Lettres, instructions et mémoires de Colbert,* ed. Pierre Clément (Paris, 1861–82), VI, 2–5, 247–9, 5–12; Esprit Fléchier, *Mémoires sur les Grands Jours d'Auvergne en 1665,* ed. B. Gonod (Paris, 1844); *Proces-Verbal des conférences tenues devant Louis XIV pour la reformation de la justice, Discours sur le conseil de justice* . . . *10 octobre 1665, Moyens de parvenir à remettre le parlement dans l'éstat où il doit être naturellement* . . . *Octobre 1665,* published in *Lettres* . . . *de Colbert,* VI, 369–91 and 14–7; *Edit portant fixation des prix des offices des cours supérieures* . . . *décembre 1665,* in *Recueil général des anciennes lois françaises,* XVIII, 66–9; Louis XIV, *Mémoires for the Instruction of the Dauphin,* ed. Paul Sonnino (New York, 1970), 116–8, 137.

8. *Procès-Verbal des conférences tenues par ordre du Roy pour l'exécution des articles de l'ordonnance civile du mois d'avril 1667 et de l'ordonnance criminelle du mois d'août 1670* (Paris, 1709); Francis Monnier, *Guillaume de Lamoignon et Colbert: essai sur la législation française au XVIIe siècle* (Paris, 1862); *Ordonnance civile touchant la réformation de la justice* . . . *avril 1667,* in *Recueil général des anciennes lois françaises,* XVIII, 103–80.

9. Floquet, VI, 37–9; Aimé-David Rabinel, *La Tragique aventure de Roux de Marcilly* (Paris, 1969); Georges Mongrédien, *Le Masque de fer* (Paris, 1952), chs. 5–6; *Edit portant règlement général pour les eaux et forêts* . . . *août 1669* and *Ordonnance pour la réformation de la justice faisant la continuation de celle du mois d'avril 1667* . . . *août 1669,* in *Recueil général des anciennes lois françaises,* XVIII, 219–311 and 341–61; Louis XIV, *Mémoires,* 43.

10. *Procés-Verbal des conférences;* Monnier; *Ordonnance criminelle* . . . *août 1670,* in *Recueil général des anciennes lois françaises,* XVIII, 371–423; Edmond Detourbet, *La Procédure criminelle au XVIIe siècle: histoire de l'ordonnance du 28 août 1670, son influence sur les législations qui l'ont suivie et notamment sur celle qui nous régit actuellement* (Paris, 1881). My interpretation differs from that of John H. Langbein, *Torture and the Law of Proof: Europe and England in the Ancien Regime* (Chicago, 1977), 50–5.

11. *Edit portant que les offices de notaires, procureurs, huissiers, sergens et archers seront héréditaires* . . . *23 mars 1672, Lettres patentes portant règlement sur l'enregistrement dans les cours supérieures des édits, déclarations et lettres patentes* . . . *24 février 1673, Declaration pour l'impression sur papier ou timbre royal* . . . *19 mars 1673,* in *Recueil général des anciennes lois françaises,* XIX, 5–8, 70–5, 89–90. The fiscal edicts may be seen in the *Catalogue des livres imprimés de la Bibliothèque Nationale: actes royaux* (Paris, 1910–60), III, 191–207. See also the *Ordonnance du commerce* . . . *mars, 1673,* and the *Règlement pour les dispenses d'âge, de service et de parenté* . . . *30 novembre 1673,* in *Recueil général des anciennes lois françaises,* XIX, 92–107 and 121–2; the *Edit portant création et attribution à tous nos officiers de nos cours et autres de 500,000 livres d'augmentation de gages héréditaires. Verifié en la Chambre des Comptes le 16 février et à la Cour des Aydes le 22 du même mois 1674,* in *Catalogue* . . . *des* . . . *actes royaux,* III, F. 21254 (16); Clément, *Police,* chs. 5–6; Saulnier, I, xxii; John J. Hurt, "The Parlement of Brittany and the Crown: 1665–1675," *French Historical Studies* IV (1966), 411–33; Boscheron des Portes, II, 198–211.

12. Georg Bernhardt Depping, *Correspondence administrative sous le règne de Louis XIV* (Paris, 1850–5), II, 195–6, 214–5, 243–4, 252, 593–5. Compare Augustin Nicolas, *Si la torture est un moyen sûr de vérifier les crimes* (Amsterdam, 1682), with Jean Domat, *Les Loix civiles dans leur ordre naturel* (Paris, 1689–94), 3

vols.; Vincenzo Guizzi, "Il diritto commune in Francia nel XVII secolo: i giuristi alla ricerca di un sistema unitario," *Revue d'histoire de droit— Tijdschrift voor Rechtgeschiedenis* XXXVII (1969), 1–46; and Christian Chêne, *L'Enseignement du droit français en pays du droit écrit: 1679–1793* (Geneva, 1982). See also Clément, *Police,* ch. 7; Mandrou, 484; *Lettres . . . de Colbert,* VI, 67–8, 407–30; Charles Gérin, *Recherches historiques sur l'Assemblée du Clergé de France de 1682* (Paris, 1869), 334–5; Dubédat, II, 313–4; and Floquet, VI, 1–184. The succession of edicts leading up to the revocation may be seen in the *Catalogue . . . des . . . actes royaux,* III, 335–487 passim, and the *Recueil général des anciennes lois françaises,* XIX, 204–534 passim.

13. Sagnac, I, bk. 2; Depping, IV, 384–5, 379, 391–4, 397–8, 402–3, and for the cited passage, 411–2; Claude Rabaud, "Procès à un cadavre en 1686," *Bulletin de la Société d'Histoire du Protestantisme Français* CXV (1969), 356–61.

14. Depping, III, 312, 313; Patrice Berger, "French Administration in the Famine of 1693," *European Studies Review* VIII (1978), 101–127; Gérin, 460–3; Lionel Rothkrug, *Opposition to Louis XIV: The Political and Social Origins of the French Enlightenment* (Princeton, 1965); *Declaration du Roi portant établissement de la capitation . . . 18 janvier 1695,* in Arthur de Boislisle, ed., *Correspondance des controlleurs-généraux des finances avec les intendants des provinces* (Paris, 1874–97), I, 565–74; Stanislas Mitard, *La Crise financière en France à la fin du XVIIe siècle: la première capitation: 1695–1698* (Rennes, 1934); Dubédat, II, 330–1; *Edit portant règlement pour la jurisdiction ecclésiastique . . . avril 1695,* in *Recueil général des anciennes lois françaises,* XIX, 243–57.

15. Depping, II, 302–3, 303–4, for the cited passage, 401–3, 462, 520–1; Charles Frostin, "Le Chancellier de France Louis de Pontchartrain, 'ses' premiers présidents et la discipline des cours souveraines: 1699–1714," *Cahiers d'histoire* XXVII (1982), 9–34; Albert Le Roy, *Le Gallicanisme au XVIIIe siècle: la France et Rome de 1700 à 1715; histoire diplomatique de la bulle Unigenitus jusqu'à la mort de Louis XIV, d'après des documents inédits* (Paris, 1892); Jacques Parguez, *La Bulle Unigenitus et le Jansenisme politique* (Paris, 1936), ch. 1 and appendix, 193–202.

16. Sagnac, II, bk. 1; Franklin Ford, *Robe and Sword: The Regrouping of the French Aristocracy after Louis XIV* (Cambridge, 1953); Francois Bluche, *Les Magistrats du Parlement de Paris au XVIIIe siècle* (Paris, 1960); Paul M. Bondois, "La Torture dans le ressort du Parlement de Paris au XVIIIe siècle," *Annales historiques de la Révolution française* V (1928), 322–37; Jules Flammermont, ed., *Remontrances du Parlement de Paris au XVIIIe siècle* (Paris, 1888), I; Dubédat, II, 229–42; Boscheron des Portes, II, ch. 5; Floquet, VI, 193–211, 251–325; Charles Berriat Saint-Prix, *Des Tribunaux et de la procédure du grand criminel au XVIIIe siècle jusqu'en 1789, avec des recherches sur la question ou torture* (Paris, 1859); Francis Delbeke, *L'Action politique et sociale des avocats au XVIIe siècle, leur part dans la préparation de la Révolution française* (Paris, 1927); Robert Anchel, *Crimes et châtiments au XVIIIe siècle* (Paris, 1933); Julius Ruff, *Crime, Justice and Public Order in Old Regime France: The Sénéchaussées of Libourne and Bazas: 1696–1789* (London, Sydney, Dover, 1984).

17. Charles de Montesquieu, *De l'Esprit des lois* (Geneva, 1748), bk. 5, chs., 9, 11, and for the first cited passage, bk. 6, ch. 2. See also chs. 6, 16, 17, and for the subsequent cited passages bk. 28, ch. 37, and bk. 39, ch. 11; Delbeke, 143–242; Athanase Coquel, *Jean Calas et sa famille* (Paris, 1928); Marc Chassaigne, *L'Affaire Calas* (Paris, 1928); David Bien, *The Calas Affair* (Princeton,

1961). Compare Cesare Beccaria, *Dei delitti e delle pene* (Leghorn, 1764), with Pierre-François Muyart de Vauglans, *Refutation des principes hasardés dans le traité des délits et des peines* (Paris, 1767).

18. *Declaration concernant l'abolition de la question préparatoire . . . 24 août 1780, Edit en faveur de ceux qui ne font pas profession de la religion catholique . . . nov. 1787, Déclaration relative a l'ordonnance criminelle, 1er mai 1788,* in *Recueil général des anciennes lois françaises,* XXVI, 373–5, XXVIII, 472–82, 526–32; Gerard Aubry, *La Jurisprudence criminelle du Châtelet de Paris sous le règne de Louis XVI* (Paris, 1971); Henri Carré, *La Fin des Parlements* (Paris, 1912); Funck-Brentano, 346, 412, 417.

SIX

The Administrative History of the Reign

JOHN C. RULE

A French royal official in the seventeenth century wrote that wherever the king was, there also was his court, and wherever was his court, there also his council. This observation was literally true until the third decade of that century, when the proportions of the government increased startlingly due to the pressures of civil and international war.[1] The middle years of Louis XIII's reign were rife with unrest precipitated in part by the siege of the Huguenot army in La Rochelle and the contagion of revolts spawned by the siege. During these times of trouble the king travelled continually, and while he was on the march he found that many advisors and officials lingered in Paris or remained but a short time with his entourage. At first he considered such absences as a dereliction of duty and threatened those councillors who were not in attendance on his person with disgrace. Partially to appease him and partially to strengthen his hold on the bureaucracy in Paris, Richelieu increased the number of royal officials, especially those in the department of the secretaries of state and of the superintendants of finance.[2] From that time on, some of these officials attended the king, while others established their residence in the capital.

Like his father, Louis XIV led a peripatetic life. In his youth he moved from Paris to the circle of royal residences that extended in an arc below the capital from Saint-Germain-en-Laye to Versailles and Fontainebleau and far into the valley of the Loire. During the campaigns of the 1650s the young king joined his army near the Flanders border, attended by the chancellor, carrying the seals of France, and by at least two secretaries of state, who were entrusted with the *cachet*, or small seal, whose imprint they attached to the king's communications to his officials. At each of the royal residences the chancellor designated a *salle de conseil d'état du roi*, where the laws were verified in a ceremony known as the Audience of the Seal. From the early 1650s onward, the secretaries of state met in a *conseil des dépêches* where the young Louis, Cardinal

Mazarin, and Anne of Austria listened to reports from the provinces. These meetings of the council of dispatches became one of the means of governing France on a day-to-day basis, but by the end of the reign its importance had waned.[3]

The year 1682 marked a watershed in the history of the king's councils. It was then that he moved his family, court, and councils to Versailles, providing them with a permanent residence. The plans for the palace at Versailles clearly showed that the rooms leading off the Cour Royale were set aside for a *conseil d'état*. They also reveal that a *cabinet de conseil* was built adjacent to Louis' bedroom on the first floor of the palace. It was there that the ministers, a small body of advisors, seldom more than six at any given point in the reign, met two or three times a week to discuss matters of state and to formulate policy. Even more conspicuous to the visitor were the so-called ministerial wings that formed the forecourt of the palace and housed the offices of the secretaries of state and the controller-general of finances. Behind the ministerial wing, to the left as one entered the palace, Hardouin-Mansart, the king's chief architect, constructed a huge apartment building known as the Grand Commun, where rooms were available to the *premier commis* and to other chief officers of the king's household. Down the narrow street from the Grand Commun were located the offices of the *surintendant des bâtiments* (superintendant of buildings). Across the broad avenue from the palace was the vast complex of the royal stables, which also housed a school for pages, a military band, the king's couriers, postal employees, and the governor of the city.[4] As the Duke de Saint-Simon exclaimed:

> [Louis XIV's] constant residence at Versailles caused a continual coming together of officials and persons employed, which kept everything going, got through more business and gave more access to ministers in one day than would have been possible in a fortnight had the court been in Paris. The benefit to his service . . . was incredible. It imposed orderliness on everybody and secured dispatch and facility to affairs.[5]

It was not only in Versailles but also at the satellite palaces that government offices were created for the chancellor and for the heads of departments. At Fontainebleau the forecourts of the palace, as can be seen in a 1682 map,[6] were set aside for the secretaries of state; and even the hermitage of Marly, hidden behind the cascades and hedges of the main palace, included a block of buildings assigned to the secretaries. If Louis was searching for a haven, *sans souci*, he did not find it at Marly.[7] Paris too provided an increasing number of buildings and *hôtels* for bureaucrats. Henri Pussort, the dean of the council of state in the 1680s and 1690s, turned one of the floors of his Paris home into offices for his *commis*, while down the street Louis de Pontchartrain, the controller-general and after 1699 chancellor, converted an entire wing of his residence to a government office. At the nearby Place des Victoires the distinguished genealogist-librarian Clairambault employed a half-dozen clerks to sort out the papers of the marine ministry and at the same time to conduct research for the foreign office. In the nearby Rue Vivienne librarians of the king's library not only had amassed one of the finest collections of books and manuscripts to be found in Europe, but were also compiling an annotated edition of treaties for the use of French diplomats. In the Louvre Louis XIV housed many of the pensioners of the crown, and in the upper reaches of the palace clerks assembled the archives of the foreign ministry. Across the Seine river in the great structure of the Invalides hospital the minister of war had the papers of his department put in order. In a sense Paris and the palaces on its fringe were drawn together, locked in a bureaucratic balance that was unified by the presence of the king.[8]

The councils of the king drew their powers from the concept of *justice retenue*, that is, justice retained in his person and embodying his authority as trustee of the kingdom, as an arbiter between subjects, and as lawgiver. As *seigneur dominant*, or *par dessus*, he held authority over his feudal vassals; as justicier of the realm he could dispense *grâces*, pardons, rights of citizenship, indemnities, and immunities. In his coronation oath, he pledged as follows: "I will command and ordain that all judgments must be based on standards of equity and clemency."[9] Thus as a public person he was the very embodiment of justice; truly he gave it life: *Rex animata lex*.

The act of giving life to royal law was entrusted to the Chancellor of France and to the *conseil d'état*, who oversaw the sealing and verification of the laws. The chancellor was the most important of the great medieval servants of the crown. He was appointed for life and could not be dismissed; if in disgrace, his office was temporarily given to a keeper of the seals. Technically the chancellor could preside over any royal court, could order the registration of royal acts, take the presidency of the Estates-General, recommend the appointment of judges, and, until the mid-seventeenth century, participate in the allotment of taxes among the provinces.

The council that served as the chancellor's highest tribunal was known as the *conseil d'état, privé, des parties, finances et directions*, or in its shortened form as the *conseil d'état, privé et directions*. It met on Mondays to verify new laws in the Audience of the Seal; on Monday afternoon it acted as a court of appeal, assuming the name of *conseil privé*, and Tuesdays it sat in special committees and bureaus.

As the king's lieutenant and deputy the chancellor gave assent and sanction to the laws in what was called the Audience of the Seal, held on Monday morning in the *salle de conseil d'état*. Such a room, as we have seen, existed in most of the major palaces. The chancellor himself sat at one end of a long table, and at the other end of the table was an empty *fauteuil*, or armchair, signifying the symbolic presence of the king. As councillors of state and other dignitaries entered the room they bowed first to the empty chair and then to the chancellor. The king himself attended the session when great ordinances or edicts were proclaimed, such as the major legal reforms of 1667, 1669, and 1670; the maritime code of 1681; and the revocation of the Edict of Nantes in 1685. Routine matters, however, were conducted by the chancellor or his deputy, and the edicts, ordinances, and regulations (often in the form of letters patent) were read by the *grand audiencier*, the official responsible for summarizing and verifying the law. The seal was then affixed, the summary was recorded, and the document was carried in a special case, with silver boxes for the seals, into an adjoining room to be checked for accuracy. Copies were made to be sent to all the sovereign courts of the land, where the *gens du roi*, the king's lawyers, presented it to the judges. Thus was the authority of the king expressed, and thus was the law given life.

The *conseil privé* was also presided over by the chancellor, assisted by *conseillers d'état* and by *maîtres des requêtes*. Wielding important powers, this council adjudicated disputes arising from decisions of lower sovereign courts, redirected cases from one court to another, and could nullify decisions of lower tribunals, including the *parlements*, as it did in the famous Calas case in the eighteenth century. The council also heard appeals from the decisions of provincial intendants, disputes among princes of the blood, peers, and other great aristocrats. Decisions emanating from the council numbered about twenty-six per session and usually took the form of an *arrêt simple*.[10]

The sixteenth century had seen the increasing power not only of the *conseil privé et directions*, but also of the chancellor himself. The apogee of his power came in the first third of the seventeenth century during the long chancellorship of Pierre Séguier (1635–1672). Cardinal Richelieu entrusted Séguier with extremely heavy responsibilites, including the suppression of the *Nu-Pied* revolt in Normandy.[11] After Richelieu's death and during the years of the Fronde, Séguier, by opposing Cardinal Mazarin and the secretaries of state, lost both prestige and power, especially in the field of finances. At the end of the century Michel Le Tellier and Louis de Pontchartrain once more raised the standing of the office, but this was principally in the more narrowly defined areas of book censorship and legal reform.[12]

In the performance of his duties, the chancellor, like the other heads of departments in the seventeenth century, built a bureaucratic network, the Grand Chancellery. This vast edifice was divided into four sections, the first being the chancellor's own *maison*, or official household, which included an inner group of secretaries, *greffiers*, reporters, attorneys-general, sealers of documents, guardians of the burgeoning lists of officeholders, plus a bevy of attendant messengers and ushers: all told a *maison* of some forty-five to fifty members, highly specialized and rather small by comparison with several of the *maisons* of the secretaries of state. The second section of the Grand Chancellery was the bureau of the four *audienciers* of France, who served quarterly. The *audiencier* on duty reported on every document that was sealed in the audience of the seal; he was also responsible for writing letters of justification, a type of official apologia, that could be read before the sovereign courts that were to register the law. The staff of the *audienciers*, several dozens in number, were composed of controllers and notaries. The third group that constituted the Grand Chancellery were a large number of councillor-secretaries, a select few of whom were present at the signing and sealing of the laws. They were very important in the social hierarchy of the old regime because their office carried hereditary nobility, and due to the inflation of honors their number had risen from 200 in the late sixteenth century to 506 in 1657. Louis XIV managed to reduce their number to 296, but the exigencies of wartime finance caused it to rise to 340 by 1715. The final group to be embraced within the Grand Chancellery were lawyers who drew up the briefs to be presented to a high court of the *conseil privé* known as the *conseil des parties*. A few of these lawyers could be present at the hearings but could not take part in the discussion. Their number was limited to two hundred, and their title of *avocat du roi* is rather like that of a queen's counsel in Great Britain today. Withal, the Grand Chancellery boasted more than six hundred members by the beginning of Louis XV's reign.[13]

Two bodies—more like colleges—that assisted the chancellor and the *conseil privé et directions*, but were not considered part of the Grand Chancellery, were the councillors of state and the masters of requests. Of these two groups the *maîtres des requêtes* were more potent politically and undertook more varied and flexible tasks for the crown. The mastership, highly prized by aspiring civil servants, often led to such prestigious offices as commissioners on leave from the council—better known in the provinces as royal intendants of justice, finance, and police—as envoys to foreign courts, and as special commissioners. They were present at many of the king's councils as legal advisors: a few were always in attendance on the chancellor at the Audience of the Seal and meetings of the Council of Dispatches and the Royal Council of Finances. In addition to their administrative duties the masters fulfilled judicial functions. At least a quarter of their body, when resident in Paris, sat as a court of appeal and were allotted their own space within the quarters of the *parlement* of Paris on the Ile de la Cité. In the 1650s the judges of the *parlement*, jealous of the masters' prerogatives, tried to expel them from their situation on the Ile. The expulsion was prevented by a royal command countersigned by Cardinal Mazarin.[14]

The masters formed their own corporation, with *avocats* and *greffiers*, to hear appeals of royal officials and of others holding the right of *committimus* to the grand seal, which meant that officers of the crown could appeal from any lower court to the judgment of the king's own lawyers resident in his *hôtel*. These officials were thus given immunity from prosecution in provincial courts. The masters themselves, when traveling in the provinces on the king's service, could invoke the right of *committimus*; they could also claim the right to preside over any royal tribunal at a level below that of a *parlement*; and they could summon such inferior courts to hear cases of interest to the king. For these reasons masters were often employed as provincial and army intendants in the seventeenth century. The office of Master of Requests was so cherished that the purchase price rose dizzyingly. For example Chancellor Boucherat, when a young man, purchased his charge for one hundred eighty-six thousand *livres* and sold it thirty years later for three hundred twenty thousand. Although the number of masters of requests varied during the seventeenth century, it grew to ninety members in 1689, a fact that represented not so much an inflation of honors as a need for their services.[15]

The second great body attached to the *conseil privé*, but not part of the Grand Chancellery, was the college of the councillors of state. Although the term councillor was used indiscriminately in the old regime, the official title, *Conseiller d'Etat du Roi*, referred to one of some thirty-six eminent statesmen and distinguished lawyers attached for life to the king's council. Of these thirty-six, three represented the clergy and three the sword; the rest were members of the robe or senior officials. The dean of the councillors, a post attained by seniority, stood close to the chancellor in honors and responsibilities and shared the supervision of several of the most important councils in the Grand Chancellery.

Councillors were often named to embassies and served as plenipotentiaries to peace congresses. They also sat on the bureaus and councils attached to the *conseil privé*. The councillors of state were considered the most distinguished of the Grand Functionnaires, and the list of their names read like an honor roll. From the *Mémoire généalogique*, compiled circa 1709, one reads the names of such eminent statesmen and councillors as Nicolas de La Reynie, former lieutenant-general of the Paris police; Amelot de Gournay, ambassador to Spain from 1705 to 1709; Achille de Harlay, first president of the *parlement* of Paris; Charles-Maurice Le Tellier, Archbishop of Rheims, son of a Chancellor of France, and brother of a famous minister; Jean Phélypeaux, brother of another chancellor and a former intendant of Paris. Among the councillors there seems to be a balance not only between masters of requests and men of *parlement*, but also among the great ministerial families. Withal the councillorships were one of the most prestigious and most highly sought-after posts under the old regime.[16]

The chancellor's authority was kept alive not only by his concern with the censorship of books and the initiation of legal reforms but by the founding of new bureaus and councils. By *arrêts* (executive decrees) of the council of dispatches for 1676 and 1679 the Bureau of the Posts was founded as the highest tribunal for the postal system. From the 1670s to 1721 two extremely active Superintendants of the Posts, the Marquisses de Louvois and de Torcy, expanded the competence of the local post offices and extended the system of roads and of royal messengers. Complaints arising from misuse of franking privileges, embezzlements, and general abuse of authority were presented to the postal bureau, which arbitrated cases and sent recommendations to the superintendant. Another bureau that increased its authority was the *conseil de chancellerie*, not to be confused with the chancellor's own *maison*. It reviewed cases concerning the abuse of the book trade and management of the royal printing office, and, in general, served as a watchdog for the licensing of books that were to carry the royal imprimatur. Chancellor Pontchartrain's nephew, Abbé Bignon, was the official most closely associated with the supervision of this office from the 1690s to the end of Louis XIV's reign. In addition, the council of commerce[17] functioned as an advisory board to the government; and though it did not actually possess lawmaking powers, it did have the right to draw up model decrees for the king's council.

Like the Bureau of the Posts and the *conseil de chancellerie*, another new council, the council of prizes, sprang up from the needs of the times. The officials on this board considered the disposition of prize ships seized during wartime under the seal of letters of marque. Technically the Admiral of France held jurisdiction over prize ships brought into French ports; but the young Count de Toulouse, Louis XIV's legitimized son, was a minor until late during the War of the League of Augsburg, and his authority was exercised by the secretary of state for the navy, who brought many of the cases before his colleagues on the council of dispatches. By late 1694 a refurbished *conseil des prises* was established. The secretary of state and admiral shared authority and were aided in their decisions by the councillors of state and the masters of requests.[18]

If the scope of the chancellor's competence was narrowed and consolidated, that of the secretaries of state was truly that of an *omnia homo*, a man for all seasons. A succinct description of his role was given in April 1700, when written instructions were sent to Phélypeaux de La Vrillière at the time he was granted his charge as secretary in succession to his father. "The secretary," according to the document, "shall read, expedite, and sign all documents leaving his office, those being, especially, ordinances [to pay], confirmation of commissions and titles, powers to act in the king's name, and all dispatches dependent on his charge."[19] The secretary could also, using the king's *cachet*, order the arrest or release of any person in the kingdom. Chancellor Pontchartrain added, writing to an official in the *parlement* at Aix, a note reminding him that the secretary of state controlled all matters of ordinary administration and justice in his province; it was the secretary who must regulate affairs, commanding in the king's name what was to be done. Thus the secretary of state by the end of Louis XIV's reign blended in his person two Roman law concepts: the first, *publicae respondendi*, "the right of giving written opinions under the seal of office," and the second, *jus honorarium*, the right "to modify, supplement, temper, and explain the will of the prince".[20]

The history of the office of secretary of state in the sixteenth and seventeenth centuries also gives us a clue as to its growing importance. The letters patent of September 1547 refer to secretaries of commandment and finance, who were responsible for "expeditions" and dispatches of state. The historian can distinguish three phases of development following the letters of 1547: the first coming in the late sixteenth century, the second in the 1650s, and the last in the 1690s.[21]

In the late sixteenth century the secretaries of state gained the right of signing *arrêts* of the council. Second, they gave continuity to their office by converting it to property, with the right of inheritance—a secretary-ship costing the enormous sum of three hundred thousand to five hundred thousand *livres*; third, they were to take their oath of office directly from the king.

The second major advance in the fortunes of the secretaries of state occurred at the end of Louis XIII's reign, when a small band of "faithful" followers of Cardinal Mazarin, mainly secretaries of state like Michel Le Tellier and the Briennes, began to function as a committee of correspondence, informing the cardinal of events relating to their own offices like foreign affairs, war, and the royal household or transpiring in the provinces. The secretaries also began meeting in what was called a council of dispatches. In this council they heard reports from the king's commissioners stationed in various posts across the kingdom and from local officials seeking redress of grievances. A reaction to the power of the "faithful" occurred in 1661, when, upon the death of Mazarin, Louis XIV pointedly informed his advisors that they would sign no document with his *cachet* until he had reviewed it.[22]

The last phase of the development of the secretary's office occurred during the years of the two great wars, from 1689 through the Spanish Succession crisis. Louis XIV, despite predictions to the contrary, did not appoint a prime minister. The secretaries of state continued to correspond with the provinces on a regular basis, using the council of dispatches, which met every ten days or so, as their debating society. Pressed by affairs in the provinces, the secretaries increased the size of their bureaucracies; and, as we have seen, their departments were allotted two large wings of the palace at Versailles. By the end of the War of the Spanish Succession, in 1713, the secretaries of state had surpassed in importance the governors of most provinces and shared their authority largely with the controller-general. Little wonder that Chancellor Pontchartrain said that those with concerns about everyday administration—that is, the appointment of officials, the building of hospitals, the disciplining of clergy, the enforcement of the revocation of the Edict of Nantes, the repair of highways, etc.—should write to the secretary and not to him.

Although the management of governmental finances became an overriding concern of the French government by the eighteenth century, its bureaucracy had grown very haphazardly in the preceding two centuries. In the early seventeenth century there was a superintendant, or sometimes there were two, who headed a finance department that included at least two controllers-general and two or three intendants of finance. Gilles de Maupeou was a famous intendant under Sully who helped shape the later development of the department.[23] Cardinal Richelieu appointed two superintendants, Claude Bullion and Claude Bouthillier, whom he referred to as *messieurs des finances*, and he constantly badgered them to raise the revenues desperately needed by a monarchy at war. Although he might speak slightingly of these *messieurs*, he listened to their advice and complaints, which at times were carried to the king's high council. It was under the administration of these two *messieurs* that the superintendants began a systematic coordination of efforts with the private tax farmers, who oversaw the collection of most of the indirect taxes on spirits, tobacco, salt, and sundries.[24]

By the 1640s the new head of the treasury, Particelli d'Emery, a friend and client of the new principal minister, Mazarin, began a systematic levying of assessments in the twenty or so generalities of France, using as his agents commissioners selected from the *conseil du roi*. So hated did these commissioners—often masters of requests—become, local officials demanded their recall at the time of the Fronde. But almost before the orders for their recall could be received, Mazarin decided not only to return them to their posts but even to reinforce their authority.

Mazarin also appointed two superintendants of finance in the 1650s, one of whom was his particular creature, Nicolas Fouquet. Fouquet possessed a lively intellect and was well connected with both the parlementary families and the financiers of Paris and Lyons. As such, he became indispensable to the state. But being no fool, Mazarin put a watchdog on Fouquet: the cardinal's own household intendant, Jean-Baptiste Colbert.[25] Suspicious of Fouquet's financial manipulations, Colbert collected a dossier on the superintendant's malfeasances. At the time of Mazarin's death, in March 1661, the Fouquet scandal was just breaking. The king and the court gossiped about his extravagances, especially the riches displayed in his palace at Vaux-le-Vicomte. The gossips of Paris spoke openly of his shady dealings with the demimonde of financiers and tax collectors; and the watchdog of the treasury, Controller-General Barthélemy Hervart, reported to the king that the superintendant had falsified his accounts. Louis XIV, convinced of Fouquet's wrongdoing, had him arrested in September of 1661 and put on trial.[26]

Fouquet's successor, Colbert, was at once a sincere reformer in the style of Sully and a venal minister in the style of Mazarin.[27] On the one hand he was genuinely interested in lowering the *taille* and relieving the plight of the peasant. He followed a course of vigorous enforcement of the law within the boundaries of royal lands: forests and estates held by the king across France, especially in the provinces of Normandy, Brittany, the Ile de France, and Provence. In order to restore the productivity of the royal estates and to increase revenues, he sent boards of inquiry to local administrative capitals, such as Rennes, Rouen, Châlons, Caen, and Aix-en-Provence. These peripatetic boards, or courts, of inquiry were usually headed by a master of requests, who often remained in the provincial capital to assume the tasks of an intendant.

Colbert had a particular interest in the navy, and under his direction new ports and arsenals were founded, old ones were refurbished, and the mercantile fleet was subsidized by the crown. Like the great cardinals, Colbert was passionately interested in the arts and sciences. His agents pursued books and manuscripts with the same ardor with which intendants hunted counterfeiters and salt smugglers. Paintings were purchased by the dozens rather than singly. These treasures, accumulated largely before the expensive wars of the last two and a half decades of the reign, formed the core of the present collections of the Louvre and Versailles. The scientific community flourished under his patronage.[28] Scholars were housed both at the Louvre and at the newly completed Royal Observatory in Paris. Colbert also extended royal protection to the production of luxury goods: tapestries, rugs, mirrors, fine cloth, and porcelain. Paris as a fashion center gained the reputation it has held until today.

On the other hand, Colbert was as venal as any minister in the seventeenth century: he shamelessly advanced the fortunes of his family, appointing many of his brothers, nephews, and "cousins" to the bureaucracy and to the army and church. For himself he accumulated a huge fortune in books, paintings, palaces, and town houses. His great country estate at Sceaux became, like Vaux-le-Vicomte before it, one of the showplaces of the century.

Colbert, like the minister of war, the Marquis de Louvois,[29] was an organizer *non pareil*. At the nerve center of his bureaucratic empire were the intendants of finance, each with his own area of competence, such as the supervision of the salt tax (the *gabelle*) or the collection of the revenues of the royal estates. The intendants of finance employed their own staffs, and when they attended the king's court they sat on the councils of the *grande* and *petite direction,* or other bureaus that required an agent of the controller-general. During the War of the League of Augsburg (1688–1697) their number increased from three to four, and during the Spanish Succession War from four to six. In effect they were heads of department within an ever enlarging ministry.

In 1661 Colbert had advised the king to revive the *conseil royal des finances* and to suppress the office of superintendent. This council was usually headed by a duke, who took precedence over the other members; but it was the controller-general who guided affairs that were placed before the councillors and the king. By 1710 the royal council had declined in power and prestige. As the Duke de Saint-Simon observed, "almost the entire time was spent by the king in signing bonds and documents, judging private quarrels . . . and hearing appeals regarding prize-money for captured ships". Larger matters were discussed in a weekly meeting of the intendants of finances, and here "everything in the nature of finance, taxes, tariffs, statutes, the levying of new taxes, and increasing those already levied was done by the controller-general [and his intendants and *premier commis*]".[30]

In the provinces Colbert relied on the loyalty and good advice of some thirty provincial intendants, some of whom also served as army intendants. In the early sixteenth century these *commissaires départis* had been charged with missions, which once accomplished triggered an immediate recall to the capital. In 1542 sixteen *chevauchées,* or circuits, were established, and the intendants made annual journeys to investigate the collection of taxes. While riding circuit they visited bureaus of finance, which usually sat in provincial capitals. At the bureaus they consulted the chief officers, the *trésoriers de France,* about the taxes that were to be levied for the next year. While traveling from town to town the intendants met with the *élus,* local tax officials, to investigate irregularities in taxation collection. But this annual visit—too often biennial—seldom allowed for extensive investigations.

In the 1630s and 1640s circumstances changed. France's participation in the Thirty Years' War sparked a crisis of enormous proportions. The central government needed revenues at once. Cardinal Richelieu reluctantly, because he did not want the intendants to become entrenched in their power, sent them out with increasing regularity. The intendants' duties became increasingly varied: they raised troops, requisitioned food and munitions, tried cases of mutiny and tax evasion. In collecting taxes they ordered several of the *trésoriers de France* to accompany them and on their travels added two or three *élus* as time and place demanded. In other words the central government intervened in local affairs more openly than ever before. Little wonder that at the time of the Fronde local officials, often urged on by the treasurers of France, demanded the intendants' recall. Mazarin, however, returned them to their posts, and Louis XIV and his ministers found them useful instruments of policy. Neither the Sun King nor his ministers displayed Richelieu's reluctance to have them settle in an area for several years at a time. By the 1670s the royal intendant had become a fixture in the provinces, and his power over justice, finance, and general administration, though limited by distance from Paris and Versailles and by the dilatory tactics of the local officials, became a recognized and important part of local life.[31]

At the pinnacle of the conciliar system of government was the *conseil d'en haut,* or high council, variously referred to as the *conseil étroit,* or restricted council, council of ministers, or secret council. In Henri IV's time the king had limited the membership of this council to his closest confidants, disregarding rank and traditional rights altogether. During Marie de Medici's regency the council increased in numbers, including princes of the blood, members of the armed forces, and several of the great officials of the crown. When Cardinal Richelieu imposed his will as principal minister after 1630, he shaped a more malleable and disciplined group by excluding all those who were not his "creatures", including the military and the princes of blood. Instead he relied on the superintendant of finance, the war minister, the chancellor, and Father Joseph, his advisor on foreign affairs. During the regency of Anne of Austria the council was broadened again to include princes, great lords, generals, and the chief civil servants, plus a prime minister (Cardinal Mazarin) and his associates. So unwieldy did this group become that Mazarin formed a shadow cabinet, including several secretaries of state and the superintendants of finance. This makeshift arrangement was falling apart at the time of Mazarin's death. But Louis XIV, following the example of his mentor, announced in 1661 that he too intended to maintain a "narrowed" council. Henceforth, only those who were summoned by his ushers each day might enter his council and have the right to be called ministers. Both Marshal de Turenne and Chancellor Séguier were generally excluded, as were the king's mother and brother. Thus, the high council remained small until Louis' death. The exclusion of the clergy, the military, the great officials, and the king's family has been termed the "ministerial revolution" of 1661.

Thus, we see that by the years from 1690 to 1715 there developed within the central government of France a delicate balance, or equilibrium, among three great agencies: the chancellery, which was responsible for the administration of justice and for legal reform; the controller-general of finance and his six intendants of finance and their agents, who were responsible for raising revenues and for reforming taxes; and the four secretaries of state and their bureaus, who were responsible for the general administration of the provinces, including police action. These three large grouping governed France in the king's name, drawing their powers from his legitimate power inherent in his public person.

There was no grand design that underlay the emergence of this tripartite division of powers. Instead, it seems that this form of government evolved over a fifty-year period, beginning with the reforms of the 1650s and 1661, culminating in the changes in the ministry of the mid-1690s. Interestingly, the three groupings of political power seldom vied with one another to frustrate administrative action or to block judicial or financial reform. For better than fifteen years the chancellor, the controller-general, and the secretaries of state cooperated with one another in an alliance that was unhappily shattered in the eighteenth century.

NOTES

1. For amplifications on the terms used in this essay the reader may wish to consult two venerable but reliable manuals: Marcel Marion, *Dictionnaire des institutions de la France aux XVIIe et XVIIIe siècles* (Paris, 1923); and François Olivier-Martin, *Précis d'histoire du droit français*, 4th ed., rev. (Paris, 1945). A briefer and more recent manual is that of Guy Cabourdin and Georges Viard, *Lexique historique de la France d'ancien règime* (Paris, 1978). For broader, more interpretive accounts of institutional history one can consult an overview by the legal historian François Olivier-Martin, *Histoire du droit français des origines à la Révolution* (Paris, 1951); and two works by Michel Antoine, *Le Conseil du roi sous le règne de Louis XV* (Paris and Geneva, 1970), and *Le Fonds du conseil d'état du roi* (Paris, 1955). See also Roland Mousnier, *Les Institutions de la France sous la monarchie absolue: 1598–1789* (Paris, 1974–80), 2 vols., English edition, *The Institutions of France under the Absolute Monarchy: 1598–1789* (Chicago, 1979–84); and Mousnier et al., *Le Conseil du roi de Louis XII à la Révolution* (Paris, 1970).
2. The best general account of the era of Richelieu and Louis XIII remains Victor L. Tapié, *La France de Louis XIII et Richelieu* (Paris, 1952). The English edition, *France in the Age of Louis XIII and Richelieu* (New York, 1974), adds an extensive survey of the literature. See also Orest Ranum, *Richelieu and the Councillors of Louis XIII* (Oxford, ·1963).
3. For a case study of the workings of the council of dispatches in the 1650s see Ruth Kleinman, "Changing Interpretations of the Edict of Nantes: The Administrative Aspect: 1643–1661," *French Historical Studies* X (1978), 541–71.
4. The most recent and readable histories of the royal palaces are Guy Walton's *Louis XIV's Versailles* (Chicago, 1986); Robert W. Berger, *Versailles: The Château of Louis XIV* (College Park, 1985); and F. Hamilton Hazelhurst, *Gardens of Illusion: The Genius of André Le Nostre* (Nashville, 1980).
5. Quoted in John C. Rule, "Le Roi-Bureaucrate," in *Louis XIV and the Craft of Kingship*, ed. John C. Rule (Columbus, 1970), 42–3.
6. David Thomson, *Renaissance Paris: Architecture and Growth: 1475–1600* (Berkeley and Los Angeles, 1984), 107–8.
7. Jeanne and Alfred Marie, *Marly* (Paris, 1947), 12 ff.
8. Leon Bernard, *The Emerging City: Paris in the Age of Louis XIV* (Durham, 1970); Orest Ranum, *Paris in the Age of Absolutism: An Essay* (New York, 1968); and Roland Mousnier, *Paris au XVIIe siècle* (Paris, 1961).
9. J. H. Shennan, *Government and Society in France: 1461–1661* (London, 1969), 79.
10. Andrew Lossky, "The Absolutism of Louis XIV: Reality or Myth?" *Canadian Journal of History* XIX (April 1984), 7; and Albert N. Hamscher, *The Conseil Privé and the Parlements in the Age of Louis XIV: A Study in French Absolutism* (Philadelphia, 1987), Transactions of the American Philosophical Society, LXVII, pt. 2.

11. Roland Mousnier, *Lettres et mémoires adressés au Chancelier Séguier: 1633–1649* (Paris, 1964), 2 vols. See also Madeleine Foisil, *La Révolte des Nu-Pieds et les révoltes normandes de 1639* (Paris, 1969).
12. John D. Woodbridge, "Censure royale et censure épiscole: le conflit de 1702," *Dix-huitième siècle* VIII (1976), 333–55.
13. See Christine Favre-Lejeune, *Les Secrétaires du roi de la Grande Chancellerie de France: dictionnaire biographique et généalogique: 1672–1789* (Paris, 1986), 2 vols. See also David Bien, "The *secrétaires du roi*: Absolutism, Corps and Privileges under the *ancien règime*," in *Vom ancien règime zur Französischen Revolution: Forschungen und Perspektiven*, ed. Albert Cremer (Göttingen, 1978), 153–68.
14. Inès Murat, *Colbert* (Charlottesville, 1984), 42.
15. Mousnier, 94.
16. Bibliothèque Nationale, *Manuscrit Clairambault* 664, "Mémoires généalogiques sur les familles des personnes qui composent les conseils du roy," fols. 721 ff.
17. Thomas J. Schaeper, *The French Council of Commerce: 1700–1715: A Study of Mercantilism after Colbert* (Columbus, 1983).
18. A. Dumas, "Le conseil des prises sous l'ancien règime," in *Nouvelle revue historique de droit français et étranger* XXIX (1905), especially 350–4; and Geoffrey Symcox, *The Crisis of French Sea Power: 1688–1697: From the Guerre d'Escadre to the Guerre de Course* (The Hague, 1974), especially 76–7.
19. Bibliothèque Nationale, *Manuscrit Français* 21564, fol. 71.
20. Justinian, *The Digest of Roman Law*, ed. C. F. Kolbert (Penguin, 1979), 13, 23.
21. Hélène Michaud, *La Grande Chancellerie et les écritures royales au XVIe siècle* (Paris, 1967), and especially ch. 4, 126–154. Also N. M. Sutherland, *The French Secretaries of State in the Age of Catherine de Medici* (London, 1962).
22. See Richard Bonney, *Political Change in France under Richelieu and Mazarin: 1624–1661* (Oxford, 1978), especially the epilogue.
23. David Buisseret, *Sully and the Growth of Centralized Government in France: 1598–1610* (London, 1968), 2–4.
24. Richard Bonney, *The King's Debts: Finance and Politics: 1589–1661* (Oxford, 1981), especially ch. 4.
25. For the Colbert family, see J. L. Bourgeon, *Les Colberts avant Colbert* (Paris, 1973). And for a recent reappraisal of his career, see Roland Mousnier et al., *Un Nouveau Colbert* (Paris, 1985).
26. Jules Lair, *Nicolas Foucquet* (Paris, 1890), 2 vols.; Georges Bordnove, *Foucquet, coupable ou victime?* (Paris, 1975); and Paul Morand, *Foucquet, ou le soleil offusqué* (Paris, 1973).
27. Daniel Dessert, *Argent, pouvoir et société au grand siècle* (Paris, 1984).
28. Roger Hahn, *The Anatomy of a Scientific Institution: The Paris Academy of Sciences: 1666–1803* (Berkeley and Los Angeles, 1971).
29. André Corvisier, *Louvois* (Paris, 1983).
30. *Historical Memoirs of the Duc de Saint-Simon*, II: 1710–1715, edited and translated by Lucy Norton (London, 1968), 104.
31. Bonney, *Political Change*, pt. 1 and 384–418. See also William Beik, *Absolutism and Society in Seventeenth-Century France: State Power and Provincial Aristocracy in Languedoc* (Cambridge, 1985).

SEVEN

The Army of Louis XIV

RONALD MARTIN

The kings of France loved their army. Henry IV, founder of the Bourbon branch of the dynasty, secured his kingdom and established his reputation in the field. His son Louis XIII loved nothing about court life as much as reviewing the household troops, and he gloried in sharing the hardships of his men, whether besieging La Rochelle or marching across the Alps. Still, the army they bequeathed the third Bourbon warrior-king had more in common with the amalgam of semifeudal levies and foreign peasant mercenaries attended by a few *commissaires des guerres* and provisioned by independent *munitionnaires* typical of sixteenth-century Valois campaigns than with the well-disciplined and neatly tailored regiments fielded by the Marshal de Saxe in the mid-eighteenth century.

Louis XIII went to war against Huguenots, Italian princelings, and finally the Habsburgs in the Thirty Years' War with a force consisting of the elite Maison Militaire du Roi; five infantry regiments evolving from the traditional Gardes Françaises and the old "bands" of Picardy, Piedmont, and Champagne, along with the newer one of Navarre; and a conglomeration of cavalry units organized into regiments between 1635 and 1638. To these he and Cardinal Richelieu added whatever they could afford, especially in the way of foreign mercenaries, and capped off the process by assuming possession of Bernard of Saxe-Weimar's entire ragtag army upon his death in 1639.[1]

With the disappearance of the office of constable (formally in 1627), the king theoretically commanded his own army, but he did so in practice by means of the colonels-general of infantry and cavalry, who, through their control over the sale of army offices, distributed positions at all higher ranks. By the mid-1630s one of the king's four secretaries of state had at least titular authority over some administrative and provisioning matters. Yet, for the most part the armies, recruited from the dregs of society, remained tribute-imposing mobs, living off the unfortunates who happened to dwell in their paths, and disciplined—if at all—by severe beatings or hangings randomly meted out for some extraordinary feat of rapaciousness.[2]

Continuous warfare from 1635 to 1659—the Thirty Years' War, the Fronde, and the lingering struggle with Spain—provided much impetus toward administrative efficiency in the army. The secretaries of state for war during most of this period, François Sublet de Noyers and his successor, Michel Le Tellier, ably seconded the efforts of Cardinals Richelieu and Mazarin to give the king an army fit to implement the Bourbon dynasty's rendezvous with destiny. At times the total number of men under arms reached one hundred fifty thousand, and the worse than hand-to-mouth acquisition of resources certainly encouraged their most careful distribution. There were some bureaucratic improvements, exemplified by the increasingly common appointment of army intendants to oversee the *commissaires des guerres* and the *munitionnaires*, as well as the virtual elimination of the colonel-general of the infantry's role in administration. It was not an abstract state, however, that demanded much from Sublet de Noyers and Le Tellier, but rather flesh-and-blood cardinal-ministers fighting to maintain position for themselves and their entourages.[3]

Le Tellier, who became war secretary in 1643, built on the principles of organization and discipline enunciated in the 1629 Code Michaud, principles that were frequently restated in later regulations and that remained little more than pious hopes. He aimed at uniformity in recruitment, payment, discipline, and effectiveness throughout the royal army. Though his efforts were limited, sporadic, and apparently almost haphazard in implementation, Le Tellier did follow a cautious pattern of administrative construction. He would attempt a tentative solution to a pressing problem, observe its impact upon those affected, and then, if it seemed to be working, issue a permanent regulation applying the solution as generally as possible. He consistently supported the institution of drill and discipline on the Dutch model, with its emphasis on each soldier's or cavalryman's following a set pattern of movements in concert with the entire unit, and by the mid-1650s each company drilled regularly once each week. During the tumultuous years of the Fronde the secretary of war's unswerving loyalty to Cardinal Mazarin earned him the sobriquet of Le Fidel, and the cardinal's victory allowed Le Tellier to create a staff of intendants, *commissaires des guerres,* and other functionaries made up almost entirely of his relatives and clients.[4]

Still, the army Le Tellier presented Louis XIV in 1661 was less a royal force than an amorphous grouping of mercenaries with the artillery functioning as a private enterprise support group. Captains purchased their authority to raise companies and then recruited individual soldiers through the inducement of signup bonuses and a promised regular pay, both reimbursed by the king; companies were grouped into regiments also purchased by their colonels. Both infantry and cavalry companies at full strength numbered around fifty men plus their officers. For tactical maneuvers the infantry operated in battalions of thirteen to seventeen companies, and while a regiment might have between one and three battalions, most had two. Three to six cavalry companies (grouped in threes as squadrons for tactical purposes) made up one regiment. Thus, an "average" infantry regiment might number fifteen hundred men at full complement and a cavalry regiment up to three hundred. In wartime, when campaigns ceased for the winter, most captains disbanded their companies and then reconstituted them the following spring. Also, regiments formed in wartime were often disbanded at the peace. At the conclusion of the Peace of the Pyrenees in 1659, for example, the number of infantry regiments was reduced from 114 to 48, many surviving regiments lost companies, and the total size of the army dropped to around fifty thousand men.[5]

If the army had gathered for a general review in 1661, it would have presented a curious spectacle to modern eyes, even discounting the disparity in numbers between units of the same category. Only a few regiments would have been in any common uniform—the notion of homogeneous dress having just emerged late in the Thirty Years' War—and those uniforms varied from unit to unit, depending on the whim of the colonel. Careful investigation would reveal that many "soldiers" were *passe-volants* (officers' valets and others) just in ranks to delude the inspectors into confirming the exaggerated numbers reported by the captains. The infantry carried pikes and cumbersome matchlock muskets in approximately equal numbers; the increasing effectiveness of firepower had led to this shift from the ratio of three pikemen for every musketeer in Henry IV's day. Horsemen were divided into the favored heavy cavalry, wearing helmet and breastplate, armed with pistols and swords, and the less-imposing light cavalry, wearing at most a breastplate and usually armed with a sword.[6]

This army had a vaguely consistent command structure. Within each company the captain maintained order with at least one lieutenant and an ensign (or cornet in the cavalry) who carried the flag. These officers were selected by the colonel of the regiment, with the theoretical approval of the king. From among the colonels (or *mestres de camp* in the cavalry) the king promoted to the general officer ranks of *maréchal de camp*, lieutenant-general, and to Marshal of France. The Viscount de Turenne served as the single marshal-general, an extraordinary rank granted for extraordinary services. The death in 1661 of the Colonel-General of the Infantry, the Duke d'Epernon, whose son, the Duke de

Candale, had possessed the right of *survivance* to the office but who had predeceased his father, made it easy for the king to abolish this position by assuming its prerogatives himself. When an army took the field it was normally commanded by a marshal, though a prince of the blood who had attained the rank of lieutenant-general could serve in the same capacity without the need for formal promotion.[7]

When taking the field in the mid-seventeenth century French armies usually formed into two lines, with the infantry in the middle of each line and the cavalry on the flanks. The infantry lined up six ranks deep with gaps between each battalion; those of the second line covered the spaces left by the first line, and behind both remained a reserve force of cavalry and infantry. Depending on the terrain, the artillery, usually about one piece per thousand men, would be placed in the gaps left by the infantry. If the army was large enough, each line was divided into a right and left wing, each commanded by a lieutenant-general, while the marshal placed himself in the most advantageous location to observe the field of battle and send instructions to his subordinates. The commander sought as his primary tactical goal to break the enemy line at some point, usually with a cavalry charge, and then penetrate the break with as large a force as possible in order to achieve a decisive victory. The beautiful picture on the battlefield contrasted sharply with the scene when it came to marching and camping, when fierce struggles frequently broke out for the places of honor based on the various pretensions of officers and regiments.[8]

The general European peace in 1661 left Louis XIV with few opportunities to match his grandfather's reputation, and he later noted regretfully, "My youth and the pleasure of leading my armies would have made me wish for a few more external affairs". What the king could do was prepare his forces for the time when his wish could be granted. Almost a century ago Ernest Lavisse observed that the eighteenth-century French army owed its form to three men, Le Tellier; his son François-Michel Le Tellier, Marquis de Louvois, who held the right of *survivance* to his father's secretaryship since 1655; and Louis XIV himself. And, while Le Tellier groomed his son for this high post, the king, three years older than Louvois, played a similar paternalistic role and authorized him to sign documents as secretary of state upon his marriage in 1662 at the age of twenty-one. Over the next five years Louis XIV and Louvois developed and strengthened a partnership in army administration while Le Tellier devoted himself more and more to his broader responsibilities as minister of state. He did not totally withdraw from army affairs, however, until elevated to the position of chancellor in 1677.[9]

Between the king's assumption of direct rule at the death of Cardinal Mazarin in 1661 and the outbreak of the War of Devolution in 1667 little changed in the organization, administration, or effectiveness of the French army, in spite of Louis XIV's later assertions. The restoration of damaged or decayed fortifications and their reprovisioning were the natural consequence of renewed peace. The creation of the infantry Régiment du Roi, which had the king as colonel, Jean Martinet for lieutenant-colonel, and rigid discipline as a life-style, was more an expression of wishful thinking that the officers and men of the rest of the infantry would imitate its practices than an innovation of any sort. Similarly, the stated intention of building up the infantry's effectiveness by granting colonelcies solely to high-ranking nobles and refusing to give positions in the cavalry to those who had not yet served in the infantry had no more impact than Louis XIV's decision to distribute "even the most minor offices in the infantry as well as the cavalry myself". Consequently, in 1666 on the eve of *his* first war and after two years of rebuilding, he could muster only about seventy-two thousand men, less than half the strength of 1659.[10]

Queen Maria Theresa's purported rights to the Spanish Low Countries provided Louis XIV with his longed-for "exterior affairs", and in May of 1667 he launched a three-pronged assault on the poorly protected Spanish territory. During the course of this war, which lasted only one year, the French armies reached a total size of nearly one hundred thirty-four thousand men and, under the command of Marshal de Turenne and the Prince de Condé, did quite well, overrunning most of the Spanish Low Countries as well as the province of Franche-Comté before the king decided to accept the Anglo-Dutch "offer" to end the war. Nevertheless, Louis XIV and Louvois discovered that troops on campaign seldom resembled those on the parade ground. As an apparent consequence, between 1667 and 1671 they initiated a series of changes designed to make the army more responsive to its master's voice.[11]

Going beyond some prior regulations designed to impose consistent discipline, curb desertion, and avoid precedence disputes while marching or camping, the king and his war secretary pushed the process of transformation into high gear. In 1667 they made Martinet inspector-general of all infantry, intending to spread his rigorous attention to drill and discipline in the Régiment du Roi throughout the infantry. Louis and Louvois also worked to bring the cavalry more directly under the king's control, despite the fact that the prestigious Turenne had been colonel-general since 1657. They placed a number of restrictions on his authority to grant cavalry commissions in 1667, the following year assigned the Chevalier de Fourilles a "Martinet" role as inspector-general of the cavalry, and then totally reorganized the service by dissolving regiments into their component companies and regrouping them into new regiments. In 1669 the king and his war secretary created two regiments of dragoons, a hybrid type of unit consisting of mounted infantry armed with carbines (shortened muskets). The dragoons were intended to move swiftly by horse to some critical location on the battlefield, dismount, and then fight as infantry. Even the semi-independent artillery service under its grand master, the Duke de Mazarin, received attention. Mazarin was inveigled into giving up his position in 1669, and Louvois' protégé the Count de Lude ended up in the slot so that the intended integration of artillery with the field armies might begin at least. To further the process in 1671 Louis XIV established the regiment of Fusiliers du Roi, the first complete unit in the French army to be equipped with the new *fusils* (flintlock muskets), and gave it the specific assignment of providing infantry support for artillery in the field.[12]

Even disabled soldiers came within the purview of the organizational reforms. Prior to the 1660s invalids found themselves remanded to the care of various monasteries as one of the orders' obligations in recompense for royal protection. The combination of monastic penury, or stinginess, and soldierly rowdiness, or debauchery, often led to conflicts between the disabled and their nominal guardians. After 1668 the king and war secretary considered alternate means of providing sustenance for those disabled in the royal service, and in 1670 he relieved the monasteries of their unwanted guests in return for annual contributions toward the construction and maintenance of the Hôtel Royal des Invalides. This showcase of Louis' concern for those wounded on his behalf—constructed on the plain of Grenelle just outside Paris and dedicated in 1674—provided both more regular care and much more effective disciplinary supervision over the disabled pensioners.[13]

The most conspicuous aspect in the French monarch's drive to impress upon his soldiers that they were indeed *his soldiers* emerged in 1670 when he decreed that henceforth all troops would be dressed in uniforms paid for and in colors determined by the king. Now the royal household troops were adorned in blue coats, the Swiss units in red, and the remainder in gray. No longer would regiments announce to the world their colonels' wealth and prestige as they marched to battle; rather, they would proclaim the king's glory for all to see.[14]

Drill, inspections, and uniforms all testified to Louis XIV's personal intention to mold an institution worthy of his foreign policy, and his 1666 statement that "I cannot understand how princes who neglect their own affairs can imagine that those to whom they entrust them should take better care of them than they" emphasized his point. Unhappily, the venality of many military offices still complicated the process of putting the most appropriate men in position, and Louis was hardly one to deprive his nobility of their property. Since the 1650s though, Le Tellier had tried to follow the policy that the second-and third-ranked captains in each regiment (the colonel being the first among the captains), who exercised the offices of lieutenant-colonel and major, respectively, be selected not by the colonel—who would generally sell the positions—but by the king, though usually from within the regiment. Louis and Louvois did likewise. The lieutenant-colonel was officially second in command and, with most colonels absent except during a campaign, bore day-to-day command responsibility. The major assisted in handling internal discipline and by 1670 had charge of all instruction in the regiment. It was among these officers that the king and his secretary of war might find potential generals who understood that the army was the king's and not the field commander's. The problem remained, however, that the venal rank of colonel was a prerequisite to becoming a general officer. A skilled captain in humble circumstances could advance no higher than lieutenant-colonel.[15]

Coincidentally, a tactical problem with existing general officer ranks developed as well. While on the march, cavalry or infantry regiments occasionally were grouped into ad hoc brigades, composed of two or three like regiments. Disputes among the regimental colonels over the right to command a brigade frequently enlivened the march. Louis and Louvois resolved both issues with a single measure. In June 1667, they created the rank of cavalry brigadier and followed it up in March of 1668 with infantry brigadiers. The brigadier was the lowest general officer and could command a brigade of either horse or foot, but not a mixed unit. He could be promoted directly from major or lieutenant-colonel without the necessity of purchasing a regiment and becoming a colonel. This was the route to general officer status taken by Martinet and later by Catinat and Vauban, both of whom achieved the rank of marshal. But, remarkably, few others had similar success.[16]

Since disputes over precedence continued to arise between general officers on campaign, the king, before launching another war in 1672, attempted to head off such problems by establishing a rigid table of rank. He, of course, would be commander-in-chief, followed by his brother Philippe, Duke d'Orléans, the Prince de Condé, as first prince of the blood, and then Turenne as the single marshal-general. In accordance with the trend toward seniority rather than social rank, the marshal-general was followed by the marshals of France in order of seniority based on the date of their elevation to the rank of lieutenant-general; next came the lieutenants-general, the *maréchaux de camp*, and finally the new brigadiers. Three of the marshals in an immediate challenge to the table of rank refused to serve as subordinates to Turenne, insisting that all marshals had equal rank. Louis XIV used them as object lessons, exiling them from court and requiring as an act of submission that each perform the functions of lieutenant-general under Turenne for fifteen days. Few officers dared defy the table of rank afterward; by the end of the reign the table and the principle of seniority were established beyond question.[17]

Drill, inspection, uniforms, and a military hierarchy subject to royal discipline—taken as a whole these reforms exemplify the Sun King's approach to his personal reign regardless of the particular arena. The object was not to revolutionize existing institutions, but rather to bring them to their "natural" perfection. Louis XIV would never dream of depriving his loyal nobility their traditional opportunity of a glorious death while sustaining his rights on the field of battle. He would insist, however, that the death be in the place and at the time of his choosing. By the late 1660s the Marquis de Louvois had developed into an effective partner in the royal enterprise. Building on the organizational foundation constructed by his father, the young secretary of war collected a group of relatives and clients who as intendants, *commissaires*, inspectors, and provisioners might enable the army to enforce the king's foreign policy, driving them with particular ruthlessness in the years between the War of Devolution and the Dutch War to create an instrument worthy of his master's satisfaction.[18]

Of all Louvois' subordinates, the engineer Sébastien Le Prestre de Vauban imposed the most visible changes on the French military through his expertise in siege warfare and fortification design. Trained under the *commissaire général des fortifications*, the Chevalier de Clerville, Vauban during the War of Devolution had directed the sieges of Tournai, Douai, and Lille under the personal observation of Louis XIV and his young secretary of war, who both were impressed with his attention to detail and his desire to keep casualties to a minimum. After the war Vauban received the assignment of repairing and modernizing the fortifications of the recently captured places, despite Clerville's intrigues against him. Spending *livres* by the millions, Vauban proceeded to create masterpieces of geometrical symmetry and mechanical perfection, especially at Ath and the new citadel at Lille. He contributed little that was theoretically new in design, generally following the geometric shape common in the mid-seventeenth century, and saved his innovations for sieges against others' fortifications. Still, inspired by Louis and Louvois' personal inspections between 1667 and 1672, he began the ring of fortresses that by the end of the reign were to adorn the frontiers of France as distinctively as the new uniforms clothed the troops. Before his death in 1707 Vauban supervised the construction or rebuilding of some one hundred sixty fortified places as well as the destruction of numerous obsolete or unnecessary ones.[19]

Louis XIV did not wait long to put his reformed army to the test. After four years of diplomatic and military preparations, in 1672 he launched an assault against the Dutch Republic, presumably with the aim of humiliating the upstart merchants who had blocked his goals in 1668 and with the expectation that somehow the Spanish Low Countries would fall into his hands by the conclusion of hostilities. In late 1671 the pace of recruitment—both foreign and domestic—picked up sharply; the following February Louvois computed the strength of the army to be around one hundred twenty thousand, while a Dutch document estimated that it would reach some one hundred sixty thousand by the beginning of the campaign. As the king lost allies and gained enemies during the course of the Dutch War, he was forced to increase the size of his armies repeatedly, and by the Peace of Nijmegen in 1678 his forces had swelled to nearly two hundred eighty thousand men, approximately one hundred sixty-four thousand of whom served in the field—the largest army in Europe since the days of the Roman Empire.[20]

Louis XIV's first *major* war stretched Louvois' administrative abilities to their utmost. The king delighted in starting each campaign with some great feat—usually a siege—before his enemies were ready to enter the field. The secretary of war, therefore, had to have men and supplies ready at an early date each year. This required that as many soldiers as possible be maintained in winter quarters within reasonable marching distance from probable assembly points and that fortresses along likely routes serve as storehouses for food and munitions. Thus emerged the renowned magazine system for which Louvois has often been credited. It should be noted, however, that the French armies seldom received more than fifteen percent of their provisions from established magazines; this would ordinarily supply only the first operations of any campaign. After that the armies would live off the land by imposing "contributions" on the unfortunate towns and villages in their vicinity and by receiving occasional ammunition convoys from France. While the manifest usefulness of dragoons led Louvois and the king to augment their numbers to fourteen regiments (about ten thousand men) by 1678, infantry regiments increasingly were standardized at three battalions each with a ratio of two musketeers for every pikeman (continuing the centurylong decline in the pike). The early entry into each campaign also meant a shortened recruitment period for officers to fill empty places in their units, and despite the secretary of war's energetic attempts to impose order, his correspondence throughout the winter months of the war was filled with complaints from local officials about the seamy tactics of recruiters.[21]

Louis was always concerned about the lives of his soldiers, and all Europe was impressed by Vauban's spectacular use of parallels and zigzag trenches at the siege of Maestricht in 1673, which reduced casualties to a minimum. When the growing coalition of enemies forced the French to go on the strategic defensive, the king and Louvois became receptive to Vauban's suggestion that they concentrate on creating a relatively linear boundary by conquering Spanish citadels interspersed among the French cities along the Spanish Low Countries' frontier. Indeed, the campaigns of 1676 and 1677 focused precisely on this goal and resulted in the acquisition of Condé, Bouchain, Valenciennes, Saint-Omer, and Cambrai. Further accumulation of territory, at the Peace of Nijmegen and later, followed this principle of incorporating solid blocks that could be protected by Vauban's lines of fortifications.[22]

With the return of peace Louis XIV reduced his army to around one hundred thirty-eight thousand men and added only about twenty thousand to it until the outbreak of the Nine Years' War in 1688. Through this decade the king overawed his neighbors and acquired territory by judicial aggrandizement, using special courts of "reunion" created to interpret recent treaties. When the Spanish protested and declared war on France in late 1683, no power came to their support, and they had to conclude a truce the following year. Nevertheless, Louis found a number of other tasks to occupy the time and energy of his soldiers. He put much of the infantry to work on Vauban's lines of fortifications, and in 1684 another thirty infantry regiments were recruited specifically for garrison duty. The king and Louvois sent various cavalry and dragoon regiments to dwell with non-Catholics in heavily Protestant regions of France as an encouragement to these Huguenots to return to the "true" faith. The ensuing 'dragonnades' resulted in thousands of more-or-less genuine conversions, as well as the total breakdown of discipline in the units used for the purpose. Finally, between 1685 and 1688, Louis and Louvois put some twenty thousand soldiers to work in a vain attempt to build an aqueduct from the Eure River to the château of Versailles, malarial fevers in the unhealthily located construction camps causing the deaths of thousands of soldiers who would soon be needed.[23]

While the infantry kept busy during the 1680s building fortifications and aqueducts, for several weeks each year Louvois sent the cavalry (that part not engaged in converting Huguenots) to four or five camps established in open areas near major rivers for instruction and practice. And, not satisfied with the existing officer training program, which simply allowed captains to sign up cadets as recruits in their companies, a process that depended on the ability and willingness of individual captains to educate their cadets, the minister of war persuaded the king in 1682 to create two training companies for cadets at Metz and Tournai. The number of cadet companies grew rapidly and officers were forbidden to sign on any new cadets in the regular units, so that by 1684 there were nine cadet companies training 4,275 aspirants. However, this proto–Saint-Cyr approach proved both expensive and a failure. The clustering of all would-be officers, both infantry and cavalry, brought together boys and men of all ages from a wide variety of social backgrounds. The cadets seldom got along with each other or their instructors and occasionally engaged in duels despite the threat of dire consequences. On one occasion after duelists were spirited across the frontier and safely away from Louis' justice, the company involved was completely disbanded and its cadets dispersed among the others. Following Louvois' death, in 1691, the king stopped accepting new cadets, dissolved the cadet companies entirely in 1694, and returned to the old system of officer training.[24]

When Louis XIV stumbled into the Nine Years' War in 1688 against a hodgepodge of states mostly associated with the League of Augsburg, he was less prepared than he had been for any of his other wars; the infantry was particularly weakened from its construction labors. Yet the impression given Europe was of a dominating force driving decisively and successfully against formidable German fortresses. The well-supplied, uniformly attired troops striking out from a barrier of Vauban citadels seemed unstoppable and stirred one of Louvois' assistants to crow, "The king finds himself in position to name commander of his army whomever he pleases without having to fear anything from the mediocre ability of the man he chooses". Three unsuccessful campaigns in a row—in 1689, 1690, and 1691—would change that assessment dramatically, giving hope to the king's enemies abroad and creating despair at home, a despair that seemed even more fitting with the sudden death of Louvois in mid-July 1691.[25]

From the beginning of this new conflict Louis XIV and his minister of war were conscious that previous resources would not be enough to sustain French armies against the coalition building up around them. In order to supplement the regular process of recruitment, in November 1688, just two months after the war began, the king issued an ordinance creating a militia of a hundred infantry regiments of a single battalion each. Every parish in France was directed to select and equip one man for service. Louis and Louvois intended the militia to replace units currently manning coastal and frontier fortifications, thereby freeing those forces for service in the field. And so long as Louvois remained alive, the militia was restricted to garrison duty. Even with this novel method of raising soldiers, when the war minister died in 1691 the army had grown by little over a hundred thousand from its peacetime strength and stood at two hundred seventy-three thousand—just under the peak attained during the Dutch War.[26]

Louvois' impact on the French army was intertwined with that of the royal master whom he served so ably. Their thirty-year partnership in army administration—characterized more by attention to minute details than by creation of grand designs—had produced the well-supplied forces that appeared so impressive at the start of the Nine Years' War. Still, there are some things for which Louvois was personally responsible. He was very interested in technological improvements that could make the army more effective and expressed great pride in the copper-covered pontoons for the boat bridge used to cross the Rhine in the first campaign of the Dutch War. He encouraged experiments with various ways of producing cannon and gunpowder and urged Vauban to make a prototype of the first practical bayonet in 1687. Over the years he endorsed attempts to reduce the size and weight of artillery carriages and munitions wagons and to improve wheel design—efforts that had considerable success by the 1690s. He consistently exhorted officers to have their men practice firing muskets during training sessions. On the other hand, Louvois strongly resisted the trend to replace matchlock muskets with the lighter and more reliable flintlock type. In 1665 he issued an ordinance confiscating all flintlock muskets, then in 1670 reluctantly permitted their use by four soldiers in each company and the following year armed the infantry regiment assigned to artillery support with flintlocks. It was only after his death that Louis XIV, hearing the Duke de Luxembourg's son tell how French soldiers at the battle of Steinkerque had thrown down their matchlocks and picked up enemy flintlocks, ordered a report on the advisability of totally replacing the obsolete matchlocks, the last of which disappeared from service in 1703 along with the pike.[27]

Since Louvois and his father were secretaries of state for war for almost half a century, the collection of relatives and clients who did their bidding developed into a bureaucracy the form of which varied little until the French Revolution. By 1680 seven distinct offices, each with its own head and staff, carried out the secretary's intentions. As one of the secretaries of state, Louvois had supervision over a number of the royal provinces. In 1673 he and the foreign minister Arnauld de Pomponne had exchanged some of these so that the war secretary received jurisdiction over the provinces along the frontier where most of the fortifications were located. Still, coastal fortifications remained part of Secretary of the Navy Jean-Baptiste Colbert's area, and Vauban, who was *commissaire général des fortifications*, had to serve two masters. In 1690, though, when Colbert's son and successor died, the king placed all construction of fortifications under Louvois as *directeur général*. Accordingly, by the time of his death Louvois had control over virtually all the services necessary to coordinate the king's military affairs.[28]

Louis XIV personally assumed direction of his armies at Louvois' death. He instructed the army commanders to write him directly, and in return the king dictated lengthy letters of instruction, occasionally attaching suggestions written by others. In effect, for the remainder of the reign Louis became his own secretary for war and relegated the titular holder of the office to purely administrative responsibilities. Louvois' son, the twenty-three-year-old Marquis de Barbézieux, was immediately confirmed in his *survivance* to the position, although he lost a number of its functions, most notably control of fortifications, which was placed in the hands of Michel Le Peletier de Souzy, who received orders to report to the king every Saturday. The young secretary energetically launched himself into the tasks left to him and, aided by the staff his father and grandfather had put together, organized the buildup of supplies and the growth of French forces that led to Louis XIV's successful siege of Namur in 1692, Luxembourg's victory at Steinkerque later that year, and the massive 1693 offensives in Flanders and Germany. In fact, by 1693 Barbézieux may have brought French army numerical strength to something slightly under four hundred thousand men, the highest it was to reach during the reign, and the king publicly announced his satisfaction with the young secretary.[29]

Still, royal commendation meant no return to the type of collaborative role enjoyed by his father. Barbézieux seems to have become frustrated by being left to secondary responsibilities and manifested the frustration in an increasingly arrogant attitude toward army officers and less attention toward business. Sometime around 1695 Louis wrote the young secretary's uncle a warning, and Barbézieux settled down to a life of administrative routine with a little quiet debauchery on the side.[30]

When Barbézieux died suddenly, in early 1701, the monarch found himself alone in the midst of preparations designed to ward off the impending War of the Spanish Succession and quickly appointed the controller-general of the finances, Michel de Chamillart, as the new secretary of war. Chamillart had no experience at all with the war administration and, for several years at least, still controlled finances. Not surprisingly, he made few changes in the mechanism passed on by the Le Tellier clan, thus ensuring its further entrenchment by the time he was replaced in 1709 by Daniel Voisin, Louis XIV's last secretary of state for war. Voisin, an experienced administrator, understood the limitations of his post and concentrated on providing the necessary supplies for the king's forces. However, in the final few years of the reign, the aging Louis seems to have turned more of the direction of his armies over to the capable secretary.[31]

What impact, then, did the Sun King have on his army in the more than two decades of his personal administration? Remarkably little, other than a sizable increase in the proportion of general officers, exemplified in the promotions of 1693, 1702, and 1704, and whose excessively elaborate field equipment burdened down the armies' baggage trains. During the War of the Spanish Succession he permitted the new militia, restricted to garrison duty during Louvois' lifetime, to become simply another means of replenishing ranks depleted by casualties and desertion.[32]

The twenty years of warfare that followed Louvois' death were both beneficial and detrimental to the French army. They were beneficial in that the king concentrated on strategy considerations and higher officer selections, intervening in lesser administrative matters rarely and then for the purpose of maintaining established policies. His last three war secretaries introduced few innovations and satisfied themselves by retaining both the personnel and the practices of the earlier years. The earlier reforms thus had the opportunity to become institutionalized. On the other hand, at a time when other countries of Europe were both copying the French army and going beyond it in the evolution of tactics that required more precise drill and more effective discipline, Louis XIV's army remained tied to the pattern developed by Martinet in the 1660s, consistently overrated the importance of cold steel (pike and later bayonet), and failed to appreciate that of firepower on the field of battle.[33]

When the armies of Louis XV marched off to battle in the War of the Austrian Succession, they made a marvelous sight to behold—far different from the ragged and tattered levies of Louis XIII. The beautiful uniformity in dress and equipment owed much to the intermediate reign. At the same time, their tendency to plunder and pillage at the first opportunity illustrated an unwanted continuity through the Bourbon period. Finally, the overnumerous, contentious, and often incompetent general officers, as well as the armies' tactical ineffectiveness on the battlefield, reflected the rigidity that had set in during the latter years of the Sun King. It was, however, hardly imputable to Louis XIV if French armies in the eighteenth century did not always march to victory.[34]

NOTES

1. Despite recent specialized studies in a few areas, the nineteenth-century generalizations remain the point of departure for any inquiry into French army institutions, beginning with Xavier Audouin, *Histoire de l'administration de la guerre* (Paris, 1811), 4 vols.; and F. Sicard, *Histoire des institutions militaires des Français* (Paris, 1831), 5 vols. For the origins and evolution of specific units, Louis Susane, *Histoire de l'ancienne infanterie française* (Paris, 1849–53), 8 vols.; and Louis Susane, *Histoire de la cavalerie française* (Paris, 1874), 3 vols.; as well as Victor Belhomme, *Histoire de l'infanterie en France* (Paris, 1893–1902), 5 vols. Camille Rousset, *Histoire de Louvois et de son administration politique et militaire* (Paris, 1861–3), 4 vols.; Louis André, *Michel le Tellier et l'organisation de l'armée monarchique* (Paris, 1906); and the same author's *Michel le Tellier et Louvois* (Paris, 1942) serve as the foundation for André Corvisier, *Louvois* (Paris, 1983). For the development of seventeenth-century military administration, Douglas Clark Baxter, *Servants of the Sword: French Intendants of the Army: 1630–70* (Urbana, 1976), is essential, and for the end of the century much can be extracted (with difficulty) from André Corvisier, *L'Armée française de la fin du XVIIe siècle au ministère de Choiseul: le soldat* (Paris, 1964), 2 vols.
2. Jules Caillet, *De l'Administration en France sous le ministère du Cardinal de Richelieu* (Paris, 1857), 362–3.
3. Baxter, 60–138; Caillet, 378–9; John A. Lynn, "The Growth of the French Army during the Seventeenth Century," *Armed Forces and Society* VI (1980), 574–5; and André, *Le Tellier et l'organisation*, 655–6.
4. Eugene Carrias, *La Pensée militaire française* (Paris 1960), 113–9; John A. Lynn, "Tactical Evolution in the French Army, 1560–1660," *French Historical Studies* XIV, No. 2 (1985), 188–90; and André, *Le Tellier et Louvois*, 42–52.
5. Ernest Lavisse, *Histoire de France depuis les origines jusqu'à la Révolution*, (Paris, 1903–11), VII, pt. II, 230–6; André, *Le Tellier et Louvois*, 314; and Henri Pichat, "Les armées de Louis XIV en 1674," *Revue d'histoire rédigée à l'Etat-Major de l'Armée* XXXVII and XXXVIII, Nos. 109–13 (1910), especially XXXVII, 180.
6. Lavisse, 231; Susane, *Histoire de l'ancienne infanterie*, 225; and Lynn, "Tactical Evolution," 179.
7. André, *Le Tellier et Louvois*, 317–27; and Lavisse, 233.
8. Lynn, "Tactical Evolution," 181, 186–7; Carrias, 122–3, 144; and Rousset, I, 233–4.
9. Louis XIV, *Mémoires for the Instruction of the Dauphin*, ed. Paul Sonnino (New York, 1970), 28; Lavisse, 232; and Carrias, 140.
10. Louis XIV, *Mémoires*, 53; Rousset, I, 206; Louis XIV, *Mémoires*, 126, 151; and Rousset, I, 97.
11. John B. Wolf, *Louis XIV* (New York, 1968), 200–3; and Lynn, "Growth of the French Army," 575–6.

12. André, *Le Tellier et Louvois*, 321, 339–41; Susane, *Histoire de l'ancienne infanterie*, 236–40; Rousset, I, 207, 224; and Lavisse, 242.
13. Rousset, I, 252–3.
14. Susane, *Histoire de l'ancienne infanterie*, 238; and Lavisse, 241–2.
15. Louis XIV, *Mémoires*, 151; André, *Le Tellier et Louvois*, 322–3; and Susane, *Histoire de l'ancienne infanterie*, 241.
16. Léon Hennet, *Notices historiques sur l'Etat-Major Général* (Paris, 1892), 149.
17. Léon Hennet, *Regards en arrière: études d'histoire militaire sur le XVIIIe siècle: l'Etat-Major* (Paris, 1911), 195–251.
18. Rousset, I, 163–255.
19. Ibid., 274–5; and Christopher Duffy, *The Fortress in the Age of Vauban and Frederick the Great: 1660–1789* (London, 1985), 71–97.
20. Bibliothèque du Ministère de la Guerre, *Ms.* 181 (*Tiroirs de Louis XIV*), fols. 76–82; Algemeen Rijksarchief, Staten Generaal 6785; Lynn, "Growth of the French Army," 576; and Pichat, XXXVII, 378.
21. Pichat, XXXVIII, 180–1; John Childs, *Armies and Warfare in Europe: 1648–1789* (Manchester, 1982), 158–9; Rousset, I, 222–5, and II, 478–9; and André, *Le Tellier et Louvois*, 330–5.
22. Henry Guerlac, "Vauban: The Impact of Science on War," *Makers of Modern Strategy: Military Thought from Machiavelli to Hitler*, ed. Edward Mead Earle (Princeton, 1943; repr. 1971), 39–47.
23. Lynn, "Growth of the French Army," 576; Susane, *Histoire de l'ancienne infanterie*, 246; and Childs, 190–7.
24. Rousset, III, 332; André, *Le Tellier et Louvois*, 325; Carrias, 143; and Rousset, III, 302–14.
25. Chamlay to Louvois, November 9, 1688, quoted in Rousset, IV, 162.
26. Susane, *Histoire de l'ancienne infanterie*, 248; and Lynn, "Growth of the French Army," 576.
27. Rousset, III, 328; Pichat, XXXVII, 366–8; Rousset, I, 190–1, and III, 330–1.
28. Rousset, III, 323, note 2; Lavisse, 244; and Carrias, 141.
29. Wolf, 464; Lynn, "Growth of the French Army," 576; and Philippe de Dangeau, *Journal du Marquis de Dangeau* (Paris, 1854–60), IV, 85–6.
30. Wolf, 464, note 2.
31. Claude C. Sturgill, *Claude Le Blanc: Civil Servant of the King* (Gainesville, 1975), 42; and Wolf, 561 and 580.
32. Pichat, XXXVII, 377–9; and Georges Girard, *Le Service militaire en France à la fin du règne de Louis XIV* (Paris, 1976), 113.
33. Childs, 69–70; and David Chandler, *The Art of Warfare in the Age of Marlborough* (London, 1976), 113.
34. Léon Mention, *L'Armée de l'ancien régime* (Paris, n.d.), 8; and Childs, 70.

EIGHT

The Navy of Louis XIV

GEOFFREY W. SYMCOX

In the French monarchy, the army was the senior service. True, the rudiments of a naval administration existed in the local admiralties created during the Middle Ages, loosely subordinate to the Admiral of France. At times, powerful naval forces were assembled; in the early sixteenth century Francis I had waged an effective maritime war against Spain. But the navy did not exist as a permanent arm of state policy. Francis I was largely dependent on the ships he could commandeer from the merchants of the great ports, on privateers, or on contingents of warships hired from maritime *condottieri* like Andrea Doria. And after this burst of activity the makeshift fleet withered away in the chaos of the Wars of Religion. Sully's dreams of maritime power likewise succumbed to the civil strife of the early seventeenth century. Throughout this period, although some of the elements of a navy existed, they were not combined into a single whole; there were no arsenals, no standing force of warships, no administrative structure, no chain of command placing the service under the authority of the central government. The French navy did not take shape until first Richelieu and then Colbert created the ships, the bases and the administration, and recruited the manpower to form a permanent fighting service.[1]

In part the development of a navy was delayed by political factors: a naval establishment had to wait until the state had evolved strong central institutions. But the process was also conditioned by the evolution of naval weaponry and tactics. The sailing warship did not emerge as a distinct type until the middle decades of the seventeenth century: the first example of the new warship built in France was Richelieu's magnificent *La Couronne* of 1638, but she had few successors until Colbert began intensive warship construction in the 1660s. Through the seventeenth century a slow but inexorable "naval arms race" developed, led at first by the English and Dutch, with France entering as a serious contender during Louis XIV's reign. The old type of warship in use in the early seventeenth century, still part merchantman, was gradually superseded by the specialized man-of-war, designed purely for combat.

Galleys were relegated to a secondary role, even in their classical homeland, the Mediterranean; although still valuable for coastal patrols and amphibious operations, they were no match for the guns of even a small sailing warship. In the middle decades of the seventeenth century the system of line-of-battle tactics was developed as the best way of coordinating a fleet's broadsides, so that naval tactics became an artillery duel between lines of warships sailing parallel courses. The old tactic of boarding was used less and less frequently, for the gun had now become the arbiter of battle. Meanwhile, naval strategy was evolving too. The concentration of force represented by a battle fleet of ships of the line opened the way for a new conception of grand maritime strategy, so that the ancient idea of "mastery of the sea" was expanded to a global scale. Traditional notions of naval warfare as primarily commerce destruction and coastal raiding, which were deeply rooted in French strategic thinking, were supplemented—though never superseded—by visions of a grand fleet powerful enough to sweep all opposition from the seas and establish a worldwide maritime empire, visions inherited from the Iberian empire builders of the previous century, and naturally acclimatized in England or Holland. These visions were repeatedly shattered by the technical deficiencies inseparable from the conditions of the time. Fleets did not put out to sea on schedule, crews fell sick in droves, ammunition ran out, wind and tide were often unfriendly. Nevertheless, this grand design for seaborne empire lay behind Richelieu's and Colbert's efforts to endow France with a navy.

The immediate object of Richelieu's naval policy was to defeat Spain in the Thirty Years' War. In this he achieved considerable success, although the decisive blows that shattered Spanish sea power were delivered by the Dutch, France's allies, rather than by Richelieu's fledgling navy. But Richelieu had a further aim: his fleet was to form the spearhead in the battle for seaborne trade and empire, "to uphold" as he put it "the dignity of our crown abroad".[2] To this end he took over the powers of the Admiral of France and assumed the title of "Grand Master and Superintendant of Navigation and Commerce", so that for the first time naval and commercial policies were unified and brought under direct state control. Richelieu was sketching out a mercantilist strategy, which Colbert would implement with greater success a generation later. The cardinal busied himself with projects for colonization and founded state trading companies—notably one rejoicing in the grandiloquent (and untranslatable) title La Compagnie sous l'Invocation de la Nacelle de St. Pierre Fleurdelysée. He founded a new base for Atlantic operations (which now took on far greater strategic importance) at Brouage in his native Poitou. He enlarged the arsenal at Toulon to accommodate the

Mediterranean fleet. He built ships and found crews for them; his neophyte officer corps learned its trade in the rude school of combat. But after his death the navy declined precipitously; his efforts were undone by the Fronde and by years of financial neglect.

When Colbert took charge of the navy in 1661, he could draw on Richelieu's example and follow the precedents he had set, but the task of building the navy from almost nothing had to begin again. In a memorandum of 1663, drafted for Louis XIV, he summed up the situation. After noting that French trade had almost ceased for lack of a fleet to support it, he went on:

> for more than ten years no more than two or three French warships have put to sea; all the naval magazines are completely empty; the total number of vessels is reduced to twenty or twenty-two, several of which are no longer fit for service, having rotted in port for lack of maintenance; the captains are inexperienced because of the long cessation of operations; the best sailors, and many others, have taken service abroad, finding no work in France.[3]

Even when we discount Colbert's natural tendency to exaggerate the chaos he found on taking office, the picture is genuinely dismal. In 1663 he had already started to rebuild the fleet and its bases, but before he could carry through the far-reaching reforms he had in mind, he needed to secure undisputed control over every aspect of naval and commercial affairs. When he took office, authority was shared between several secretaries of state—of whom Colbert was only one—and the titular Admiral of France, who was the ex-Frondeur Duke de Beaufort. It took years of patient bureaucratic maneuvering on Colbert's part before the other secretaries could be made to relinquish their naval attributions, and only in 1669, with the providential demise of Beaufort at the siege of Candia, did he bring the entire gamut of naval affairs under his own control.

Here a word should perhaps be said about Louis XIV's role in the development of French naval power. The king took a polite, if somewhat distant, interest in naval matters, but he never favored the fleet with the same passion that he displayed for his land forces. He appears to have visited a naval arsenal only once; otherwise his practical experience was limited to watching the evolutions performed by the model warships that Colbert thoughtfully provided to decorate the canals of Versailles. But it would still be unfair to argue, as some historians do, that Louis XIV was hostile to the navy. He supported Colbert's vigorous program of naval expansion and was gratified by the fleet's victories. Nevertheless, it seems clear that the king's attitude to maritime power— a view shared by Colbert himself, as his policy during the Dutch War would demonstrate—was that although the fleet might be a desirable instrument of policy, it was only a luxury when compared with France's primary requirement for a strong army. This view was hardly the outcome of caprice or ignorance, for France was a continental power with long land frontiers menaced by invasion. So during the years of relative financial stability prior to the Nine Years' War, Louis XIV backed Colbert and his successors in their drive to turn France into a great naval power. But in the 1690s, when the cost of maritime greatness became more than the state's overburdened treasury could afford, Louis was forced to cut the naval budget and concentrate whatever money was available on the land war.

Throughout his career as secretary for the navy, Colbert seems to have retained his master's confidence, the essential condition for success. Royal favor encouraged him to regard the secretaryship as a kind of fiefdom vested in himself and his family, so that to a considerable extent his conduct of affairs was motivated by a search for dynastic prestige, just as his rivals the Le Tellier clan advanced their interests through successful management of the bureau of the army. In the classic bureaucratic tradition of the old regime Colbert secured the *survivance* of the secretaryship for his son, the Marquis de Seignelay, in 1676. Seignelay succeeded his father in 1683, but when he died in 1690 his young son was passed over and the dynastic line was broken. Apparently at Louis XIV's insistence the secretaryship of the navy was purchased by Louis Phélypeaux, Count de Pontchartrain, the Controller-General of the Finances, whose family held the office until 1715, and thereafter, with interruptions, for most of the eighteenth century.[4]

Dynasticism at the top was reproduced in structures of clan and clientage pervading the entire naval administration. Colbert and Seignelay, and the Pontchartrains after them, filled the service with men whose careers depended on their favor. Some of these in turn advanced relations or clients of their own and founded administrative dynasties; a good instance is provided by the Bégon family, intendants at Rochefort for several generations.[5] Such a system of private loyalties could pose a serious obstacle to efficiency; incompetents were promoted, and often shielded from the consequences of their failures.[6] But the naval administration (except for the financial bureau of the *trésoriers généraux*) was never based upon venal office holding, so that it was largely free from the built-in inertia characteristic of venality, and though advancement might not have been purely dependent upon merit, it was still probably more accessible to unsupported talent. One obstacle to administrative efficiency remained, however, in the old system of local admiralties, whose multifarious duties included the regulation of fishing and mercantile shipping, and jurisdiction over privateers. These came under the orders of the Admiral of France, and were thus outside the secretary's direct control. Colbert found a temporary solution to this problem by persuading Louis XIV to confer the title of Admiral of France, after the death of the Duke de Beaufort, on one of the king's illegitimate sons, and later on another, but Colbert was unable—if not unwilling—to press for outright abolition of the admiral and the officials dependent on him. Until the titular admiral came of age in 1695, Colbert and the other secretaries discharged his duties, above all presiding over the *conseil des prises* (the supreme prize court) and directing the operations of French privateers. But in the 1690s the admiral's influence began to reassert itself. The navy was feeling the strain of intensive operations and budget cuts, and privateering began to occupy a central role in the war at sea. After 1695 the Count de Toulouse as Admiral of France personally chaired the *conseil des prises* and assumed a growing part in directing policy; in 1704 he commanded the fleet in person at the battle of Velez-Malaga. The importance of the local admiralties rose as the central bureaus of the fleet declined. This administrative dualism, with the possibilities it provided for inefficiency and corruption, thus survived Colbert's centralizing reforms and was to persist through the last century of the old regime.

From the moment he began to direct naval policy in 1661 Colbert mapped out an ambitious program for developing French maritime power that went far beyond Richelieu's original design. The scale of operations was grander, the administration more sophisticated, the logistical services far more extensive. He also created the chartered companies—the East India Company, the Levant Company, and so on—which he hoped would carry French commerce to the four corners of the world, backed by the fleet. For Colbert, the creation of a powerful navy was an infinitely complex problem to be tackled simultaneously on many fronts; there was far more to it than merely building new warships. One especially critical matter was the choice of suitable bases. Richelieu's dockyard at Brouage had silted up; Le Havre and the newly acquired port of Dunkirk could not accommodate ships of any size; Toulon was cramped and its installations inadequate. Colbert sent out agents to survey the entire coastline of France in search of more promising sites. He evidently chose to avoid the main port cities, like Marseilles, Bordeaux, and Saint-Malo, presumably because he did not wish to become embroiled in disputes with their local councils, for municipal autonomy could seriously compromise the efficiency of a naval base. (Until the 1680s, for instance, the council of Toulon alone had the authority to raise or lower the chain that blocked the harbor's mouth.)[7] Dunkirk and Toulon were the only places of consequence that Colbert turned into major arsenals; for the rest, he chose small towns or empty sites where he could plan from the ground up. Lorient on the Atlantic coast was founded as the base for the new East India Company and gradually became a naval arsenal too; not far away Rochefort developed from a waste site into a regularly planned new town centering on the royal dockyard.[8] In the Mediterranean Colbert enlarged the facilities at Toulon; Marseilles remained the base for the galley fleet but was not given any significant naval installations. Rochefort, on which Colbert had pinned great hopes, proved a disappointment; its harbor was too far inland, prone to silting up, and too small to accept large warships. So from the mid-1670s, spurred on by the navy's need for a big Atlantic base from which to fight the Dutch, he began to develop the magnificent natural harbor at Brest, which he had neglected until then. Future lines of growth were now clear: Brest would serve as base for the Atlantic division of the fleet, with Rochefort as a secondary arsenal, while Toulon would accommodate the Mediterranean division. In the 1680s Vauban endowed Dunkirk with elaborate fortifications and docks, making it a valuable point from which to threaten English and Dutch trade, although it could never shelter capital ships. Saint-Malo, the other great privateering port, likewise could not accept large vessels, so that the French fleet never possessed an adequate base in the English Channel closer than Brest, far to the west. This was a grave disadvantage in the wars against Britain and the Dutch Republic that lasted well into the eighteenth century.

At first Colbert was forced to create his new fleet by purchasing vessels from abroad, but he soon initiated a building program that ranks among his most successful achievements as secretary for the navy. This program began just as the implications of the changes in naval tactics were becoming clear, and the line-of-battle system was gaining general acceptance. In fact, the French may even have benefited from entering the naval arms race relatively late: the warships they built were of the most modern type, so that the French fleet was not encumbered by a legacy of obsolete vessels, as the Dutch were. French designers and shipwrights were grouped in *conseils de construction* at the chief ports, under the direction of the naval intendant, and they were encouraged to pay careful attention to the principles of design and to hydrodynamics, which they studied with the most advanced scientific techniques available. The same kind of scientific study was also devoted to problems of navigation, cartography, and ballistics. Colbert deliberately encouraged this pioneering rationalism, which helped French shipbuilders to establish a lead over their English and Dutch rivals with their more rule-of-thumb methods. French warships not only tended to be faster and more maneuverable than their English and Dutch counterparts, they also were larger; by comparison, English and Dutch ships were often cramped and carried too many guns for their size, to the detriment of their sailing qualities. French designers were thus in the forefront of warship design in the later seventeenth century, and a further sign of their inventiveness was provided by the development of the bomb-ketch, conceived by the French engineer Renau d'Elicagaray about 1680, and soon copied by other navies.[9]

Colbert's building program rapidly expanded the French navy, until by about 1680 it had achieved rough parity with the fleets of the maritime powers. To sustain this vast enterprise an entire system of supply and procurement had to be created, almost from nothing. Timber was the first requirement; much was imported, particularly from the Baltic through the factors of Amsterdam, but Colbert strove for self-sufficiency and systematically exploited France's own timber reserves. Hence the Edict of Waters and Forests of 1669, intended to conserve France's resources in order to satisfy the fleet's voracious appetite for timber. In this way a growing proportion of the fleet's needs were met from domestic sources, and in this respect the French were better off than the Dutch, who had to import all their timber, or the English, whose resources were fast running out.[10] Artillery for the fleet, which was mainly cast iron, and the iron fittings used extensively to reinforce the framework of ships' hulls were supplied by a group of specialized contractors, subsidized and protected to develop France's mines and to set up foundries. Supply was never adequate, and the quality of the guns these contractors produced was uneven, but they went a long way to answering the need for the fleet's essential equipment.

Colbert's infrastructure of new bases and logistical services had important effects on French society and on the economy; they should be viewed as part of his wider program of industrial development. The new arsenal cities contributed significantly to the urbanization of French society. Brest grew from a fishing village to a bustling port of fifteen thousand inhabitants between 1670 and 1700.[11] Rochefort became a city of several hundred thousand in the same period; Toulon expanded, and so did Dunkirk. Demand for vast quantities of iron stimulated the growth of metallurgical industries in Limousin, Périgord, the Nivernais, and Dauphiné. Immense tracts of forest land in the Alps, the Pyrenees, and Auvergne were opened up to systematic exploitation. The naval victuallers purchased huge quantities of grain and livestock, often far from the ports, bringing the pressure of market forces into the country-side. Colbert's naval armament program thus contributed to long-term economic change and helped to call forth a group of state entrepreneurs and contractors, some of whom amassed impressive fortunes. The navy was an integral element in Colbert's mercantilist policies, for not only did it serve to open the seas to French trade, but it also stimulated demand and development within the French economy.

Equally profound in its impact on French society was the system of maritime conscription that Colbert instituted.[12] In a broad sense we can regard this as one part of the absolute state's constant striving to discipline an inchoate social reality and to assert central control over the communities of its periphery. Colbert's original intention was to assure a steady supply of trained men for the fleet, while at the same time allowing commercial shipping to carry on. In practice, however, there were not enough men to go around, so that the system never worked as he had hoped. No state in the seventeenth century could maintain a large force of professional seamen, as a modern navy does, but Colbert's system of recruitment marks a significant step in this direction. Between about 1668 and 1673 he sent commissioners to the coastal provinces to draw up a census of every sailor. The men were listed in rolls and divided into "classes"—each of which had to serve its turn aboard the king's ships; if not immediately required, the men were to remain in readiness in their home ports. If more sailors were needed, additional "maritime classes" could simply be called up—at least in theory. The classes not required for service on the fleet were at liberty to sign on with merchantmen or fishing vessels, thus meeting the needs of civilian shipping as well as those of the fleet. But Colbert never had enough trained men on the rolls to meet every need. The maritime classes functioned well enough in peacetime, but when war broke out and twenty or thirty thousand sailors were urgently needed for the fleet, the system failed to deliver them. Then the officials of the classes had to resort to the old methods of the press, closing the ports, rounding up every available man, and paralyzing commerce and the fisheries. But despite these shortcomings, the maritime classes provided a solid nucleus of trained men for the fleet, and certainly worked better than the old system of the press-gang. Naval officials in England and Holland regarded the system with envy, but never managed to emulate it for themselves.

The maritime classes were far from popular in France; sailors preferred merchant shipping or fishing, which were less dangerous and not subject to such rigorous discipline as the king's service. So they evaded or resisted the *commissaires aux classes*; not infrequently they were aided and abetted in this by the local admiralties, which resented the encroachment on their administrative domain represented by these new officials.

Although the maritime rolls might contain the names of large numbers of trained seamen—between fifty and sixty thousand in the 1680s and early 1690s, when the system was functioning at peak efficiency—not all these men could actually be found. From the 1690s the system fell into increasing disarray. The rolls were not kept up to date, and the irregularity of pay for service aboard the fleet made it harder than ever to enforce the sailor's obligation to serve. By the end of the War of the Spanish Succession, the system of maritime classes was barely functioning. Lack of manpower was a central factor in the decline of French naval strength in the second half of Louis XIV's reign.

In 1661 France did not possess a professional naval officer corps; Colbert had to create one by luring French skippers back from service under foreign flags, attracting merchant captains into the king's service, and transferring officers from the army. A large group of ready-made officers was provided by the French members of the Order of Saint John, who were experienced in galley warfare against the Turks.[13] One of them, the Count de Tourville, rose to become Louis XIV's greatest admiral. Infusing discipline and *esprit de corps* into this heterogeneous group was an enormous task, but Colbert made it clear that the king's service had no place for the wayward arrogance of nobles or the self-seeking individualism of ex-corsairs. He insisted that promotion be accorded only to merit and seniority, and demanded obedience even from the well-born; every order, he said, was to be followed as if it came from the king himself. Here the state was imposing a new, impersonal code of obedience on men whose loyalties were still largely personal, in the old chivalric sense. In this way, Colbert laid the foundations of the officer corps that would lead the French navy down to the Revolution, and in a sense even beyond, for its traditions lived on into the nineteenth century. To maintain a flow of new officers, Colbert set up training schools at the chief ports, where naval cadets learned basic seamanship, navigation, and gunnery before going to sea, and French officers probably received a more systematic professional grounding than their English or Dutch counterparts. In Louis XIV's reign officers still gravitated into the navy from the merchant marine or from privateering—one need only mention Jean Bart or Du Guay-Trouin—and the naval officer corps remained far less aristocratically exclusive than the army. But as the navy built up its own traditions and became a regular service, a more aristocratic tone began to appear, so that in the next century the officer corps became predominantly aristocratic in origin. From the beginning there were severe social tensions within the corps, but the sea officers as a group were united in their hostility to the clerks and administrators who ran the ports. Colbert was careful to keep the two branches of the service separate, to minimize the chances of corruption, but the result of this division was a constant enmity between *plume* and *épee*, which at times could have serious consequences.

Such then was the great mechanism of naval power that Colbert created for Louis XIV in twenty years of unflagging effort. He also succeeded in supplying the essential element that alone could make the wheels of this complex mechanism turn: money. During the first half of Louis XIV's reign, until the 1690s, the navy generally received the funds it needed, but from the onset of the Nine Years' War, which coincided with a period of severe economic depression, the navy's financial situation began to change dramatically. As tax revenues reached their limits and the state debt mounted, the land war took first priority. The fleet's decline was thus part of the general fiscal and economic crisis afflicting France in the latter part of Louis XIV's reign, but it was also to some degree the result of flaws in the navy's financial administration. When Colbert took over the secretaryship, he inherited the old system of naval accounting and disbursement run by the two *trésoriers généraux de la marine*, venal officials originally instituted in 1517.[14] Their function was to receive the revenues due to the navy, hold them in a central treasury, and disburse them at the secretary's orders. But because the revenue earmarked for the fleet was often in arrears, their task was far more complex. The key to their power was their personal wealth and credit. When funds were short, the *trésoriers généraux* would meet payments from their own private fortunes or by borrowing on their own account; conversely, when the navy's coffers were full, they might use the surplus for private speculation. They were in fact typical of the financial entrepreneurs on whom the French monarchy depended to compensate for the inadequacies of its own fiscal structure—tax farmers, contractors, bankers dealing in state loans, and so on. Colbert tried to bring them under closer control, but he never managed to assure a regular flow of funds into the naval treasury, and so he had to rely on the cushion of private credit that the *trésoriers généraux* provided. His successors were far more beholden to them. As the state's fiscal crisis deepened, the support provided by the *trésoriers généraux* became crucial, and by choosing which payments to disburse they assumed a de facto role in policy-making that rivaled and undercut the secretary's. The authority that Colbert had centralized in the office of secretary was thus diluted and diffused; financial chaos brought conflicts and delays to the execution of policy that were fatal to efficiency.

Another reason for the decline of French naval power was an absence of clear strategic thinking to give direction to policy. If the navy had managed to carve out a convincing role for itself as a vital instrument of state policy, Louis XIV would perhaps have been more reluctant to cut its budget as he did in the Nine Years' War and the War of the Spanish Succession. But there was never a clear notion of how the navy served France's geopolitical interests; neither Colbert nor any of his successors really defined what the fleet was for. It was held to be desirable for a number of reasons, but none of these was crucial for the state's survival. France could exist without colonies, without mastery of the seas, and with a minimum of seaborne commerce; all of these were of secondary importance when compared with the need for secure land frontiers. The problem of what purpose the navy was supposed to serve was further complicated by its very recent appearance as a permanent force. Naval strategy was slow to gain a place in France's overall geopolitical priorities. There the concept of global empire had to accommodate itself to the older tradition of naval policy that centered on coastal raiding and commerce destruction. In times of budgetary plenty, the two strategic doctrines could coexist, but when money ran short the more expensive ideal of a grand fleet had to be abandoned. Moreover, Colbert and his successors had little idea of how to exploit victory once it had been achieved, and the history of French naval operations under Louis XIV is littered with missed opportunities, from Du Quesne's victories in the Sicilian campaigns of the 1670s, to Beachy Head and the war for Ireland in 1690. In many ways Admiral Tourville, who commanded at Beachy Head, epitomized the strengths and weaknesses of French maritime thinking. Seignelay criticized him as having "a brave heart but a cowardly head", and the judgment might be extended to most of his fellow commanders, with notable exceptions, like Jean Bart, who within his own chosen sphere was a master of both tactics and strategy. The verdict might even be applied to the king himself, who on various occasions—for instance, in the campaign of 1689—seems to have intervened to tie his commanders' hands with orders not to risk combat.[15]

It is also true that the failure to exploit tactical success was often due to the usual technical deficiencies of the time. But whatever the cause, in each of Louis XIV's wars, fleet operations proved indecisive, and critics began to question the strategic premises on which they were based. In each war, the initial phase of battle fleet operations led to an impasse, which coincided with serious financial difficulties. For strategic and financial reasons, the emphasis in the war at sea then shifted to a *guerre de course*, a policy of commerce destruction, which according to its advocates offered a surer road to victory at less cost, since it would be waged by privateers rather than by the king's ships.

The first such reappraisal of French naval strategy came early in 1674. Two campaigns against the Dutch fleet had proved inconclusive, and in February the defection of Louis XIV's ally, Charles II, tilted the balance of forces against France. In the meantime the war on land was expanding dangerously, and Colbert was forced to wind down naval operations and cut back the naval budget; as he admitted, with only forty French warships available, "the Dutch will be the masters of the sea".[16] Over the summer months he planned further reductions in the fleet in order to devote more funds to the war on land, while stepping up the privateering war against Dutch trade.[17] But at this moment the situation suddenly changed, when the city of Messina in Sicily revolted against Spanish rule. Fleet operations were quickly resumed; the earlier trend toward abandonment of the battle fleet in favor of exclusive reliance on the *guerre de course* was reversed, at least in the Mediterranean where the French fleet enjoyed the advantage of proximity to its base at Toulon. Early in October 1674 a French squadron raised the Spanish blockade of Messina, beginning a series of convoy actions of growing scale and intensity that culminated in Du Quesne's victory over De Ruyter off Augusta in April 1676.[18] But the Sicilian campaigns were only a diversion, and despite Du Quesne's victories, Messina was finally abandoned to its fate. And in the Atlantic theater main fleet operations were largely replaced by the *guerre de course* for the remainder of the war.

In the decade between the Dutch War and the Nine Years' War the French fleet grew steadily until by 1688, when the war broke out, it was stronger than the combined fleets of England and Holland, France's opponents. The revolt of the Catholic Irish against English domination, late in 1688, provided Louis XIV with a chance to deploy this superior force to good advantage. For the first three years of the war the French navy convoyed aid to the rebels, but the strategic possibilities offered by the Irish theater, which promised great advantages if exploited with audacity and determination, were never realized. The French victory at Beachy Head in 1690 over the Anglo-Dutch fleet achieved no more than brief command of the Channel; Ireland was left to its fate. In 1692 the Anglo-Dutch fleet, now stronger than the French, thanks to a feverish building program, won a crushing victory at the battle of La Hogue, and though Tourville put to sea again with a powerful fleet in the following year, the emphasis in French naval strategy began to shift to the *guerre de course*. The economic crisis of 1693–1694 forced Louis XIV to reduce naval expenditure, while criticism of the apparent futility of grand fleet operations was growing more insistent. The campaign of 1695 completed the change of direction in French naval policy. Several big privateering ventures were undertaken, including one by the Sieur de Gennes to Africa and Cape Horn, which pointed the way for the expansion of the *course* far beyond European waters. And in the same year Marshal Vauban—who had close financial ties to the privateers of Dunkirk and Saint-Malo—gave the *guerre de course* its definitive theoretical formulation in his *Mémoire sur la caprerie*. Commerce destruction, he argued, was the logical way to defeat the English and Dutch, whose economies depended so heavily on seaborne trade. The grand fleet had achieved little to justify the vast sums expended upon it, in his view; the state would benefit far more from unrestricted commerce raiding. This was the strategy that France pursued for the rest of the war, and even if it did not produce the results Vauban had expected, it inflicted serious damage on allied shipping and so hastened the end of hostilities.[19]

The latter part of the Nine Years' War marks the start of French naval decline under Louis XIV, and with the resumption of hostilities in 1700 the process accelerated. By now the French fleet was starved of funds; ship construction had virtually ceased, pay for officers and men was in arrears, and the dockyards could barely function. The disaster at Vigo in 1702, the loss of Gibraltar, and the indecisive combat at Velez-Malaga in 1704 completed the sad tale of decline; from this time the fleet never again put to sea in force. The allied attack on Toulon in 1707 destroyed what was left of the French Mediterranean squadron; in the Atlantic bases, the ships rotted for lack of maintenance, and the crews could not be found to man them for lack of pay. The land war consumed all of France's resources, and there was no surplus to spare for the fleet. Such offensive action as France undertook after 1704 was restricted to commerce destruction, now prosecuted with greater determination and efficiency than ever before. The captains and *armateurs* of Dunkirk and Saint-Malo scored a series of notable successes, but these served merely to underline the fact that the sea war had largely slipped out of the state's control; the secretary of the navy's function was now to coordinate the operations of privateer owners, rather than to direct policy and execute it through the means of a great fleet. The sea war had become decentralized and privatized, as part of the general erosion of central authority characteristic of Louis XIV's last years. In the realm of overseas trade too, private capital was called in to compensate for the decline of state power, superseding the grand design of trading companies and naval power that Colbert had built up. The old state companies were foundering, and the new ones that arose to take their place were different in form: the initiative for them came from local trading interests, and only secondarily from the government. A leading role in these new companies was played by the potent shipowners of Saint-Malo, the leaders in the privateering war, who reached the apogee of their wealth and power during the War of the Spanish Succession.[20] Ships from Saint-Malo, outfitted as privateers and merchants, opened up the route to South America and China via Cape Horn and reaped huge profits from illicit trade with the Spanish colonies.[21] The geographic scope of privateering operations extended dramatically as the Malouins sought wider horizons and richer prizes: Du Guay-Trouin's sack of Rio de Janeiro in 1711 is only one episode in the saga of long-range privateering that characterized the Malouins' operations in the War of the Spanish Succession.

The spectacular successes won by French privateers in Louis XIV's later years would seem to refute the premises of grand fleet strategy and state-sponsored commerce on which Colbert's policies had been based. But it would be wrong to dismiss his schemes as entirely futile. It would perhaps be more accurate to argue that Colbert stimulated France's considerable maritime potential to a new level of endeavor. Colbert laid the foundations of a great naval tradition that encouraged France to measure itself against the established maritime states. It would be difficult to attribute the growth of French trade in the later seventeenth and eighteenth centuries to spontaneous individual enterprise alone. State sponsorship created opportunities and established structures that private entrepreneurs—who were frequently linked to the state, as the great Malouin privateer syndicates were—could exploit for themselves. Nor did Colbert's great system of naval administration collapse in the chaos of Louis XIV's later years. Amid financial disorder and physical decay, the institutional structure of the navy survived. The central administration with its bureaus under the secretary's orders continued to function; the traditions of the officer corps were maintained; the administration of the ports struggled to preserve ships and installations from complete ruin; the mechanism for recruitment subsisted, even though it now served only to drum up crews for privateering voyages. All stood ready to revive when a better budgetary climate and energetic ministerial initiative were restored. Ships could be built anew, crews could be recruited afresh: the system of naval power that Colbert established would last throughout the old regime, and even today the French navy looks back to him as its founder.

NOTES

1. The best general history of the French navy in this period is still Charles de La Roncière, *Histoire de la marine française* (Paris 1899–1932), 6 vols. Alfred T. Mahan, *The Influence of Sea Power on History, 1660–1783* (Boston, 1890; numerous reprints), is a classic that can be read with profit. Didier Neuville,

Etat sommaire des archives de la marine antérieures à la Révolution (Paris, 1898), is actually far more than a catalog, and contains an excellent introduction to the French naval administration in the old regime. A summary of recent work on Louis XIV's navy is in my paper, "Louis XIV's Navy: Problems and Perspectives," in *Changing Interpretations and New Sources in Navy History*, ed. Robert W. Love (New York, 1980).

2. The standard work remains Georges Lacour-Gayet, *La Marine militaire de la France sous les règnes de Louis XIII et Louis XIV*, I, *Richelieu, Mazarin: 1624–1661* (Paris, 1911); see also La Roncière IV, 590 ff.

3. Published in *Lettres, instructions et mémoires de Colbert*, ed. Pierre Clément (Paris, 1861–82), II, pt. 1, 50–1.

4. Colbert's grooming of Seignelay to succeed him as secretary can be followed in Clément's collection of papers, cited above, and in his edition of *L'Italie en 1671: Relation d'un voyage du Marquis de Seignelay* (Paris, 1867). On the Phélypeaux family, see J.-L. Bourgeon, "Balthazar Phélypeaux, Marquis de Châteauneuf, secrétaire d'état de Louis XIV," in Roland Mousnier et al., *Le Conseil du roi de Louis XII à la Révolution* (Paris, 1970).

5. Yvonne Bézard, *Fonctionnaires maritimes et coloniaux sous Louis XIV: les Bégon* (Paris, 1932).

6. Examples of incompetent or corrupt officials who were tolerated for a long time but eventually dismissed would be the intendants Arnoul at Toulon and Demuin at Rochefort. The naval correspondence shows that they were guilty of a long series of gross errors.

7. Octave Teissier, *Histoire des divers agrandissements et des fortifications de la ville de Toulon, accompagnée d'un mémoire inédit du Maréchal de Vauban* (Paris and Toulon, 1873), 48.

8. See the study by René Mémain, *La Marine de guerre sous Louis XIV: Le matériel: Rochefort, arsenal modèle de Colbert* (Paris, 1937).

9. On naval tactics in this period, see Geoffrey W. Symcox, *The Crisis of French Sea Power: 1688–1697: From the Guerre d'Escadre to the Guerre de Course* (The Hague, 1974), 32–71. For galley warfare, see John F. Guilmartin, Jr., *Gunpowder and Galleys: Changing Technology and Mediterranean Warfare at Sea in the Sixteenth Century* (Cambridge, 1974); and Paul W. Bamford, *Fighting Ships and Prisons: The Mediterranean Galleys of France in the Age of Louis XIV* (Minneapolis, 1973). On Renau and the bomb-ketch, see Alphonse Jal, *Abraham du Quesne et la marine de son temps* (Paris, 1873), II, 412–21.

10. See Paul W. Bamford, *Forests and French Sea Power: 1660–1789* (Toronto, 1956).

11. Joseph Konvitz, *Cities and the Sea: Port City Planning in Early Modern Europe* (Baltimore, 1978), 92–3.

12. On recruitment, see René Mémain, *Matelots et soldats des vaisseaux du roi: levées d'hommes au département de Rochefort: 1661–1690* (Paris, 1937); and Eugene L. Asher, *The Resistance to the Maritime Classes: The Survival of Feudalism in the France of Colbert* (Berkeley and Los Angeles, 1960). University of California Publications in History, vol. LXVI.

13. Paul W. Bamford, "The Knights of Malta and the King of France 1665–1700," *French Historical Studies* III (1964), 429–53.

14. The only study of naval finance for this period is Henri Legoherel, *Les Trésoriers généraux de la marine (1517–1788)* (Paris, 1965). On problems of funding, see Symcox, *Crisis*, 143–50, and appendix 1.

15. Symcox, *Crisis*, 89. Seignelay's criticism of Tourville is quoted on p. 69.
16. Colbert to Frontenac, May 17, 1674, published in *Lettres . . . de Colbert*, III, pt. 2, 575; La Roncière, V, 577–9. For the naval budget, see his figures on p. 331, note 1, which show that from a total of nine million *livres* in 1673 the budget fell to six million in 1675.
17. Colbert to Demuin, August 13, 1674, published in *Lettres . . . de Colbert*, III, pt. 1, 523. For the intensification of privateering, see La Roncière, V, 667 ff. On the reversal, compare his letters to Arnoul of September 25 and of November 16, 1674, published in *Lettres . . . de Colbert*, III, pt. 1, 528 and 534–5.
18. On the Sicilian campaign, see F. Laloy, *La Révolte de Messine, l'expédition de Sicile et la politique française en Italie: 1674–1678* (Paris, 1929), 3 vols.
19. On De Gennes' pioneering voyage, see F. Froger, *Relation d'un voyage . . . aux côtes d'Afrique . . . par une escadre . . . commandeé par M. de Gennes* (Paris, 1698). An incomplete version of Vauban's *mémoire* is in E. A. de Rochas d'Aiglun, *Vauban: sa famille et ses écrits* (Paris, 1910), I, 454–61. On the background, see Symcox, *Crisis*, 177–87.
20. See, for instance, C. Madriolle, *Les Premiers voyages français à la Chine: la Compagnie de Chine: 1698–1719* (Paris, 1901). See also F. Froger, *Relation du premier voyage des François' à la Chine fait en 1698, 1699 et 1700 sur le vaisseau "l'Amphitrite"*, ed. E. A. Voretzsch (Leipzig, 1926).
21. Malouin trade to the South Seas is studied exhaustively in a series of works by Erik W. Dahlgren: *Les Relations commerciales et maritimes entre la France et les côtes de l'Océan Pacifique*, I, *Le Commerce de la Mer du Sud jusqu'à la paix d'Utrecht* (Paris, 1909); "Voyages français à déstination de la Mer du Sud avant Bougainville (1695–1749)," in *Nouvelles archives des missions scientifiques et littéraires*, XIV, pt. 4 (1907); "Le Comte Jérôme de Pontchartrain et les armateurs de Saint-Malo: 1712–1715," in *Revue historique* LXXXVIII (1905); and "L'Expedition de Martinet et la fin du commerce français dans les mers du sud," in *Revue de l'histoire des colonies* I (1913).

NINE

The Diplomatic History
of the Reign

JOHN T. O'CONNOR

For centuries the kings of France engaged in a series of wars in which the interests of the state and those of the dynasty were often inextricably linked. These kings were anxious about the exposed position of Paris and sought to lengthen the distance between the capital and the frontier. In the early modern period, Spain, of course, was the principal enemy. France was virtually surrounded by territories of the Spanish monarch: to the southwest, Spain itself; to the north, the Spanish Low Countries (roughly the Belgium and Luxembourg of today); to the east, Franche-Comté. For generations, the Habsburg rulers of Spain had allied themselves with their cousins, the Austrian Habsburgs, who, in addition to their holdings in Central Europe, possessed territories in Alsace and in the Rhineland. These same Austrian Habsburgs were repeatedly elected Holy Roman Emperors. With good reason, therefore, the kings of France feared encirclement and the snuffing out of their independence.

Like many other rulers of the early sixteenth century, Francis I made some limited institutional improvements and began a system of resident ambassadors. Yet his system of carrying out foreign policy remained unwieldy. These affairs were handled by several secretaries of state, each of whom dealt with a certain geographical department, a mixture of areas in France and various foreign countries. Of the four secretaries during Francis II's reign, one handled Poland, the Holy Roman Empire, Switzerland, the Grisons, Lorraine, Burgundy, Champagne, and Brie.[1] This arrangement led to a great deal of duplication and inefficiency. In 1624, at the outset of his ministry, Cardinal Richelieu could not find the instructions to the various French ambassadors abroad and had to ask them for copies.[2] Richelieu was a believer in perpetual negotiation, but he and Louis XIII had to do a lot of revamping, if not complete reorganizing, in order to launch their ambitious diplomatic program. One reform in 1626 finally ended the practice of having multiple secretaries in charge of foreign affairs. A *règlement* of 1626 for the first time gave permanent jurisdictional form to the departments of foreign affairs and war, and entrusted one secretary with all foreign correspondence. The latter, like the secretary for war and the superintendant of finance, collaborated closely with Richelieu and took part in meetings of the supreme advisory council, the *conseil d'en haut*, in which foreign affairs were regularly discussed.[3]

Tax money was collected and pressed from the people until revolts and sometimes provincewide rebellions intervened, but regardless of the domestic cost, the priority was always assigned to foreign affairs. A vehement debate took place at the court in 1630 as to whether domestic reforms should be postponed or shelved in favor of military opposition to Spain.[4] The peace party argued that the quest for funds would trigger explosions of popular revolts. Louis XIII supported Cardinal Richelieu: alliances were contracted with various German princes, with Sweden, and with the Dutch; war was declared against both the Spanish and the Austrian Habsburgs. When the revolts occurred they were brutally repressed.

Following the death of Cardinal Richelieu in 1642 and of Louis XIII in 1643, the same emphases were continued by the regent Anne of Austria and by her prime minister, Cardinal Mazarin, on behalf of the minor Louis XIV. Tax collection amounted to fiscal brigandage as Mazarin made use of any and all expedients. The young king witnessed a perpetual emergency. No sooner was the war against the Austrian Habsburgs ended in 1648 than a five-year civil war, the Fronde, erupted in France. Though twice forced into temporary exile, Mazarin kept in close touch with both Louis and Anne. All the while, the war with Spain dragged on. It was precisely during this period that, under Mazarin's guidance, Louis got his training in the craft of kingship. He attended council meetings, listened to dispatches, and observed the briefings of French ambassadors about to depart for foreign capitals.[5]

One feature of French diplomacy in the seventeenth century that greatly impressed contemporaries was that "negotiations were carried on in a twilight atmosphere created by the opaque art of secrecy".[6] That art implies methods of obtaining information, including the use of spies and informers. Much is still unknown in this area of politics and diplomacy, but it should be noted that in the seventeenth century espionage was viewed differently from the way it is in today's world. It has been fairly said that "espionage at that time did not have the same brutal significance that resulted from administrative centralization and the fixing of frontiers between rival countries. It was often a question of utilizing voluntary agents, among whom might be found persons of the highest rank".[7] Tangled inheritances and overlapping jurisdictions often made informants of men who owned property in Breisgau or in Flanders as well as in France and who were compelled to remain in the good graces of the French crown.

Yet while voluntary agents were always welcome, it was money and more money that smoothed the way on countless occasions. *Pensions* and *gratifications* were liberally dispensed at foreign courts. The recipients were not only the princes and major figures at these courts but minor functionaries and valets as well, anyone who could influence decisions or provide information on those who made them. The fact that a man accepted money (and sometimes from more than one side) did not necessarily mean that he was going to tie his hands for the future. Even in the case of direct subsidies attached to a formal treaty, a prince would follow the provisions only insofar as they served his interests: for a ruler to fulfill treaty obligations in spite of changing circumstances was usually equivalent to disaster. This, of course, depended on the proximity of the French army. Fear could sometimes do more than money in dealings with foreign rulers. The combination of the two was usually most persuasive.

Like most statesmen on the continent, Cardinal Mazarin was obsessed with events in Europe, and he doubtless fostered the same streak in his pupil. The larger goal to which particular efforts were subordinate was frequently alluded to in the cardinal's letters to young Louis: "You can become a great king . . .", "God has given you talents . . .", "You owe your God and your *gloire* . . ."[8] *Gloire*, the word and the ambition, was intimately a part of French culture in that age; it recurs frequently in the plays of the period, notably in those of Corneille. As a term or concept, *gloire* cannot simply be translated into English as "glory". It was thought of as a lifelong quest by an aristocrat, something well above the ambitions of mere commoners. In practice, it meant testing your mettle, rising to challenges, attempting to fulfill your potential. If you succeeded, it might be said of you at the end of your life that you had achieved your *gloire*. Your reputation would then resonate among your descendants, inspiring them to emulate your striving and your successes. A concern for *gloire* would be ever present in the Sun King's handling of foreign affairs.

By the time Louis was twenty years old, Cardinal Mazarin was on the verge of achieving his own *gloire* as he sought to end the seemingly interminable war with Spain. He joined with Cromwell's England in a military alliance against Spain and stitched together an intricate network of treaties with German princes, the League of the Rhine, to block Austrian assistance to Spain. At this time, he also sounded out the

Germans on the possibility of electing Louis XIV emperor, but that step, from the point of view of German princes, seemed tantamount to surrendering their precious independence and was rejected. The union of England and France was sufficient to defeat Spain militarily, and Spain had to surrender some territory to the victors. England got Dunkirk and the island of Jamaica; France acquired towns and enclaves of territory on her northern borders, as well as territory in the region of the Pyrenees. Mazarin was the principal French negotiator at the Peace of the Pyrenees in 1659. The peace treaty included a provision for the marriage of Louis XIV to a daughter of the King of Spain, the *Infanta Maria Theresa*, Mazarin calculating that by marrying a daughter of Philip IV, Louis could engage in some fence mending for the present and perhaps stake a claim to more Spanish territory in the future. This, of course, would later become one of the major diplomatic themes of the reign.

On Cardinal Mazarin's death, in March 1661, Louis immediately announced that he would no longer have a prime minister, and if proof be needed of the efficacy of Mazarin's lessons, it is manifest in the king's first significant action of his personal reign—the dramatic arrest of Nicolas Fouquet in September 1661. Mazarin's influence is likewise evident in the number of his aides and protégés whom Louis kept on as his principal ministers. From the outset, however, he sharply limited the membership in the *conseil d'en haut*. He might invite anyone to a given session, but regular attendance was limited to a chosen few ministers, with no minutes kept and secrecy at a premium.

In the first decade of the reign, the secretary of state for foreign affairs was Hugues de Lionne. Hailed by Saint-Simon as the greatest minister ever to serve the Sun King, Lionne had spent much of the 1630s in Italy, especially in Rome, working in close concert with Mazarin. Fluent in Italian and competent in Spanish, he had been entrusted by Mazarin with key assignments in the 1640s and 1650s and possessed an extraordinarily broad knowledge of European affairs. Lionne was fifty at Mazarin's death and was an astute and resourceful advisor on countless affairs of state, but—never to be forgotten—his role was to do the king's bidding. Lionne was stricken with dread upon the arrest and trial of his good friend Fouquet and required Louis' assurances that no harm would befall him as well. Whether or not Lionne agreed with a given policy may be open to conjecture or, on occasion, confirmed by evidence, but that he was expected to carry out that policy is beyond question. This must be emphasized, especially since it is often assumed that after Lionne's death, in 1671, the king's mind was "changed" or "overly influenced" by the bellicose Louvois. If Louvois as secretary of war exerted an influence on his master, it was precisely because his arguments reinforced dispositions and desires that were there from the outset.

In the first year of his personal reign, Louis XIV issued a clear warning that he expected precedence over other monarchs. In August 1661, in a dispatch to his ambassador in England, he noted that "the king's ambassadors must make it known that the king never is content with equality but should have pre-eminence over all other kings and is in possession of it".[9] Several months later, when he learned that the adherents of the Spanish embassy in London, exploiting their superiority in numbers, had forced their way ahead of the French at a diplomatic function, Louis threatened an invasion of Spain unless apologies were rendered and a solemn pledge made that such an incident would never happen again. Since the Spanish were in no position to defend themselves militarily against France, they were obliged to send an ambassador to Paris with explicit and profuse public apologies. A Gobelins tapestry was commissioned to record the scene for posterity. Soon thereafter, a skirmish in Rome between members of the French ambassador's household and papal guards resulted in an exchange of shots; a page attached to the embassy was killed. Louis threatened a land and sea invasion of the papal states unless a formal apology was rendered. The result was similar: a cardinal was received by the king in the presence of the court and the diplomatic corps. Another Gobelins tapestry was commissioned; both may be seen at Versailles today. Louis adopted as his symbol the sun and as his motto, "*Nec pluribus impar*" (not inferior to many). In his *Age of Louis XIV*, Voltaire would write: "Europe feared Louis XIV even before he went to war".[10]

The king justified his first major war, the War of Devolution (1667–1668), on a questionable extrapolation from certain private laws of inheritance in the Spanish Low Countries onto the public rights of his queen to inherit territories in this area from her recently deceased father. The pettifoggery was transparent. More to the point was a remark by Vauban to Louvois that perfectly distilled the French legal position: "No judges are more equitable than cannons".[11]

It was while attempting to defend herself in this war under the reign of the minor and sickly Carlos II that Spain was forced to concede Portugal's right to independence. In securing a peace treaty, the Portuguese relied on England, not on France, despite the assistance rendered to their cause by French officers, including Count von Schomberg. Although outmaneuvered by the English in the diplomatic skirmishes, Louis XIV acted magnanimously in the aftermath; for example, he assisted the new regime in negotiating with the papacy.

The War of Devolution also served as a backdrop for a highly secret negotiation between France and the Austrian Habsburgs on the subject of partitioning the Spanish monarchy if , as seemed very likely, Carlos II were to die without heir. In this, the first partition treaty of the reign, Louis and his heirs stood to inherit the Spanish Low Countries, Franche-Comté, Navarre with its dependencies, the Philippines, Naples, Sicily, and fortifications on the coast of Morocco. Leopold of Austria and his successors would receive Spain and Spanish colonies in the New World, Sardinia, Milan, the Balearic and Canary Islands, and territory and ports in Tuscany. The treaty was signed in January 1668. The Spanish Council of State was informed of the treaty and made aware of Austria's inability to aid in the war against France. The council felt constrained to accept the partition arrangement and to cede to France a number of fortified places lost during the previous year.[12]

The partition agreement must be viewed on several levels. For each side, the prospect of obtaining so much territory without fighting for it was tantalizing. It disentangled the emperor from a ticklish political and military situation, though it by no means improved his relations with Spain. It is in the context of this treaty that we must judge French reaction to the almost simultaneous Triple Alliance of England, the Dutch Republic, and Sweden, the intent of which was to preserve the Spanish Low Countries from French conquest. The three powers offered to mediate the Franco-Spanish conflict, but in a secret article pledged to enter the war on the side of Spain if France proved obdurate. Since Carlos II might die soon and Louis was not disposed to become entangled in a drawn-out war against an enemy coalition, he elected to accept peace with Spain. Naturally, one is left to speculate on the probable reaction of the English and Dutch if Carlos II had died shortly thereafter. Could they have successfully blocked France from taking the Spanish Low Countries without having Spain or Austria as allies? Apart from that eventuality, it is not farfetched to view the treaty as a brilliant move on the part of Lionne and of his Austrian counterparts to entice Louis out of the war and to obviate future conflict over the Spanish inheritance.

Louis was also confronted with the supplications of Pope Clement IX that the Christian states cease fighting each other and concentrate all their forces upon the Turks. For months, the king had been ignoring these pleas, but now he made a great show of deference. Louis went so far as to exclaim that "weapons fell from his hands when the nuncio of His Holiness asked for a suspension" of hostilities.[13] The treaty of Aix-La-Chapelle extended French frontiers at the expense of Spain, but the settlement left much "unfinished business" for Louis and his ministers.

Louis himself was torn between his own desire to continue the conquest of the Spanish Low Countries and the great difficulties that stood in the way of this objective. His ministers, especially Colbert and Lionne, were reluctant to engage him in any war at all. However, handsome subsidies eventually persuaded Charles II of England secretly to desert the Dutch and to ally with France against them. It seemed like a good compromise idea. Lionne and Prince Wilhelm Egon von Fürstenberg arranged some alliances with various German princes who were to provide a boulevard for the invasion of the republic. The emperor shrewdly pledged neutrality, subject to French troops' avoiding Spanish territory. When Lionne died, in September 1671, he was succeeded by the extremely moderate Arnauld de Pomponne, who was then in Sweden. The king made one last-ditch effort to turn the war upon the Spanish Low Countries. The English would not hear of it, and Louis had to be satisfied with attacking the Dutch—for the time being.[14]

The invasion of the Dutch Republic in 1672 proved a spectacular success. The French armies captured over forty outlying Dutch strongholds in a single campaign; and with only the Elector of Brandenburg as an ally, the Dutch came to the king's camp with humiliating offers in a desperate bid for peace. But he was waiting for the Spanish to enter the fray, and thus his own terms were even harsher. The lynching of the De Witts and, subsequently, William of Orange's plucky refusal to sell out to the French and English were harbingers of a reversal of fortunes. The impasse became even greater in 1673 after the Elector of Brandenburg pulled out, yet the expected withdrawal of French troops from Imperial territory did not take place. Attempted explanations by French diplomats were looked upon as mere word spinning by their German counterparts. With rumors that the emperor might come to the defense of the empire, all Europe waited to see what would happen next.

Under Swedish aegis, a peace congress had begun to meet in Cologne in 1673. The congress served as a cockpit for polemicists as well as diplomats, and it witnessed a remarkable event, the armies of Louis XIV, under the great Marshal de Turenne, being outmaneuvered by the Imperial general Montecuccoli, forcing the abandonment of most of the conquests of 1672. When the Spanish finally intervened, the English pulled out. The congress itself was blown apart by a stunning *coup de théâtre* in February 1674: Wilhelm Egon von Fürstenberg, an accredited delegate representing the Electorate of Cologne, was seized in the neutral city of Cologne on orders from Emperor Leopold and spirited off to a prison in Austria. Since Fürstenberg was also the leading partisan of France in the Empire, there was the threat of a treason trial and execution hanging over him. Though that threat was never carried out—such a trial would have opened a crab basket of problems for the Austrians—Fürstenberg was kept in prison till the war's end in 1679. As the Diet of the Empire declared war on France on May 28, 1674, Louis XIV deployed his diplomatic corps in all areas of Europe to secure Fürstenberg's release or, at least, to have him transferred into the custody of the pope. The Fürstenberg case was a veritable textbook example of the violation of diplomatic immunity; because of it, the king refused to consider a city in the empire as the site for the peace conference. After considerable haggling, Nijmegen in the Netherlands was chosen as the site for the peace negotiations, with England and the papacy as mediators.[15]

The French delegation at Nijmegen was effectively led by Colbert de Croissy, soon to replace Pomponne as secretary of state for foreign affairs. The Dutch were the first to be detached from the coalition; the separate peace included generous economic provisions on their behalf. French claims in Alsace were reinforced, and considerable territory, including Franche-Comté, was surrendered by Spain. Yet Louis had not conquered the Spanish Low Countries.[16]

No sooner was the Dutch War concluded than French diplomacy began to concentrate on a thoroughly legalistic approach, as seen in the infamous policy of "reunions". Precision was conveniently supplied by various judicial bodies; one of them, the Chamber of Reunions at Metz, provided the name that would soon be applied to all such proceedings. French archivists reported to French judges, who instructed French troops to occupy what was defined as French sovereign territory. The French did have some valid legal claims, but the *manner* in which they acted led to alarm and hostility in the Spanish Low Countries, Liège, and numerous German states, especially since there was no clear sense of just when and where the process would end.

Louis XIV surely would have agreed with Frederick the Great's dictum that diplomacy without force is like music without a score.[17] Most statesmen and political theorists, past and present, would concur. But to an increasing number of his contemporaries, Louis appeared to believe that force—or intimidation, or intimidation sweetened with subsidies—could serve as a substitute for diplomacy. Perhaps he thought that other states might forever be bludgeoned into accepting his demands as so many faits accomplis. As a Spanish delegate to a reunion conference in 1681 ruefully admitted, "Spanish reasons are never worth anything compared with those of the French, supported . . . by one hundred thousand infantrymen and twenty-five thousand cavalry".[18]

Though financial and military resources gave the king an undeniable advantage in dealing with other states, some of his expectations and

very same time, he sought to undermine attempts by Maximilian's brother to become Elector of Cologne. The French supported Wilhelm Egon von Fürstenberg, by now Bishop of Strasbourg and a cardinal. Still a staunch ally of France, Fürstenberg was unalterably opposed by the emperor, who conveyed those sentiments to Rome. Leopold spoke menacingly of the disarray in the empire should Fürstenberg ever become the Elector of Cologne, but that rhetoric was largely the ink of the squid. The emperor's chief objection flowed from his conviction that Fürstenberg would never vote for a Habsburg in the next Imperial election. As it turned out, no candidate at Cologne received the requisite number of votes. The decision was left to Pope Innocent, who chose Maximilian's brother, Joseph Clement.

The fear of Austrian military victories' tipping the balance of power, the rage and frustration in the face of collaboration between Rome and Vienna in the Cologne affair, and the gamble that a Dutch invasion of England to oust James II would afford French troops ample time to invade the western empire without fear of an enemy riposte—all these conspired to produce a momentous decision at Versailles in August 1688. The ensuing invasion of the Palatinate in September and October included barbarities perpetrated on orders from Louis and Louvois; no diplomatic efforts could ever efface the stain on France's reputation for the remainder of the Sun King's reign. But instead of a short, successful war that might have transformed the Truce of Regensburg into permanent reunion gains, Louis found himself enmeshed in a war of nine years' duration that sapped the human and material resources of all the combatants.

In the course of this draining war, Louis' hopes for a neutral "third party" among the northern German states never materialized.[25] Ultimately, he picked off Savoy from the allied coalition in 1696 at the Treaty of Turin. He paid a high price: the fortifications of Casale and Pinerolo, key elements in the French strategic frontier in northern Italy. The remaining members of the coalition came to terms in the following year at Ryswick. Though the Austrians were not able to wrest Toul, Metz, or Verdun away from France or reverse earlier cessions in Alsace, the French came close to forfeiting Strasbourg. They did have to surrender many of the reunion gains, together with Luxembourg, Freiburg-im-Breisgau, Philippsburg, and Breisach—the last three key positions in the French strategic frontier in the western empire. It was the first war in Louis' reign that had led to a surrender of French possessions. Not on the agenda at Ryswick was the most critical issue then facing European statesmen: the disposition of Spanish territories when the King of Spain, Carlos II, died without an heir.

During the Dutch War, Austria had renounced the partition agreement concluded in 1668. An alternative plan in 1698 hatched by France, England, and the Dutch Republic, provided for the young Joseph Ferdinand of Bavaria to inherit all Spanish possessions except for Naples, Sicily, and the province of Guipuzcoa in Spain (assigned to the dauphin of France) and the Duchy of Milan (assigned to Emperor Leopold's younger son, Charles). Leopold opposed this settlement, desiring the entire inheritance for his own family, but the death of the young Bavarian prince made another scheme necessary.

The next partition plan was proposed jointly in 1699 by Louis XIV and William, King of England and stadholder in the Dutch Republic. This would have left the bulk of the Spanish inheritance to Charles, the son of Leopold; Spanish territories in northern and southern Italy would be transferred to Louis XIV's son, the dauphin. Those territories in Italy might then conceivably be exchanged for other territories. Thus, the Duke of Lorraine might be given Milan and Lombardy, with Lorraine going to France; and the Duke of Savoy could acquire all of southern Italy and Sicily in exchange for Piedmont and Savoy, which would enable France to round off her frontiers in the southeast. William and Louis may have accepted this plan, but the Spanish and the Austrians did not. The Spanish did not want to lose their Italian territories; Leopold wanted the Italian territories to be controlled by Austria.[26]

Just before Carlos II died, he signed a remarkable will, leaving all of the Spanish inheritance to a grandson of Louis XIV, a seventeen-year-old boy who would become Philip V of Spain. If the Bourbons declined to accept this arrangement, then the entire inheritance would instead go to Charles of Austria. Would Louis try to keep the partition agreement with William? If so, he would be at war with Spain as well as Austria. If he accepted the will, he faced war with Austria. Could England and the Dutch be kept out of the struggle? Louis decided to accept the will; in a historic moment at Versailles, he introduced his grandson to the assembled court as the King of Spain. Soon Bourbon family connections were used to advance French merchant interests in the Spanish colonial world and to make moves in the Spanish Low Countries, which unsettled the Dutch. When the fighting began, Louis again found a broad allied coalition ranged against France; his only allies throughout the war were Spain, Bavaria, and the Electorate of Cologne.

During this longest and bloodiest war of the reign, the French crown subsidized an ambitious propaganda campaign to influence opinion across Europe. Books, pamphlets, and even forged political testaments were put to use in the very effective operation led by the capable secretary of state for foreign affairs, Colbert de Torcy.[27] In his lucid study of the royal propaganda campaign, Joseph Klaits notes that Torcy's office gave him "censorship authority over all literary material concerning diplomacy and foreign relations", and that he "wielded his administrative control over censorship regularly and systematically".[28] Torcy also directed the work of resourceful pamphleteers and sometimes served as an editor for their publications. In addition to his activity as minister, advisor to the king, and diplomat, he drafted many of the key public pronouncements issued by Louis. This was especially the case during the nadir of the tragic and exhausting struggle, the terrible famine of 1709, one of the worst in the history of France from the early medieval period to the present day.

When the king indicated a willingness to compromise, the enemy coalition raised its terms, even demanding that Louis participate in driving his grandson out of Spain. Caught in what must have seemed a recurring nightmare, the king wrote letters to officials across France, letters that were printed and distributed broadside. But the death of Emperor Joseph, son of Leopold and brother of the Habsburg claimant to the Spanish throne, infused new fervor into the peace party in England. If Charles (the would-be Carlos III) succeeded as Holy Roman Emperor and at the same time were King of Spain, the sixteenth-century empire of Charles V would be revived, with the likelihood of plunging Europe into a bloodbath for a whole generation. The final treaties at Utrecht in 1713–1714 included an extensive reshuffling of territories connected with the partition of the Spanish Empire.

Philip V of Bourbon continued to rule in Spain and in Spain's American colonies, but the Spanish Low Countries, as well as many of Spain's holdings in Italy, were transferred to Austria. England obtained Gibraltar and Minorca from Spain, as well as Canadian territories from France: Newfoundland, Nova Scotia, and vast tracts of land around Hudson Bay. The *asiento* clause in the treaty accorded the English a monopoly in the provisioning of African slaves to Spanish colonies in the New World, as well as the right to send a trading ship each year to Spanish America, opening up lucrative opportunities for smuggling. England thus received the lion's share of the spoils and had begun to undermine France's position in Canada. Both England and Austria made significant gains in power by comparison to the status that each had held vis-à-vis France at the beginning of Louis' reign in 1661. Not the least of the results of the coalition wars against France is that they established the basic guidelines for the balance of power in international relations in the eighteenth century.

At Louis XIV's death in 1715, France remained the most populous and one of the most fertile, resourceful, and resilient states in Europe. The chain of fortifications designed by Vauban protected her frontiers and enclosed the territorial gains made during the reign, especially Franche-Comté and Alsace. By the standards of the time, Louis may be said to have achieved a great measure of the *gloire* that he pursued relentlessly throughout his long career. All the same, the king's quest for hegemony had fallen short of his aspirations. Moreover, that quest had exacted exorbitant human and material sacrifices from the French people. On his deathbed, Louis advised his successor, "Do not imitate me in war; try always to maintain peace with your neighbors, to spare your people as much as you can which I have had the misfortune not to be able to do because of necessities of state".[29] By referring to "necessities of state", the king was still seeking to justify his choices, his actions, and all that flowed from them. His heir was his great-grandson, Louis XV, who was five years old, the same age as Louis when his father died in 1642. Beginning with Louis XV, only two more Bourbon kings would reside at Versailles before the events of 1789 restored Paris as the capital.

In the course of the eighteenth century, the French crown was perpetually attentive to the balance of power in Europe, with less overt concern for dynastic matters than in the age of Louis XIV. At the end of his reign, the Sun King had pondered a possible rapprochement with the House of Austria, but that historic turning point came only in 1756 with the famous "diplomatic revolution". France continued to lose colonial territory in its wars with England; by 1763 the French had been driven from Canada. Subsequent French support for the American revolutionaries carried with it a catastrophic burden of debt that accelerated the calling of the first Estates-General since 1614, a step that Louis XIV had managed to avoid. A century that began with the spectacle of Barcelona as the last outpost of Habsburg Spain, besieged and conquered by a Castillian army under Bourbon command,[30] would see a Bourbon monarch of France encouraging a war against the Austrian Habsburgs in the vain hope that France might be defeated.

Armies may have fought under different banners, but the essential elements current in seventeenth-century high politics remained in force. There remained plentiful reserves of enmity to fuel future conflicts and occasions to ignite them, such as the desperate nationalist struggle to oust a Bonaparte dynasty from Spain and to restore the Bourbons (and the Inquisition) to power. Such an eventuality might have taxed the imagination of a Louis XIV, but, once briefed, he would surely have approved.

NOTES

1. Orest A. Ranum, *Richelieu and the Councillors of Louis XIII* (Oxford, 1963), 49.
2. Garrett Mattingly, *Renaissance Diplomacy* (Baltimore, 1964), 199.
3. Ranum, 55, 61.
4. See Georges Pagès, "Autour du 'grand orage', Richelieu et Marillac: deux politiques," *Revue historique* CLXXIX (1937), 63–97; and J. H. Elliott, *Richelieu and Olivares* (Cambridge, 1984).
5. Mazarin's role in preparing young Louis for his future career is analyzed in John B. Wolf, "The Formation of a King," *French Historical Studies* I (1958), 40–72. This analysis is developed in the first part of Wolf's splendid biography, *Louis XIV* (New York, 1968).
6. August Franzen, "Französische Politik and Kurkölns Beziehungen zu Frankreich unter Erzbischof Max Heinrich (1650–1688) in römischer Sicht," *Römische Quartalschrift für Christliche Altertumskunde und Kirchengeschichte* VI (1957), 180–1.
7. Gaeton Guillot, "Leopold Ier et sa Cour, 1681–1684," *Revue des questions historiques* (April, 1907), 406.
8. Wolf, *Louis XIV*, 71.
9. Cited by Louis André, *Louis XIV et l'Europe* (Paris, 1950), 55.
10. Ibid., 61.
11. Vauban to Louvois, August 13, 1668. Cited by Nelly Girard d'Albissin, *Genèse de la frontière Franco-Belge: les variations des limites septentrionales de la France de 1659 à 1689* (Paris, 1970), 113–4. Bibliothèque de la Société d'Histoire de Droit des Pays Flamands, Picards, et Wallons, vol. XXVI.
12. See Jean Bérenger, "Une Tentative de rapprochement entre la France et l'empereur: le traité de partage secret de la succession d'Espagne du 19 janvier 1668," *Revue d'histoire diplomatique* LXXIX (1965), 291–314. English translation, "An attempted *Rapprochement* between France and the Emperor: The Secret Treaty for the Partition of the Spanish Succession of 19 January 1668," in *Louis XIV and Europe*, ed. Ragnhild Hatton (London and Columbus, 1976), 133–52.
13. Charles de Terlinden, "La Diplomatie pontificale et la paix d'Aix-La-Chapelle de 1668 d'après les Archives Secrètes du Saint-Siège," *Bulletin de l'Institut Historique Belge de Rome* XXVIII (1952), 261.
14. Paul Sonnino, *Louis XIV and the Origins of the Dutch War* (Cambridge, 1988).
15. See Paul Sonnino, "Arnauld de Pomponne, Louis XIV's Minister of Foreign Affairs during the Dutch War," *Proceedings of the Western Society for French History* I (1974), 49–68; Carl J. Ekberg, *The Failure of Louis XIV's Dutch War* (Chapel Hill, 1979); and John O'Connor, "French Relations with the Papacy during the Dutch War," *Proceedings of the Western Society for French History* XIII (1986), 51–60.
16. See the excellent collection of essays stemming from a symposium commemorating the negotiations at Nijmegen: *The Peace of Nijmegen: 1676–1679: Proceedings of the International Congress of the Tricentennial, 14–16 September 1978* (Amsterdam, 1980).
17. Cited by Maurice Keens-Soper, "François de Callières and Diplomatic Theory," *Historical Journal* XVI (1973), 507.
18. Cited by Camille Rousset, *Histoire de Louvois et de son administration politique et militaire* (Paris, 1861–3), III, 216.

19. There is a suggestive discussion of French-Swedish relations in Basilio Cialdea, *La crisi nelle alleanze nord-orientali della Francia, 1697–1703* (Milan, 1943). Pubblicazioni dell'Università Cattolica del Sacro Cuore, Serie nona: Scienze Politiche, vol. V.

20. Andrew Lossky, "The General European Crisis of the 1680s," *European Studies Review* X (1980), 187.

21. George von Rauch, "Moskau und die europäischen Mächte des 17. Jahrhunderts," *Historische Zeitschrift* CLXXVIII (1954), 39.

22. In the course of reviewing two volumes (on Prussia and Savoy) in the instructions to ambassadors series, Max Immich noted the danger of latter-day historians' absorbing the mind-set of seventeenth-century French diplomats and judging the politics of other states accordingly. See the *Historische Zeitschrift* XC (1903), 498.

23. Zbigniew Wojcik, "From the Peace of Oliva to the Truce of Bakhchisarai: International Relations in Eastern Europe: 1660–1681," *Acta Poloniae Historica* XXXIV (1976), 263–4. In connection with Turkish designs, Wojcik especially cites the works in Polish of the historian Z. Abrahamowicz.

24. Numerous aspects of the Huguenot diaspora are treated in the superb collection of essays *Le Refuge Huguenot*, ed. Michelle Magdelaine and Rudolf von Thadden (Paris, 1985).

25. Janine Fayard, "Les Tentatives de constitution d'un 'tiers parti' en Allemagne du Nord: 1690–1694," *Revue d'histoire diplomatique* LXXIX (1965), 338–72. English translation, "Attempts to Build a 'Third Party' in North Germany, 1690–1694," in *Louis XIV and Europe*, ed. Ragnhild Hatton (London and Columbus, 1976), 213–40.

26. See Ragnhild Hatton, *Europe in the Age of Louis XIV* (New York, 1969), 100–8; and Mark A. Thomson, "Louis XIV and the Origins of the War of the Spanish Succession," in *William III and Louis XIV: Essays 1680–1720 by and for Mark A. Thomson*, ed. Ragnhild Hatton and J. S. Bromley (Liverpool, 1968), 140–61.

27. For an overview of Torcy's career, see John C. Rule, "King and Minister: Louis XIV and Colbert de Torcy," in *William III and Louis XIV*, 213–36.

28. Joseph Klaits, *Printed Propaganda under Louis XIV: Absolute Monarchy and Public Opinion* (Princeton, 1976), 40.

29. Cited by William F. Church, "Louis XIV and Reason of State," in *Louis XIV and the Craft of Kingship*, ed. John C. Rule (Columbus, 1969), 393.

30. R. A. Stradling, *Europe and the Decline of Spain: A Study of the Spanish System, 1580–1720* (London and Boston, 1981), 204.

TEN

The Religious History
of the Reign

JOHN H. GREVER

The kings of France, recalling their services to the pope, gloried in the titles of "eldest son of the church" and "most Christian king". But the French monarchy had also inherited a tradition of conflict with Rome. Around 1300 Philip the Fair had violently attacked Pope Boniface VIII, denying papal authority over the temporal power of the crown. One century later, at the Council of Constance, Jean Gerson, chancellor of the University of Paris, defended the "liberties of the Gallican church", the religious autonomy of France, and the doctrine of conciliarism, i.e., the subordination of the pope to a general council.[1] Soon thereafter, in 1438, the conciliarist ideas were enshrined in the meeting of French bishops chaired by Charles VII that produced the Pragmatic Sanction of Bourges. Through this royal edict the pope lost most of his influence over the appointment of bishops, who were instead elected by ecclesiastical chapters. Francis I, however, depended on papal support to protect his Italian possessions. Therefore, in 1516 he negotiated the Concordat of Bologna with Pope Leo X. While the concordat granted the king the right to nominate the bishops, the pope had to confirm the nominees through the bulls of investiture. The *parlement* of Paris, which had turned into a bulwark of Gallicanism, registered the concordat only under protest and after repeated threats by Francis I.[2]

The most serious crisis of the French church came during the Wars of Religion, when the Huguenots, the French Calvinists, rapidly expanded their religious and political influence. After three decades of civil war, Henry IV, the leading Bourbon pretender to the French throne, came to the conclusion that Calvinism would always remain the faith of a minority, in violation of the current ideal of religious uniformity. He decided to convert to Catholicism and soon obtained widespread recognition as the legitimate king of France. Aware of the necessity to pacify the country, he formally ended the Wars of Religion in 1598 with the Edict of Nantes, which granted religious, political, and even

159

considerable military rights to the one or two million Huguenots in France. This edict did not establish a "state within a state", but rather accorded a privilege within the kingdom. It was not an act of toleration, but a temporary admission of weakness by the government. The edict rendered the Huguenots vulnerable in the sense that it could be revoked whenever the king's authority became more firmly established.[3]

This uneasy truce in the conflict with the Huguenots marked the beginning of the Catholic revival in France. It came half a century after the Council of Trent, although some cities, like Lyons, had felt its impact decades earlier. While the Council of Trent provided the model for Catholic reform, its decrees were accepted by the clergy, the first estate, only during the meetings of the Estates-General of 1614. The *parlement* of Paris viewed the decrees as a threat to the "liberties of the Gallican church". The impact of Gallicanism gave the Catholic revival in France a unique character and brought it into conflict with the papacy. At one point, Cardinal Richelieu even sought to become the patriarch of an autonomous Gallican church and to make himself abbot of all the Benedictine congregations in France.[4]

Though restrained by the Gallican tradition, the reform movement in the French church followed Tridentine standards. In keeping with these standards, it centered upon raising the level of clerical education, with the bishops holding a pivotal position as the chief shepherds of the local church. Their most influential role model was Carlo Borromeo, the Archbishop of Milan, who was canonized in 1610. His example was emulated in particular by such French prelates as Anthime Denis Cohon, the Bishop of Nîmes, and Alain de Solminihac, the Bishop of Cahors.[5] But episcopal reform had its political limitations. With the church so closely interwoven into the fabric of premodern society, the king had a political interest in the appointment of bishops, who themselves served not only royal but local interests. The provincial assemblies included two archbishops and four bishops as *ex officio* presidents and forty-three bishops as regular members.[6]

For the reform of the lower clergy, the bishops depended on the religious orders. One of these was the Jesuits, who favored a more humanistic and integrated understanding of the Christian's role in society. By supporting Molinism, the Jesuit theologians argued that efficacious grace depended on a free act of the human will, while their moral doctrine of probabilism lightened the obligation of scrupulous observance.[7] In France, new congregations emerged to direct successful seminaries. Cardinal Bérulle introduced the Oratorians, who quickly became the educational rivals of the Jesuits and later underwent Jansenist influence. A former Oratorian, Jean Eudes, created his own congregation, the Eudist Fathers. He concentrated on western France, where one of his seminaries, located in Rouen, yielded a record harvest of 656 ordinations in the period 1665–1669.[8] Vincent de Paul not only established the Lazarists (or the Vincentians) to staff the diocesan seminaries, but also organized retreats and held weekly Tuesday conferences to reawaken the pastoral zeal of the Parisian clergy. The seminary that had the widest impact on shaping a French model of the ideal priest was Saint-Sulpice in Paris, founded by Jean-Jacques Olier.

Some of the congregations in charge of the seminaries, like the Vincentians and the Eudist Fathers, also participated in a growing missionary movement to bring about a renewal of the sacramental life of the laity. The Eudist seminary of Rennes and the Vincentian seminary of Saint-Meen closed their doors for half a year, so that the priests could evangelize the countryside.[9] The main method used consisted in organizing missions, periods ideally of seven to eight weeks during which a team of missionaries visited a parish. Through a series of sermons delivered with disarming simplicity or resounding with dramatic damnations, and through elaborately staged liturgical celebrations and processions, the whole parish community underwent a spiritual reawakening that aimed at a more frequent and fervent reception of the sacraments of confession and communion. In the rural parishes, where most of the missions were held and where local *curés* seldom bothered to explain the main tenets of the faith, the sermons often resembled catechetical instructions.[10] At first, Jesuit missionaries in Britanny, like Michel Le Nobletz, encountered clerical resistance, but his successor, Julien Maunoir, who preached three hundred twenty-five missions in the Diocese of Quimper, was careful to gain the cooperation of the secular clergy. As a result, his missions began to attract large crowds. In Landivisau, thirty thousand persons received communion on one day.[11] In general, however, bishops resented the papal privileges that allowed Catholics to acquit themselves of their annual confession through a member of the regular clergy. This conflict became one of the issues in the religious Fronde during the 1650s.[12]

The missionary movement not only reached the dark corners of the kingdom, as in the case of Brittany, but also spilled across the oceans to touch the distant shores of Southeast Asia. In 1653 Alexandre de Rhodes, a Jesuit missionary in Indochina, arrived in Paris with a papal mandate to invite French priests to help him in the formation of a native clergy in Indochina. After a warm reception at court, he received the most eager response among the members of Jean Bagot's Association of Friends, an elitist group of former Jesuit students. Although Rhodes' mission failed, several members of the association initiated lengthy negotiations in Rome with the Congregation of the Propagation of the Faith, which in 1663 led to the foundation of the Paris Foreign Mission Society.[13] The missionary movement revealed the growing influence of the Company of the Holy Sacrament, a secret organization of *dévots* that met monthly in committee to promote the cause of foreign missions. This secret organization helped to establish in 1660 the China Company, which was to fit out a ship to take the French missionaries to Indochina. Although Cardinal Mazarin supported this project, he began to fear the secret power of the company with its many aristocratic members. Ultimately, the *parlement* of Paris prohibited all unauthorized assemblies, a prohibition that dissolved the company in the capital, though not in provincial cities like Lyons.[14]

These missionary initiatives were the charismatic results of a generation of saints. Yet the religious rejuvenation also expressed itself in a creative outburst of theological reflection. One of its chief expressions would be the rise of Jansenism, denounced by some as a danger greater than the Huguenot heresy, because it undermined the internal unity of the French church.[15] The Catholic revival had inspired a return to the purity of the early church, to the writings of the church fathers, and, above all, to those of the anti-Pelagian Augustine. It was this preoccupation with one period in the history of the church and with one phase in the life of one prestigious church father that explained both the appeal of Jansenism and the violent resistance it encountered.[16] The preoccupation derived from Cornelius Jansen's monumental work on Saint Augustine, the *Augustinus*, whose ambitious goal was to solve the intractable problem of the relation between grace and free will through a historical presentation of Augustine's theological concepts. In contrast, Jean Duvergier de Hauranne, Abbé de Saint Cyran—his friend and former fellow student—had mainly pastoral interests, aiming at a lasting reorientation of the Christian life, based not on fear but on an unconditional love of God. His mentor was Bérulle, who saw spiritual renewal as a response to Christ's call to reach through His incarnation the majestic power of God Himself. As spiritual director of the convent of Port-Royal in Paris, the saintly Saint-Cyran spread this austere spirituality through the *dévot* circles in Paris, while his protégé, Antoine Arnauld, awakened an admiration for the rigorist penitential ideals of the early church.[17]

Such an exclusivist Augustinianism and rigorist spirituality ran into particularly strong opposition from the Jesuits, who were extremely influential at the court of Louis XIV as well as in Rome. The king's later Jesuit confessor, Father Annat, was the author of anti-Jansenist tracts. While in Rome, he had collaborated with Francesco Albizzi, the fiercely anti-Jansenist assessor at the Holy Office. The Jesuit historian of the

Council of Trent, Sforza Pallavicino, was a close friend of Pope Alexander VII, while his colleague, Jean de Lugo, had taught many members of the Roman curia.[18]

The Jansenists also encountered episcopal opposition. On the basis of a strategy suggested by Albizzi, ninety-three French bishops eventually signed in 1651 a letter drawn up by Isaac Habert, the Bishops of Vabres, requesting Pope Innocent X for a ruling on five of seven propositions, indirectly associated with Jansen, that had caused an unresolved dispute at the Sorbonne. In the meanwhile, the trouble-making Jean-François-Paul de Gondi, Coadjutor of Paris and about to be Cardinal de Retz, was exploiting pro-Jansenist feeling during the Fronde.[19] Thus with Mazarin's backing, in 1653 Innocent X issued the bull *Cum occasione* which condemned the five propositions.[20] The Jansenist conflict, however, did not end there but became more subtle and complex because of the Roman approach, which was to rule on propositions and to render verdicts without explanations.[21] This imprecision enabled the Jansenists to draw a distinction between the "question of faith" (i.e., accepting the condemnation of the five propositions) and the "question of fact" (i.e., denying their presence in Jansen's work). The anti-Jansenists retaliated by obtaining Arnauld's exclusion from the Sorbonne, a move his father blamed on a Jesuit plot.[22] The Jansenists, however, carried the day in the battle for public opinion, when Blaise Pascal's *Lettres provinciales* came to their defense, sparkling with brilliant satires on Jesuit moral theology.

Exasperated with the public's enthusiastic response to Pascal, Mazarin appealed to Pope Alexander VII through the Assemblée Générale du Clergé, a quinquennial meeting of delegates elected by bishops and lower clergy, for a definite ruling on the "question of fact". When, in 1656, his bull *Ad sacram* explicitly linked the five propositions with Jansen's work, Arnauld reacted by denying papal infallibility in textual questions. Although the bull was registered by the *parlement* of Paris with some reservations, the wily Mazarin, fearful of too much ultramontane influence, neglected to enforce the signing of a formulary that required the clergy's adherence to the papal decision. He did remain, however, hostile toward Jansenism and bequeathed this hostility directly to Louis XIV.

The other threat to the religious and political unity of the realm was the Huguenot presence. When, after the fall of La Rochelle in 1629, the Huguenots were deprived of their military power, they had adopted a posture of loyalty to the crown. Both the king and the hierarchy, however, were unwilling to accept the notion of religious separatism. Under the impact of the Catholic revival, plans to remove the Huguenot menace in one way or another multiplied. Since, however, the religious vitality of the Huguenot community proved more than a match for peaceful persuasion, the main method left was to enforce, through the intendants, a strict interpretation of the Edict of Nantes on the local level. But Mazarin's domestic and foreign preoccupations saved the Huguenots from a consistent policy of harassment. Between 1643 to 1660 the *conseil des dépêches* issued ninety-three unfavorable decisions involving Huguenots, with most of the seventy-nine favorable ones occurring during the Fronde and during important negotiations with England.[23]

Mazarin's pragmatic policy toward the Jansenists and Huguenots ended abruptly in 1661 with the start of the personal reign of Louis XIV. He was determined to rule firmly and to eliminate any form of disorder, including religious dissent. He had little knowledge of religious questions and little empathy with the sincerity of differing religious viewpoints. Early in his personal reign, a council decision ordered the clergy to sign the controversial formulary. But between 1662 and 1664, the Créqui affair, which disrupted relations with Alexander VII, punctuated in 1663 by the Six Articles of the Sorbonne, which withheld support for the doctrine of papal infallibility, prevented successful enforcement. Even after 1665, when the bull *Regiminis apostolici* explicitly required the signing of the formulary, the conflict between the Roman and the Gallican churches about the appointment of episcopal judges remained an obstacle to the successful prosecution of four recalcitrant bishops. With a more flexible pope, Clement IX, an episcopal intervention that excluded the Jesuits, and Hugues de Lionne's patient ingenuity, the four bishops finally accepted an ambiguous compromise. This compromise initiated in 1669 the "Peace of the Church", which closed the Jansenist question until the end of the century.[24]

The king's initial policies toward the Jansenists were paralleled by his policies toward the Huguenots. At first, he hoped through a strict interpretation of the Edict of Nantes to achieve a steady reduction in Huguenot influence. As a result, the Huguenots saw thirty-five out of thirty-eight council decisions in 1661 go against them; in 1663 the negative record was nineteen out of twenty. Languedoc's Huguenot towns were obliged to include Catholics in the municipal government. Of the fifty Protestant churches in Poitou that were asked to produce their legal titles, twenty-seven were obliged to close.[25] At the same time, he encouraged peaceful methods, which were crowned in 1668 by the dramatic conversion of Marshal de Turenne. One of the chief contributors to Louis' success with such methods at his own court was Bishop Bénigne Bossuet, renowned for his moving sermons and funeral orations. Yet the success was only skin deep. Conversions were rare:

between 1652 and 1680 in all of Bordeaux a mere one hundred thirty. Moreover, the policy of harassing the Huguenots ended in 1669, largely for the sake of diplomatic interests. The preparation and the outbreak of the Dutch War, which rapidly developed into a continental alliance against France, preoccupied the king so much that from 1669 till 1679 there were hardly any council decisions affecting the Huguenot community. The only major effort was the creation of Paul Pellisson's conversion fund, established in 1677 to support former Huguenots. This religious bribery—niggardly administered—was a dismal failure in the Diocese of Nîmes.[26]

Although the Jansenist controversy deeply divided the French church, it did not end the Catholic reform movement. The French episcopate kept gaining in theological erudition and pastoral experience. Before their appointment, most bishops served as vicars-general in another diocese. Of the 247 episcopal nominees in the period 1611–1660, 110 had university degrees, and this number rose to 185 out of 261 in the period 1661–1715. The bishops also selected their own vicars-general, a right that limited the king's choice of episcopal nominees. Within the episcopate the proportion of bishops who had served the king or his sovereign law courts fell from sixty-five percent in 1661 to thirty-nine percent in 1715.[27] The drop reflected the rising share of the nobility of the sword, infusing an aristocratic spirit into the hierarchy. One such aristocratic prelate was Henri de Laval, Bishop of La Rochelle and a member of the Montmorency family, who combined firmness of faith with assiduity at court.[28] But, in general, episcopal absenteeism declined. Nearly each diocese opened a seminary. In part through local initiative, in part with royal prompting, thirty-six were opened in the period 1652–1660, seventy-six during the personal reign. In 1695 Louis XIV increased his bishops' jurisdiction over the lower clergy. Episcopal absolutism was a perfect mirror of royal absolutism.[29]

Although the quality of the episcopate improved, political appointments continued to be made for such key positions as Archbishop of Paris. This was certainly the case with François de Harlay, Archbishop of Rouen and one time champion of the Estates of Normandy. In 1660, after a background check by Colbert, Mazarin selected Harlay as the president of the Assemblée Générale du Clergé. In 1664, during the subscription campaign for the French West India Company, he ingratiated himself with Colbert by forcing Rouen's reluctant merchant community to open its purse.[30] Seven years later, he became Archbishop of Paris, serving as sole and permanent president of the assemblée, and as one of the king's closest ecclesiastical advisors. Harlay quickly acquired a reputation as a schemer, a sycophant, and a corrupt prelate.[31] It was only his successor, the saintly Cardinal de Noailles, who, through his frequent pastoral visits, introduced the Tridentine reforms in the rural parishes. For the first time, Noailles required all candidates for the priesthood to attend one of the five seminaries in Paris.

Bishops, however, still depended on the religious orders to introduce the spirit of Catholic reform among the laity. In 1669 Henri de Béthune, the Archbishop of Bordeaux, invited six Jesuits to hold missions in his diocese. The Jansenist Bishop of Angers, Henri Arnauld, allowed a mission led by the celebrated Capuchin, Honoré de Cannes. Even the disreputable Harlay, in Paris, set up a massive mission directed by one hundred sixty priests. He also arranged for Jean Eudes' two missions at the court of Louis XIV. The Bishop of Quimper, François de Coëtlogon, obtained the services of the Capuchins, who were assisted by twelve additional confessors from the local secular clergy. In the Diocese of Coutances, the Eudist Fathers covered most parishes over a period of forty-four years. Inspired by the missionary movement, the participation of the secular clergy increased, yet it was the religious orders that had become the backbone of the spiritual renewal. They also reinforced the king's authority, as in the case of Maunoir's missions after the revolt of 1675 in Brittany.[32]

A recurrent problem with the religious orders was the jurisdictional disputes with the bishops about the obligation of an annual confession. In such conflicts the king was called upon to act as arbitrator. In 1666 Claude Joly, the newly appointed Bishop of Agen, revived the old conflict, when he limited to one year the right of regular clergy to hear confessions. The religious orders appealed to the *parlement* of Bordeaux and to Rome, while Joly sought the protection of the king. An *arrêt du conseil* initially upheld the bishop, but after a vigorous protest from the papal nuncio, the king proved willing to adjust his Gallican maxims. A special committee, appointed by the king and consisting of the Archbishops of Paris and Rheims, of Father Ferrier, the king's confessor, and of Jean-Baptiste Colbert, recommended a compromise: the bishops approved the right to hear confession for one to three years, but only if the superiors of the religious asked for an extension.[33] The king enforced this compromise, showing his willingness to strike a delicate balance between episcopal authority and the privileges of the religious orders. He did not, however, compromise in the dispute about the separate jurisdiction of the abbey of Saint-Germain-des-Prés, a seventeenth-century center of monastic erudition. Supported by the king, the Archbishop of Paris did finally succeed in 1668 in establishing his spiritual jurisdiction over the abbey.[34]

The king and Colbert also became involved in the French missionary movement in East Asia. Pope Alexander VII had established vicariates apostolic in China and Indochina and appointed in 1658 members of the Association of Friends as titular bishops, like François Pallu, who had already conducted "domestic" missions, and Pierre de La Motte, the benefactor of the Lisieux mission of 1653 and the cofounder of the Eudist seminary in Rouen.[35] This first major project of the French missionaries served not only the centralizing policies of the Propaganda but also Colbert's plans for a colonial empire in Asia. Here Pallu emerged as the revealing link with the volatile world of financiers and tax farmers. His brother, Bertrand, and his rich uncle, Thomas Bonneau, participated in the revenue farms and tax contracts, arranged by Nicolas Fouquet, the superintendant of finances. After Fouquet's dramatic downfall, both tax farmers joined Colbert's circle of clients and helped to finance the trading companies of the 1660s. Such connections explained Pallu's regular correspondence with Colbert, in which he coupled the prosperity of the French East India Company with that of the East Asian missions.[36]

After a decade of moderation in religious affairs, and coinciding very closely with the end of the Dutch War, around 1680 the policy of inflexibility and interventionism reemerged, this time lasting till the end of the reign. The king, advised at first by his confessor La Chaise and by Harlay, became deeply involved in a series of religious conflicts: the extension of the *régale*, the revocation of the Edict of Nantes, the disputes about Quietism, and the final attempt to destroy second-generation Jansenism.

Louis' inflexible attitude first appeared in his conflict about the *régale*, which led to a bitter confrontation between Gallican and Roman principles of church government. This conflict originated in the declarations of 1673 and 1675 that extended the *régale*, a right to collect the revenues and control the benefices of vacant bishoprics, to fifty-nine dioceses in southern France, thus making it universal throughout the kingdom. But the extension yielded limited benefits. The intervening revenue was invariably turned over to the new bishop, and the right of nomination was limited. Mysteriously, Rome initially remained silent about this unilateral violation of the concordat.[37] The quarrel broke out only when Pope Innocent XI—rigorist in piety and politics—intervened to protect the right of appeal to Rome by Nicolas Pavillon and François Caulet, two bishops who had refused to accept the extension of the *régale*. This intervention pointed in the king's mind to a conspiracy between the Holy See and the Jansenists. The two bishops were among the four who had refused to sign the formulary. Opponents of the *régale* were also among the most enthusiastic supporters of the pope's plan to organize a crusade against the Turks, not at all in keeping with the diplomatic interests of Louis XIV.[38]

To Innocent's request for a revocation of the edicts, the king countered with a defense of the inalienable rights of the crown, an argument he stubbornly repeated for fifteen years. When in 1680 a papal brief threatened him with censures, the Assemblée Générale du Clergé stood firmly by his side. But he was not yet ready to throw the Gallican clergy into the breach. Instead, he sent Cardinal d'Estrées on a diplomatic mission to Rome; who in the face of the pope's obvious inflexibility, began to support the extreme threat of a national council in order to blackmail him into surrender. Such an approach coincided perfectly with the mentality of Charles-Maurice Le Tellier, brother of Louvois, Archbishop of Rheims, and a doctrinaire Gallican of the first order. It also fitted in with the thoughts of Harlay. At his suggestion, Louis convened about forty bishops in Paris to seek their advice. They, in turn, agreed to convene a special meeting of the Assemblée Générale. When this decision failed to intimidate Innocent, the king allowed it to open on October 27, 1681.

This assembly was not completely under Louis' thumb. Indeed, it exploited the situation in order to gain royal concessions. Its committee on the *régale*, chaired by Le Tellier, approved its extension, as did the assembly, provided the king renounced his right to make nominations to certain benefices. This raised the hackels of some members of the *parlement* of Paris, but the king was willing to go along. Rumors soon spread, however, that the pope intended to issue bulls of excommunication. Possibly to counter this threat, a commission on the Six Articles of the Sorbonne began to examine the rights of the Gallican church. Through the editorial intervention of the celebrated Bossuet, the first three articles were compressed into one, so that the assembly approved on March 19, 1682, the famous Four Articles, which denied papal authority over the temporal power of the king and made the pope subject to a general council.

Innocent's reaction to the actions of the assembly was the brief *Paternae caritati*, which harshly condemned the conduct of the bishops. To avoid the danger of a total break, D'Estrées and the pope agreed to an armistice of silence. The king ordered the separation of the assembly. Yet this tactical move did not pacify Innocent. When Louis submitted two signatories of the Four Articles as episcopal nominees, the pope refused to issue the bulls of investiture. D'Estrées retaliated by no longer submitting any nominations. The result of this stalemate was that by the year 1687, thirty-three dioceses were without bishops. The conflict escalated relentlessly when Innocent deprived the ambassadors in Rome of most of their extensive *franchises*, or extraterritorial privileges. His death did not at once resolve the conflict. Although the king, facing a host of enemies in the Nine Years' War, surrendered the *franchises*, the new pope, Alexander VIII, kept insisting on the withdrawal of the Four Articles. Such a drastic concession was still too much for Louis; but during the subsequent pontificate of Innocent XII, the king allowed episcopal nominees who had not signed the Four Articles to request the papal bulls of investiture. After his statement in 1693 that the Four Articles would not be enforced, the conflict about the *régale* faded away in the same mysterious manner as it had started.[39]

While relations with the papacy were going from bad to worse, the French episcopate hailed Louis as a new Constantine, efficiently whittling away the civil and religious rights of the Huguenots until in 1685 they were all swept aside by the revocation of the Edict of Nantes. The first abrupt change took place in 1678, with the exclusion of all Huguenots from the municipal government of Montauban. There followed an avalanche of council decisions against the Huguenots. There were general orders such as the suppression of the Chambers of the Edict, which had guaranteed the Huguenots some legal protection. But, more frequently, the council decisions engaged in piecemeal destruction. The number of Huguenot churches on the demolition lists of Angelo Ranuzzi, the papal nuncio in Paris, sadly illustrates this form of religious torture: twenty-eight in 1681, forty-eight in 1682, forty-five in 1683, and sixty-five in 1684. Ruvigny's personal intervention with the king remained fruitless.[40] In the opposite camp, Daniel de Cosnac, Bishop of Valence, erected the ruins of the Huguenot churches into glorious monuments to Louis' zeal for the true faith. The church even paid for the wrecking crews and for the printing of the orders.[41] During the rising waves of persecution, Harlay held high expectations that he could convince the Huguenots to abandon their "errors". When the king decided in 1682 to close the controversial Assemblée Générale, Harlay concluded it triumphantly by having it approve a letter that combined florid exhortations and underlying threats to the Huguenot churches. Louis instructed his intendants to avoid violence and to have it read, but within three years, he was ordering *dragonnades*, the billeting of soldiers in Huguenot households, which started in the spring of 1685 in Bearn and moved into the Midi during the summer. Misleading reports by overzealous intendants about a rapid increase in the number of converts apparently convinced him that only a few Huguenots remained. Whatever the immediate cause, the Edict of Fontainebleau, which revoked the Edict of Nantes on October 17, 1685, still came with surprising swiftness. The Assemblée Générale of 1685 had not asked for it, but once it came the entire French church welcomed it with a hurrah. Innocent XI was more blasé. He simply placed the king's reward into the hands of "Divine Mercy".[42] Although the deleterious economic effect of the revocation has been exaggerated, through the efforts of Huguenot refugees such as Jurieu, it was hardly a boon to Louis' image in Europe.

While the revocation of the Edict of Nantes was an act of direct royal intervention, the divisions that appeared soon thereafter within the French church caused the king to appeal to papal authority, in violation of his Gallican maxims. The first conflict involved Quietism, primarily a bitter quarrel between Bossuet and Fénelon over the role of mysticism in Catholic spirituality.[43] At the court of Louis XIV, Fénelon had joined an aristocratic circle of *dévots*, which included the Dukes de Beauvillier and Chevreuse, and their wives, both daughters of Colbert. In this circle, Fénelon met both Mme. de Maintenon, who was married in secret to the king, and Mme. Guyon, the developer of a form of mysticism based on the notion of "pure love", through which one moves beyond an intellectual understanding of religious doctrine toward a more experimental awareness of union with God. When Beauvillier became the governor of Louis' grandson, the Duke de Bourgogne, Fénelon received the influential position of tutor.

This spiritual Camelot of Sunday conferences and dinners ended suddenly in 1693, when Mme. de Maintenon turned against her protégée, Mme. Guyon, out of envy and fear of her influence upon Saint-Cyr, a school for aristocratic girls, close to Versailles. Fénelon defended her and advised her to seek the help of Bossuet. It was a disastrous suggestion. Bossuet lacked the remotest sensitivity to mysticism. He reflected, on the contrary, a prevailing antimystical sentiment, reinforced by Rome's recent condemnation of the Spanish writer Miguel de Molinos. Bossuet, therefore, rejected Mme. Guyon's ideas, but he did organize a conference at Issy to examine her writings in conferences with Louis Tronson, Superior General of Saint-Sulpice, and Noailles, Bishop of Châlons. The outcome was a protocol signed in 1695 by the participants, as well as by Fénelon, who had supplied some supporting documents. During the same year, Fénelon became Archbishop of Cambrai, and Noailles, recommended by Mme. de Maintenon, Archbishop of Paris; but while Bossuet and Noailles published the protocol with a pastoral instruction, Fénelon refused to follow suit, in spite of Mme. de Maintenon's insistence.

The whole issue of Quietism soon developed into a personal contest between Bossuet and Fénelon. Both prelates wrote treatises to defend their positions. Fénelon managed to have his, the *Maximes des Saints*, published first, but it did not do him much good at court. There were good political reasons for this. The first to warn the king about Fénelon had been Count de Pontchartrain, Controller-General of the Finances, who resented the criticism of the government's mercantilistic and militaristic policies made by Fénelon to the Duke de Bourgogne. With the king's permission, Fénelon decided to appeal to Innocent XII, and although Louis urged the pope to condemn the *Maximes*, such was the shift of public opinion in Fénelon's favor that Rome hesitated to censure him. Bossuet produced his ultimate weapon when he composed his *Relation sur le Quietisme*, which hinted at an improper relationship between Fénelon and Mme. Guyon. Surrendering to persistent lobbying by Louis and by Bossuet's young nephew in Rome, in 1699 Innocent XII finally issued the brief *Cum alias*, which condemned twenty-three propositions from the *Maximes*. At this point Fénelon submitted, showing his firm belief in the infallibility of the church.[44]

Although he denied the motive of revenge, Fénelon's conflict with Noailles, which was an offshoot of the Quietist controversy, would recur as a significant element in the king's most serious conflict, his attempt to destroy the second generation of Jansenists. For three decades, the issue of Jansenism had remained dormant. After the "Peace of the Church", the Jansenists had concentrated on liturgical reform and on developing a biblical spirituality, both based on making the Scripture available in French translations. They also studied the the writings of the church fathers. Here Pasquier Quesnel of the Oratory made a reputation through his publication of the works of Pope Leo the Great, even though in 1676 the Holy Office condemned it because of its Jansenist commentary. In 1668 Quesnel had begun to publish a short series of meditations on biblical texts, which he repeatedly expanded, until in the 1690s they had become a large work, known under the short title of *Réflexions morales*. Gradually, Quesnel had moved away from the rigorism of early Jansenism in favor of a christological spirituality that centered upon the human heart and the mystical body of Christ.[45] In 1696 Tirso Gonzales de Santalla, the Jesuit general, warned La Chaise about the growing influence of Jansenism. Louis himself became alarmed when, in 1703, in the midst of the War of the Spanish Succession, the capture of Quesnel's papers in Brussels suddenly revealed the wide range of his connections. The king made up his mind to destroy this new Jansenist menace, with the Jesuits and with Fénelon, who objected both to the Jansenists' quibbling and to their intellectuality, collaborating in the assault.[46]

Besides their long standing emnity, the French Jesuits had an additional motive to attack the Jansenists, because the Jesuit mission in Peking, which they had started in 1688 under royal protection, had become involved in the Chinese rites controversy. The Jansenists were constantly criticizing the missionary methods of the Jesuits as another example of their willingness to compromise on Christian moral principles.[47] The Jesuit Michel Le Tellier, who in 1709 became Louis' confessor, and Louis Le Comte, the Duchess de Bourgogne's confessor, had both published works defending the policy of cultural accommodation. Le Tellier's book, which was attacked by Quesnel, was not allowed a reprint by the Holy Office because of an intervention by Henri Dorat, the Roman agent of Caulet, the Jansenist and antiregalian bishop of Pamiers.[48] In 1700 the Sorbonne condemned Le Comte's publication, under pressure from Bossuet, the Archbishops of Paris and Rheims, and the Paris Foreign Mission Society. It was a member of the same society, Charles Maigrot, the Vicar Apostolic of Fukien, who had reopened the controversy in 1696 when he had forbidden the use of Chinese terms for God. Since Jacques Brisacier, the long-term superior of the Paris Foreign Mission Society, had sided with Mme. de Maintenon in the Quietist controversy, Fénelon strongly supported the Jesuit position. Louis, however, did no more than to insist on the impartiality of the Roman judges who were to examine the question, and in 1704 Pope Clement XI decided to confirm Maigrot's decision.[49]

It was within this atmosphere, charged with religious rivalries and personal conflicts, that the Jansenist question was reopened. One of the first partisan acts was the examination of Quesnel's confiscated papers in the lion's den of the anti-Jansenist movement, the Collège Louis-le-Grand, by the Jesuit Louis Doucin, Le Tellier's former student, and Jacques Philippe Lallemant, who maintained close contacts with Guillaume Daubenton, the order's Assistant-General of France in Rome.[50] Irritated with the unexpected existence of a Jansenist network, Louis had appealed to the pope to destroy it. The hesitant reply, in 1705, was the bull *Vineam Domini*. But the only major result of the bull was the complete destruction of Port-Royal-des-Champs, an act that merely increased public sympathy for the Jansenist cause.

Directed by Fénelon, the anti-Jansenist campaign now began to move against Quesnel's *Réflexions morales*, a work that had been approved by Noailles. After constant and impatient pressure by the king, Clement in 1713 issued the bull *Unigenitus*, which condemned one hundred one propositions from the *Réflexions morales*. The condemnation was the outcome of a thorough but not impartial examination. One consultor, the Augustinian provincial Pierre-Lambert Ledrou, who showed himself more lenient toward Quesnel, suddenly withdrew after three weeks of meetings. The partisan team of Le Tellier and Daubenton had assisted in the drafting of *Unigenitus*, which by condemning propositions seventy-nine through eighty-three even prohibited the unsupervised reading of the whole Scripture by all Catholics. Louis, however, was only worried about Roman tricks to slip anti-Gallican maxims into the bull. Once satisfied with its contents, he confidently expected episcopal and judicial support. He was sorely mistaken. Noailles, enraged by this attack upon a work that he had personally approved, proclaimed the king's conscience unsafe under the guidance of Le Tellier.[51] The *parlement* of Paris delayed registration of the bull, calling for an examination by provincial synods. The king responded by convening a special meeting of bishops. But while thirty-nine bishops agreed to accept the bull, nine bishops, led by Noailles, refused. On Fénelon's suggestion, Louis planned to convene a national council to end their resistance. His death intervened.[52]

Religion in the personal reign ended the way it had started: the Jansenist problem still unresolved, even given a new lease on life. Eighteenth-century Jansenism would gather so much strength as a symbol of political opposition against the government that through a few Jansenist sympathizers in the *parlement* of Paris, it would score in 1764 its greatest triumph: the expulsion of the Jesuit Order from France.[53] But before their expulsion, the Jesuits had helped to arouse the *philosophes'* fascination with Chinese culture through the *Lettres édifiantes*, missionary letters filled with glowing progress reports about the Chinese church in order to defend their missionary methods. During this period of rising religious relativism, which was partly caused by the exposure to non-European cultures, the Jansenists lost their hold upon an educated reading public, which instead welcomed the rule of reason and the pursuit of human happiness. The reaction of an anonymous inhabitant of Montpellier was typical: he heaved a sigh of relief about the disappearance of the "disputes over Calvinism, Molinism, and Jansenism".[54] It was the same shift in public opinion that led to a growing support for religious toleration, culminating in 1787 with the Edict of Versailles, the restoration of the civil rights of the Huguenot community. The authority of the hierarchy had also been undermined through the long and bitter campaign to impose *Unigenitus* upon a divided clergy, and through a growing spirit of solidarity among the *curés*, who wanted to curtail the autocratic powers of the bishops.[55] Yet the missionary movement, which had suffered a setback abroad through the expulsion of the Jesuits, continued to flourish at home. The greatest measure of its success was that the *curés* adopted its methods and goals in the style of preaching and in liturgical celebrations.[56] Although the Quietist controversy had ruined the mystical tradition, the spiritual life of the French church remained richly textured. It was only in the eighteenth century that the devotion to the Sacred Heart of Jesus spread throughout the kingdom. The religious history of the reign was most certainly a history of intolerance, doctrinal disputes, and conflicts with Rome, but it also built up a vital legacy of clerical reform, spiritual renewal, and missionary fervor.

NOTES

1. J. Favier, "France: La Fin du Moyen Age," *Dictionnaire d'histoire et de géographie ecclésiastiques*, XVII, col. 48.
2. R. J. Knecht, *Francis I* (Cambridge, 1982), 51–65.
3. Mark Greengrass, *France in the Age of Henry IV: The Struggle for Stability* (London, 1984), 68, 76–9, 83; N. M. Sutherland, *The Huguenot Struggle for Recognition* (New Haven and London, 1980), 299, 332.
4. J. H. Elliott, *Richelieu and Olivares* (Cambridge, 1984), 75; Philip T. Hoffman, *Church and Community in the Diocese of Lyons: 1500–1789* (New Haven and London, 1984), 52.
5. Jean Delumeau, *Catholicism between Luther and Voltaire* (London, 1977), 33; Donald Weinstein and Rudolph M. Bell, *Saints & Society: The Two Worlds of Western Christendom, 1000–1700* (Chicago, 1982), 225–6; Louis Chatellier, *Tradition chrétienne et renouveau catholique dans l'ancien diocèse de Strasbourg* (Paris, 1981), 220; Robert Sauzet, *Contre-Réforme et Réforme catholique en Bas-Languedoc: le diocèse de Nîmes au XVIIe siècle* (Louvain, 1979), 239.
6. Roland Mousnier, *Les Institutions de la France sous la monarchie absolue* (Paris, 1974–80), I, 255, English edition, *The Institutions of France under the Absolute Monarchy* (Chicago, 1979–84), I, 323; Michel Peronnet, "Pouvoir monarchique et épiscopat: le Roi et les évêques députés nés des Etats de Languedoc à l'époque moderne," *Parliaments, Estates and Representation* III (1983), 115, 120; *Histoire religieuse de la Bretagne*, ed. Guy-Marie Oury (Chambray, 1980), 130–1; Jean-François Soulet, *Traditions et réformes religieuses dans les Pyrénées Centrales au XVIIe siècle* (Pau, 1974), 110–8.
7. Bernard Häring, "Moral Systems," in *Sacramentum Mundi*, ed. Karl Rahner (New York, 1968–70), IV, 131.
8. *Le Diocèse de Rouen-Le Havre*, ed. Nadine-Josette Chaline (Paris, 1976), 140, 182.
9. *Le Diocèse de Rennes*, ed. Jean Delumeau (Paris, 1979), 132, 140.
10. Jean de Viguerie, "Quelques aspects du catholicisme des Français au dix-huitième siècle," *Revue historique* CCLXV (1981), 338, 342.
11. *Histoire religieuse de la Bretagne*, 180–5.
12. Richard M. Golden, *The Godly Rebellion: Parisian Curés and the Religious Fronde: 1652–1662* (Chapel Hill, 1981), 97.
13. Lucien Campeau, "Le Voyage du Père Alexandre de Rhodes en France," *Archivum Historicum Societatis Iesu* XLVIII (1979), 67–70; Guillaume de Vaumas, *L'Eveil missionnaire de la France au XVIIe siècle* (Paris, 1959), 379, 414–7.
14. Ibid., 423; *Correspondance de Fénelon*, ed. Jean Orcibal (Paris, 1972–6), I, 65–8; Hoffman, 74.
15. Jacques Gaudin, *Oraison funèbre de Messire Hardouin de Péréfixe de Beaumont* (Paris, 1671), 20–1.
16. Pietro Stella, "Augustinisme et orthodoxie des congrégations De auxiliis à la bulle *Vineam Domini*," *Dix-sèptieme siècle* XXXIV (1982), 174–9; Bruno Neveu,

"Augustinisme janséniste et magistère romaine," Ibid., 202, 205–09; Alexander Sedgwick, *Jansenism in Seventeenth-Century France: Voices from the Wilderness* (Charlottesville, 1977), 28, 51–2.

17. Ibid., 28; *History of the Church*, ed. Hubert Jedin (New York, 1965–81), VI, 28–30; Lucien Ceyssens, "L'Authenticité des cinq propositions condamnées de Jansénius," *Antonianum* LV (1980), 370.

18. Lucien Ceyssens, "François Annat, S.J., avant son confessorat: 1590–1654," *Antonianum* L (1975), 497, 515–28; Stella, 173.

19. Sedgwick, 68, *History of the Church*, VI, 45–6; Albert N. Hamscher, "The Parlement of Paris and the Social Interpretation of Early French Jansenism," *Catholic Historical Review* LXIII (1977), 401–5; Golden, 132–3; Pierre Blet, *Le Clergé de France et la monarchie* (Rome, 1959), II, 301.

20. *History of the Church*, VI, 37–40; Ceyssens, "Authenticité," 369.

21. Neveu, 196.

22. Paule Jansen, *Arnauld d'Andilly: défenseur de Port-Royal: 1654–1659* (Paris, 1973), 78.

23. David Parker, *La Rochelle and the French Monarchy* (London, 1981), 21, 33; Elizabeth Wirth Marvick, *The Young Richelieu: A Psychoanalytic Approach to Leadership* (Chicago, 1983), 68, 133; Ruth Kleinman, "Changing Interpretations of the Edict of Nantes: The Administrative Aspect: 1643–1661," *French Historical Studies* X (1978), 545, 552–61.

24. Paul Sonnino, *Louis XIV's View of the Papacy: 1661–1667* (Berkeley and Los Angeles, 1966), 79–81, University of California Publications in History, vol. LXXIX; *History of the Church*, VI, 46–9; B. Robert Kreiser, *Miracles, Convulsions, and Ecclesiastical Politics in Early Eighteenth-Century Paris* (Princeton, 1978), 5.

25. Ibid., 265–71; Solange Deyon, *Du Loyalisme au refus: les Protestants français et leur député général entre la Fronde et la Révolution* (Villeneuve-d'Ascq, 1976), 75, 87–8.

26. Ibid., 92, 94, 97, 118, 121; Yves Congar, "Turenne et la réunion des chrétiens," *Revue d'histoire de l'église de France* LXII (1976), 315–6, 321; Sauzet, 392.

27. Peronnet, 117, 119; René Tavenaux, *Le Catholicisme dans la France classique* (Paris, 1980), I, 37; *Histoire des Catholiques en France*, ed. François Lebrun, (Toulouse, 1980), 223.

28. Louis Pérouas, *Le Diocèse de La Rochelle de 1648 à 1724* (Paris, 1964), 228–9.

29. *Histoire religieuse de la Bretagne*, 134; Hoffman, 81; Mousnier, I, 342, 347, 349; Tavenaux, I, 147; *Recueil des instructions données aux ambassadeurs et ministres de France*, XVII: *Rome* (Paris, 1911), 146; Kreiser, 23.

30. Richard Bonney, *Political Change in France under Richelieu and Mazarin, 1624–1661* (Oxford, 1978), 357; Blet, *Clergé*, II, 256; Bibliothèque Nationale, *Mélanges Colbert* 123bis, fols., 771–3, Harlay to Colbert, September 9, 1664.

31. Jeanne Ferté, *La Vie religieuse dans les campagnes parisiennes, 1622–95* (Paris, 1962), 25–7, 167, 226, 313; Delumeau, *Catholicism between Luther and Voltaire*, 28–9, 187; Maarten Ultee, *The Abbey of St. Germain-des-Prés in the Seventeenth Century* (New Haven and London, 1981), 180; *Correspondance de Fénelon*, I, 165; V, 45.

32. Charles Berthelot du Chesnay, *Les Missions de Saint Jean Eudes* (Paris, 1967), 32, 51, 338; *Le Diocèse de Bordeaux*, ed. Bernard Guilleman (Paris, 1974), 116, 128; Jacques Maillard, "La Mission du Père Honoré de Cannes à Angers en

1684," *Annales de Bretagne et des Pays de l'Ouest* LXXI (1974), 502–7; Tavenaux, I, 195; Delumeau, *Catholicism between Luther and Voltaire*, 192–3; *Le Diocèse de Rennes*, 124; *Histoire des Catholiques en France*, 147–8; *Histoire religieuse de la Bretagne*, 176–85.

33. Pierre Blet, "Les Jésuites et la querrelle de la confession au temps de Louis XIV," *Archivum Historicum Societatis Jesu* XLIX (1980), 203–17.
34. Ultee, 176–80.
35. Vaumas, 423; Berthelot du Chesnay, 343; Henri Chappoulie, *Rome et les missions d'Indochine au XVIIe siècle* (Paris, 1943–48), I, 114, 124, 139–44.
36. Ibid., 278–82; Daniel Dessert, "Finance et société au XVIIe siècle: à propos de la Chambre de Justice de 1661," *Annales E.S.C.* XXIX (1974), 854–5.
37. *Correspondance du nonce en France, Frabrizio Spada: 1674–1675*, ed. Ségolène de Dainville-Barbiche (Rome, 1982), 70.
38. *Correspondance de Fénelon*, I, 94–95.
39. Compare the account of this conflict in Pierre Blet, *Les Assemblées du Clergé et Louis XIV de 1670 à 1693* (Rome, 1972), with Paul Sonnino's review essay on this book in *Reviews in European History* I, No. 3 (December 1974), 319–22.
40. Deyon, 140–42, 150; Blet, *Assemblées*, 425–6, 437–42.
41. Ibid., 474–85.
42. Ibid., 433–7.
43. For Quietism, see Lionel Rothkrug, *Opposition to Louis XIV: The Political and Social Origins of the French Enlightenment* (Princeton, 1965), 249–98; and the two biographies by Louis Cognet: "Fénelon," *Dictionnaire d'histoire et de géographie ecclésiastiques*, XVI, cols. 958–87; and "Madame Guyon," *Dictionnaire de spiritualité*, VI, cols. 1306–36. A gold mine of information are the notes in the *Correspondance de Fénelon*, I–V, edited by Orcibal.
44. Ibid., V, 51.
45. J. A. G. Tans and H. Schmitz du Moulin, *Pasquier Quesnel devant la Congrégation de l'Index* (The Hague, 1974), xxii–xxxiv; J. A. G. Tans, "Port-Royal entre le reveil spirituel et le drame gallican; le rôle de Pasquier Quesnel," *Lias* IV (1977), 102–3; Kreiser, 7–8.
46. Cognet, cols. 982–83; Lucien Ceyssens, "Jacques Philippe Lallemant: champion de l'antijansénisme," *Antonianum* LVI (1981), 754.
47. William V. Bangert, *A History of the Society of Jesus* (Saint Louis, 1972), 248–9, 279–80, 336–7; *Lettres édifiantes et curieuses de Chine par des missionnaires Jésuites*, ed. Isabelle and Jean-Louis Vissière (Paris, 1979), 20.
48. Lucien Ceyssens, "Le P. Louis Doucin, S.J.: 1652–1726," *Antonianum* LVIII (1983), 450–53; J. Carreyre, "Quesnel et le quesnellisme," *Dictionnaire de théologie catholique*, XIII, col. 1468.
49. *Recueil des Instructions*, XVII: *Rome*, 215; Henk Hillenaar, *Fénelon et les Jésuites* (The Hague, 1967), 229–41; Ceyssens, "Jacques Philippe Lallemant," 756; *Correspondance de Fénelon*, V, 160.
50. Ceyssens, "Le P. Louis Doucin," 449–50, 460–1, 464, and "Jacques Philippe Lallemant," 757–8, 764–5; Hillenaar, 148–9.
51. Ibid., 256–7; J. Carreyre, "Unigenitus," *Dictionnaire de théologie catholique*, CXLIV–V, cols. 2112–5; Albert Le Roy, *Le Gallicanisme au XVIIIe siècle: la France et Rome de 1700 à 1715: histoire diplomatique de la bulle Unigenitus jusqu'à la mort de Louis XIV, d'après des documents inédits* (Paris, 1892), 362–4; Lucien Ceyssens and J. A. G. Tans, "L'*Unigenitus* à Rome: 1712–1713," *Lias* VIII

(1981), 3; Lucien Ceyssens, "Le Cardinal Charles-Augustine Fabroni: 1651–1727," *Bulletin de l'Institut Historique Belge de Rome* LII (1982), 189.
52. *History of the Church*, VI, 381–7; Sedgwick, 191–2.
53. Dale van Kley, *The Jansenists and the Expulsion of the Jesuits from France: 1757–1765* (New Haven and London, 1975), 229–30.
54. Quoted in Robert Darnton, *The Great Cat Massacre* (New York, 1984), 139.
55. Kreiser, 395; *Histoire des Catholiques en France*, 157.
56. Viguerie, 343–4; Hoffman, 139–40, 151–65.

ELEVEN

Science in the Reign
of Louis XIV

SEYMOUR L. CHAPIN

Although the medieval university, following in the traces of Aristotle, Ptolemy, and Galen, erected the basic framework for man's collective actions in the scientific field, it was the Italian "Renaissance", more Pythagorean, Platonistic, and Cabbalistic, that either reshaped or supplanted the methods of the past. Probably the most persistent note sounded by the Italian humanists was their anti-Aristotelianism. There were two variants of this theme. On the one hand, there was a broad rejection of the authority of "The Philosopher" in favor of the newer trends. Such a supplantation required new institutions, and the Italian princes obliged the "Renaissance" humanists by creating academies and professorships from which these alternatives could be developed. As opposed to this total rejection, there was a continuation of a late medieval attack upon specific weak points within the traditional systems, pursued largely in the established universities, such as Padua. Botanical gardens and theaters for the public performance of dissections were typical features of these revitalizing centers.[1]

As the "Renaissance" spirit spread beyond Italy, the northern humanists and their stylish monarchs imitated the Italian example. Such was the case in France, where in 1530 Francis I appointed a group of "readers", which quickly became known as the Collège Royal de France. The collège gave no examinations and awarded no degrees, being more like a research center in which chairs of mathematics and medicine were included almost from the outset; and not surprisingly, Pierre de La Ramée (or Ramus), one of its first professors of philosophy, relentlessly debunked Aristotle. While this new center was in the forefront of the newest trends, the University of Paris, unlike its Italian counterparts, resisted them. Long after Vesalius' *On the Structure of the Human Body*, published in 1543, challenged Galenist anatomy on numerous points, it continued to reign supreme on the Left Bank of the Seine. But the University of Montpellier, closer to Italy, embraced the study of chemical

179

pharmacopeia and created a botanical garden in order to further the medicinal use of plants.[2]

Copernicus' *On the Revolutions of the Heavenly Spheres*, also published in 1543, posed an even greater threat to established patterns of thought. Though in many ways simply reshuffling the work of Ptolemy, Copernicus nevertheless revolutionized it by insisting that the earth travels around the sun and that the sun and stars, to which he attributed greater nobility, are immobile. The great advantage of this approach, in his own view, was that it restored an Aristotelian axiom regarding uniform circular motion. The great drawback of the theory, in the view of his critics, was that it contradicted every other axiom of Aristotelian physics. In France the Sorbonne rejected him, while Ramus issued a call for an "arithmetical" astronomy that would merely add up heavenly motions rather than force them into a Ptolemaic or Copernican strait-jacket. A mathematical orientation in French scientific endeavor thus emerged quite early.[3]

By the early seventeenth century, the Italians were beginning to establish academies devoted specifically to the study of science. In 1603 the Roman nobleman Cesi formed the Accademia dei Lincei, whose reputation quickly spread. Its most renowned member was Galileo. His previous work on the motion of bodies had been a decisive step in the direction of a new physics necessary to buttress Copernicanism, and his subsequent astronomical observations furnished less-conclusive albeit more spectacular support to the modern system. Galileo wrote no treatise on method. Yet his contribution to methodology was probably his greatest contribution to science. In this connection, he insisted upon a distinction between the primary and secondary qualities of matter. It was only the former—like shape and weight—with which he concerned himself. The latter—such as taste, smell, and color—he ignored. The reason was clear: it was only the primary qualities that could be treated mathematically. His desire to achieve the rational geometrizing of problems and his experimental program of rolling balls down inclined planes led him to the concept of uniform acceleration. That discovery, in turn, led him to enunciate an almost modern doctrine of inertia, which stated that a body in motion will continue in a circular line until something intervenes to slow or deflect it. His vision was too clouded by a predilection for circular motion to hit upon Kepler's more radical idea of elliptical orbits, but Galileo remained an outspoken advocate of original Copernicanism until silenced by the Inquisition in 1633.[4]

In France the gifted amateur Fabri de Peiresc, whose vocation was in the *parlement* of Aix, undertook activities similar to those of Cesi, forming a loose scientific network in the southern part of the country. The most important adherent of Peiresc's group was the atomist Pierre Gassendi. Upon Peiresc's death, in 1637, Gassendi moved to Paris, where he bacame both a professor at the Collège Royal and a participant in the circle of the Minim friar Marin Mersenne. Gassendi's transfer to Paris symbolizes the emergence of the capital's and the state's scientific dominance. Already in 1626 Louis XIII had established a botanical garden, the Jardin du Roi, there; and in 1635 Richelieu had created the Académie Française for the purpose of standardizing the French language. Mersenne's group included the mathematician Pierre de Fermat and the young prodigy Blaise Pascal, who collaborated to lay down the basis for modern probability theory. There were also in Paris at this time public lectures and a free clinic associated with the Bureau d'Adresse, run by Théophraste Renaudot, a Montpellier product.[5]

The most celebrated member of Mersenne's entourage was René Descartes. His *Discourse on Method* of 1637 was both his manifesto rejecting the past and his program for the deductive, mathematical, and experimental road to the future. The *Discourse* served to introduce three specific scientific treatises, one of which created the new tool of analytical geometry. And although he was delayed in part by the condemnation of Galileo, Descartes, with his *Principles of Philosophy*, ultimately brought out his entire mechanistic, nonteleological system of the world. His position was that God had originally set matter (extension) in motion and that the universe conserved this same amount of motion for all time. Here was an effort to retain the "plenum" of the Aristotelians while rejecting their motive forces inherent in matter. Here, too, was a more ambitious version of Galileo's doctrine of inertia. In describing how this simple mechanistic conception could account for the complicated facts of observation, Descartes elaborated his controversial theory, according to which there had to exist an extraordinarily fine "first matter," located in a number of "vortices" in the heavens. The sun and its surrounding planets remained respectfully, in the light of Galileo's condemnation, motionless, each carried around in its particular vortex. Descartes even reduced all living things to the level of automata, with the sole exception of human consciousness; small wonder that he so warmly embraced the theory of the circulation of the blood put forward in 1628 by William Harvey, with its picture of the human heart as a mechanical pump and its rejection of Galenic spirits. This approach serves to underline Descartes' metaphysical dualism, his separation of the world into one part made up of an immense machine extended in space, the other made up of unextended thinking spirits, mysteriously employing their pineal glands in order to direct the motions of their bodies. The main problem with Cartesianism is that although it claimed to be so mathematical, some of its mechanisms—e.g., vortices or the pineal gland—were so obscure that they removed from mathematical consideration precisely those characteristics of the phenomenal world that Galileo had been struggling to quantify. Indeed, Gassendi criticized the Cartesian plenum, while the University of Paris rose to the defense of Galenism. Still, in spite of the apparent contradiction between its dualism and the Catholic doctrine of transubstantiation, Cartesianism established a tremendous hold over generations of French scientists.[6]

The death of Mersenne, in 1648, coincided roughly with the coming of the Fronde, that haphazardly organized uprising against young Louis XIV, Anne of Austria, and Cardinal Mazarin. The scientific community was disrupted, but with the restoration of order, new centers of scientific activity appeared. Gaston d'Orléans, the king's uncle, set up a considerable establishment at Blois, featuring an astronomical observatory and a botanical collection. Henri-Louis Habert de Montmor, *maître de requêtes* and member of the Académie Française, placed his town house in Paris at the disposal of Gassendi, and regular meetings of an "academy" were held there as early as 1654. The monarchy, too, resumed its patronage of the arts and sciences. Mazarin utilized the ambitious intendant, later superintendant, of finances, Nicolas Fouquet, who himself worked through the poet Gilles Menage, the historian Paul Pellisson, and the mathematician Pierre Carcavi, in order to establish a coterie of intellectuals. It met in the excellent library of Fouquet's house at Saint-Mandé, which was opened to the public in 1657 and rapidly became a setting for scholarly research. Mazarin also utilized the financial director of his own estate, Jean-Baptiste Colbert, for the collection of intellectual talent. The death of Mazarin, in 1661, and the beginning of Louis' personal reign, as is well known, saw the arrest of Fouquet and the triumph of Colbert, who eventually became controller-general of finances and secretary of state for the navy. Quickly, most of Fouquet's clients switched their allegiance. One of the principal defectors was Carcavi, who obtained some of Fouquet's books for the Royal Library, which in 1663 became the site for the meetings of a *petite académie*. Another significant refugee was the architect Charles Perrault, who became its secretary. Still another of its members, Jean Chapelain of the Académie Française, drew up a long list of scholars deserving state support.[7]

In this period new scientific societies under princely protection were sprouting up all over Europe. In 1657 Grand Duke Leopold of Tuscany founded the Accademia del Cimento, while in 1662 Charles II of England granted a charter to the Royal Society. Membership did not bring payment, but, in contrast, the private Montmor club in France was floundering in amateurish disputations, and in 1663 Samuel de Sorbière, its secretary, addressed a discourse to Colbert maintaining that only kings and princes could effectively underwrite scientific endeavors. This was certainly in line with the statist conceptions of Colbert, who felt that an official scientific society not only would enhance the prestige of the Sun King, but also would serve as a consultative body for the ambitious economic and colonial policies of the government. Colbert was himself attempting to attract the Dutch Protestant Christiaan Huygens, inventor of an accurate marine chronometer, to France, and another sign of beneficent interest in science was the granting of a privilege to the *Journal des Savants*, whose first issue, with its announcements and reviews of books, along with its indications of new inventions and discoveries, appeared in January 1665. About this same time Adrien Auzout, an aspiring astronomer and perfector of the micrometer, offered up a splinter group of experimentally minded scientists that had been meeting in Paris at the home of Melchisédich Thévenot for incorporation into a royal society.[8]

Not surprisingly, the members of the *petite académie* were in the best position to anticipate Colbert's intentions, and in the beginning of 1666 Charles Perrault proposed the creation of a general academy, munificently staffed by paid *pensionnaires*, to consist of sections for *belles-lettres* (grammar, eloquence, poetry), history (general, geography, chronology), philosophy (anatomy, botany, chemistry, experimental physics), and mathematics (algebra, astronomy, geometry), each of which was to meet twice weekly in the Royal Library. By this time Colbert was ready to move. In April Huygens took up residence in Paris, and in the following month Colbert began selecting pensioners for the new body. He was careful. He did not want it to represent a threat to established groupings. Thus he started with "mathematicians", such as Huygens; Carcavi; Auzout; Bernard Frénicle de Bessy, councillor in the *cour des monnaies*; Jacques Buot, professor at the Grande Ecurie; and Gilles Personne de Roberval, professor at the Collège Royal. Colbert then proceeded to the "philosophers", Marin Cureau de La Chambre, physician ordinary to the king; Jean Pecquet, who had discovered the body's lymphatic system; Claude Perrault, architect, physician, and brother of Charles; Louis Gayant, a rather obscure surgeon; Nicolas Marchant, onetime apothecary to Gaston d'Orléans; Claude Bourdelin Ier and Samuel Cottereau-Duclos, physicians and chemists. By the end of November, however, Colbert had decided not to push matters further, and he abandoned the two other sections. Instead, in addition to those already established he appointed five unpaid *élèves*, or students. Finally, the

Oratorian priest Jean-Baptiste Du Hamel was named perpetual secretary. His minutes of the first plenary meeting, held on December 22, 1666, reveal that the society was to gather every Wednesday and Saturday, with mathematics being discussed on the first day and physics on the second. Though not originally possessed of a royal charter per se, this organization quickly became known as the Académie Royale des Sciences. Du Hamel's minutes also reveal that the academicians initially expected to be working in concert, an intention made even clearer by the purchase, in March 1667, of land adjoining the Luxembourg gardens for its new home, which was to lodge its members, its equipment, and its observatory. As it turned out, the remote location and the frequent impracticability of the common program led to the land's being used exclusively for the Royal Observatory, which began its astronomical life in September of 1671.[9]

During the earliest sessions, Auzout set forth a program calling for a wide variety of observations both at home and abroad by means of scientific expeditions, a remarkable innovation that meshed splendidly with Colbert's desire to achieve the accurate mapping of the kingdom. This emphasis brought two additions to the academy. One was Jean Picard, the closest approximation to a professional astronomer then to be found in France, the other Giovanni Domenico Cassini, lured from Italy in 1668 by a handsome royal pension. And it was in the field of astronomy that the academy scored its greatest successes. On land, it carried through a revolution in observational astronomy made possible by Huygens' astronomical pendulum clocks, Auzout's micrometer, and the combination of telescopes with large-scale graduated instruments appropriate for the measuring of small angles. It was with this equipment that Picard undertook to determine the length of a degree of latitude on the meridian of Paris. Marked by a precision thirty to forty times greater than any previously achieved, that eminently successful experiment became the basis on which the desired rectification of French cartography could be carried out. At sea and abroad, in 1668 and 1669, the *élève* Delavoye made two successful voyages to the Mediterranean to test Huygens' clocks, the outcome of which stimulated in 1670 the sending of his fellow student Richer on a less-successful voyage to Acadia. Then, in 1671, Picard traveled to the site of Tycho Brahe's Danish observatory, and Richer was dispatched to Cayenne. The former aimed at establishing the longitudinal separation of Uraniborg from Paris in order to correct Tycho's observations, while the latter, aside from making longitudinal observations of his own, hoped to deduce, by means of corresponding observations of Mars made by Cassini in Paris, a new and improved figure for the parallax of the sun. Picard brought back with him Ole Römer, who engaged in Paris in his study of the deviation of the eclipses of Jupiter's satellites from their predicted times, leading him in 1676 to enunciate the finite velocity of light and provide a reasonably accurate figure for it. As to Richer, he found it necessary to shorten a seconds-pendulum that had been accurately adjusted in Paris, thus providing the first hint that the earth is not a perfect sphere, though Cassini charged the discrepancy to Richer's carelessness. This thrust toward scientifically determined locating continued into the early 1680s. Picard completed his work on Tycho's observations, a massive edition of which went to press in 1682, and made plans for a voyage to Alexandria for a similar study of Ptolemy's. Cassini, for his part, trained a Jesuit going to China and engineers going to the West Indies in the methods of astronomical observation and was making plans for a southward extension of Picard's earlier arc measure. Unfortunately, all of these projects came to naught, succumbing either to the death of Picard, in 1682, or to the passing of Colbert the following year.[10]

The role of Auzout in the mathematical section was paralleled by that of Claude Perrault in the philosophical one. He was a leading instigator of an extensive program of dissection that began in April of 1667. He had for collaborators such original appointees as Pecquet, Cureau de La Chambre, Gayant, and a new member, Edmé Mariotte. One of the first dissections was that of a young woman who had died at Versailles, although dissections of animals were more commonplace. The results of these activities were summed up in the *Mémoires pour servir à l'histoire naturelle des animaux,* on the appearance of which in 1671 Louis had the members of the academy presented to him. While paying due Cartesian attention to the mechanism of anatomical features and destroying many popular myths, this work added little new knowledge, except perhaps to provide more exact illustrations and lay the groundwork for some of Perrault's subsequent publications. It had nothing to do, on the other hand, with Mariotte's independent discovery of the blind spot in the eye. Perrault also proposed the preparation of a "Histoire des plantes", an effort in which he was to be joined by Marchant, Bourdelin, and Duclos. Although this project was later abandoned, Denis Dodart, a second botanist added to the academy in 1673, published many of its descriptions in his *Mémoires pour servir à l'histoire des plantes,* while Joseph Pitton de Tournefort, who worked mainly in the Jardin du Roi and joined the academy only in 1691, elaborated a completely new system of plant classification in his *Elémens de botanique.*[11]

Finally, Mariotte engaged in notable researches in physics. His failure to confirm the experiments Isaac Newton described in his first letter on light and color greatly delayed the acceptance of these ideas on the continent. On the other hand, Mariotte came up with the same conclusions as Robert Boyle on the relationship between volume and pressure, this law in France being known as Mariotte's law.[12]

Although the most important scientific work done in France during the first three decades of Louis XIV's personal reign was under the aegis of the academy, this does not mean that it was the sole site of scientific endeavors. A whole generation was growing up on Descartes' philosophy. In the 1650s Jacques Rohault, an early member of the Montmor circle, had begun to hold weekly lectures on Cartesianism at his own house, and his *Traité de Physique,* published in 1671, quickly became the standard textbook of Cartesian physics. Among his listeners, or readers, must have been Molière's pseudo-intellectual *Femmes Savantes,* whose learned considerations upon vortices attest to the currency of this theory in polite society. A more serious convert was Father Nicolas Malebranche, an Oratorian priest and Professor of Mathematics who saw himself as the chief mediator between theology and Cartesianism. A mediator was certainly needed, for as he developed his ideas, his own Oratory and many French universities stubbornly prohibited the teaching of the new philosophy. But he overcame the reluctance of the censors and published his *Recherche de la vérité,* which was followed, in his own name, by his pupil Jean Prestet's *Elémens des mathématiques.*[13]

The death of Colbert, in 1683, ushered in some significant changes. His longtime rival Louvois, secretary of state for war, immediately took the academy under his wing, but he tended to limit his scientific vision to the activities of Vauban and a corps of some two hundred military engineers. The astronomers who had left for the extension of the meridian were called back, and the publication of Tycho's observations was halted. Moreover, although Louvois agreed to finance the publication of a book on the astronomical and geodetical voyages of the academy, he gave it no great encouragement. The deaths of Carcavi and Mariotte, both occurring in 1684, and the revocation of the Edict of Nantes in 1685, which led the Protestants Huygens and Römer to leave France, may also have contributed to this trend. Instead, the labors of the astronomers were directed to projects nearer to the king's heart, such as the surveying for an aqueduct that would conduct the waters of the river Eure into the fountains of Versailles. All in all, during Louvois' stewardship presentations on astronomy decreased some thirty-eight percent, while those on mechanics and mathematics disappeared almost entirely.[14]

In contrast to the decline of research in the exact sciences, there was an increase in works on anatomy and natural history. Louvois, who had also agreed to support a book on rare animals, gave this project his strong personal endorsement. It seems as if one motivation for this new emphasis on the life sciences was its relationship to the health of the royal family. In 1682 Louis suffered his first attack of the gout, and the following year he dislocated his elbow, experienced lymphangitis, and was struck by the sudden death of his queen from staphylococcal septicemia, these being but preludes to his upsets of 1686, a bout with malaria and a very painful anal fistula. Louvois not only set up a center in Paris for experimentation on fistulous subjects, he also consulted on this matter with the academy. He was still no Colbert. After 1686 Louvois took virtually no more interest in the academy, which tended to degenerate from lack of direction. The carrying of the torch of science seemed to be passing to such popularizers as Bernard de Fontenelle, whose *Entretiens sur la pluralité des mondes* extolled a Cartesian mechanistic view of the universe for the society at large to contemplate.[15]

The death of Louvois, in 1691, ushered in still more changes. Control over the academy now passed into the hands of Louis Phélypeaux, Count de Pontchartrain, whose position as controller-general of the finances and secretary of state for the navy hinted at a return to the days of Colbert. Pontchartrain seemed to have the best intentions in this regard. One of his initiatives was the establishment of a monthly periodical, the *Mémoires,* in order to bring the academicians' work more promptly before the eyes of the public. Another was to create the entirely new post of president and to place in it his own nephew, Abbé Jean-Paul Bignon. But although these alterations may have restored a new sense of dignity to the activities of the academy, the Nine Years' War, with its many financial and other exigencies, prevented anything like a brilliant recrudescence of the sciences from taking place. The *Mémoires* proved short-lived, while the project to extend the meridian, though supported in theory, could not be funded until 1700. And, like Louvois, Pontchartrain did not rely exclusively on the services of the academy. In 1696 he established, as part of the secretariat of the navy, the Dépôt des Cartes et Plans. Made up of cartographers, engineers, and such military experts as Vauban, this bureau continued, after the war, to plan France's New World development, including Iberville's voyage of 1698 to the mouth of the Mississippi. A clear distinction between the academy's systematic researches and the practical pursuits of the military technicians thus emerged at this point.[16]

Whether inspired by Colbert, Louvois, or Pontchartrain, the achievements of French astronomers continued to be largely observational and did little to advance astronomical theory, thanks in part to their attachment to Cartesian principles. Mariotte's failure to confirm Newton's key experiment on the refraction of light led to the rejection of his theory of colors. Similarly, his discovery of the law of universal gravitation, enunciated in his *Principia*, went completely unappreciated in France, his concept of action at a distance being incompatible with the dominant mechanistic philosophy. On the contrary, Leibnitz' new calculus was greeted with immense enthusiasm by such French mathematicians as Malebranche, L'Hospital, and Varignon. Still another sign of popularity of Cartesianism was the appointment, in 1697, of Fontenelle as perpetual secretary to replace the retired Du Hamel.[17]

Although the Newtonian achievement made leadership in science pass to England in the last decades of the seventeenth century, French science was given a considerable boost by the reorganization of the academy in 1699. With several years of experience under his belt, Abbé Bignon undertook to reorganize the academy with a set of official regulations. They considerably expanded the academy's membership, adding to the old *pensionnaires* and *élèves* such new classes as *honoraires*, *correspondants*, and *associés*, although only the last were to contribute significantly to the academy's scientific production. Of their number of twenty, eight were to be foreigners, Leibnitz and Newton being among the first named. The twelve French associates were distributed equally across six disciplines, each of which also featured three *pensionnaires* and two students chosen by them. This hierarchy ultimately meshed with a financial arrangement in which *pensionnaires* received salaries on one of three scales, associates possessed only limited possibilities for lesser payments, and *élèves*—later to be designated *assistants*—continued in their unremunerated status. Still, the monetary support was very important and was carried over into a provision for the annual publication of the *Mémoires*. Moreover, the new statute gave to the academy and its members several rights and privileges, such as censorship and the examination of machines, which made of it and them one corporate body placed at the center of French scientific endeavor. Although these changes made for greater specialization, they also retained certain common elements, like the presentation by academicians of works before their peers. These practices facilitated a confrontation between Cartesian and Newtonian principles that saw the stubborn retreat of the first and the relentless advance of the second.[18]

Newton's discoveries on light and color were summed up in his *Optiks*, published in 1704, a Latin edition of which appeared in 1706. Malebranche lost no time in integrating them with his own ideas, a process pursued by three of his disciples, Reyneau, Privat de Molières, and Mairan, the first French scientist to repeat some of Newton's experiments on color. But Mairan's work still did not overcome the skepticism of the French scientific community. Following a challenge issued by Leibnitz in the *Acta eruditorum*, the demonstrations were verified in London in April 1715 under the direction of Desaguliers, a Huguenot refugee. A delegation of French scientists carefully noted the precautions that were required, thus permitting the same experiments to be repeated successfully in France in the presence of members of the academy. The *Optiks* was translated into French, and by the time of Fontenelle's 1727 *Eloge* of Newton, that work had come to be accepted in France as the very model of experimental science. Newton's laws of motion, on the other hand, had greater difficulty in gaining adherents. One of the members of the 1715 delegation to London was the Chevalier de Louville, a recent astronomical addition to the academy, who is probably best known for having applied a micrometer to a quadrant. Having already worked on the apparent path of the sun, he was also in London to observe a solar eclipse, and his interest culminated in 1720 with his presentation to the academy of a *mémoire* on the construction of solar tables. It was the first such exposition in France to make use of gravitational principles. Unlike the situation with the *Optiks*, however, there was not, in this other area, a single crucial or even a series of specific experiments that could be performed in order to gain the allegiance of the scientific community. This had to be done, therefore, through a demonstration that Newtonian principles could "save the phenomena" better than those of Descartes could. Maupertuis, who during his trip to London in 1728 was converted from Cartesian vortices to Newtonian mechanics, became the foremost proponent of the Newtonian system in France, employing it in studies of the shape of the earth and of tides. His position brought him into conflict with Giovanni Cassini's son, Jacques, on whom it had fallen to carry out the extension of Picard's arc measure, and who had published results that contradicted Newton. The issue was joined in the middle of the 1730s by the academy's dispatch of expeditions to Peru and to Lapland, the latter suggested and headed by Maupertuis. The results, of course, vindicated the Newtonian position.[19]

While Newton's worldview was slowly infiltrating the academy, Voltaire, in his *Philosophical Letters* of 1734, was disseminating both Newton's laws of motion and Locke's sensationalist psychology among educated French men and women generally. This work was followed by Voltaire's *Elements of Sir Isaac Newton's Philosophy*, by Abbé Condillac's further development of Locke's epistemology, and by the Marquise du Châtelet's French translation of the *Principia*. The scientific spirit in the Newtonian and Lockian sense was thus becoming the spirit of the entire "Enlightenment".[20]

In some ways the academy thrived amid the spreading recognition of science that characterized the eighteenth century, serving as a model for the academies founded in Berlin (1700) and Saint Petersburg (1724), as well as the large number of provincial academies that sprouted up throughout France. The Paris academy also allowed the plates prepared for its own *Description des arts et métiers* to be used in Diderot's *Encyclopedia*, the greatest combined scientific effort of the age. Yet the academy occasionally felt threatened by this same process and fell prey to the common malady of exclusivity and ossification. In the 1730s the academy engineered the suppression of the promising Société des Arts, and in the 1780s the academy attempted, this time unsuccessfully, to prevent the reorganization of the observatory. Moreover, the academy refused to expand its membership at a time when the number of capable scientists was growing by leaps and bounds, and was slow to accommodate new areas of scientific inquiry, such as the electrical studies that were becoming so popular. The French Revolution put an end to the academy and, temporarily at least, to its corporate approach to science. That a more democratized science was able to survive the academy and the revival in our own age of government-directed scientific endeavors is a testament to the enduring legacy of Colbert's creation.[21]

NOTES

1. Paul Lacroix, *Science and Literature in the Middle Ages and the Renaissance* (New York, 1878); Herbert Butterfield, *The Origins of Modern Science* (London, 1949); A. C. Crombie, *Augustine to Galileo: The History of Science: A.D. 400–1650* (London, 1952); *History of Science: The Beginnings of Modern Science from 1450–1800*, ed. René Taton (New York, 1964); *Actes du seizième colloque international: Platon et Aristote à la Renaissance* (Tours, 1975); *The Emergence of Science in Western Europe*, ed. Maurice Crossland; George Sarton, *Six Wings: Men of Science in the Renaissance* (Bloomington, 1957); Marie Boas, *The Scientific Renaissance: 1450–1630* (New York, 1962).

2. Louis Sedillot, *Les Professeurs de mathématiques et de physique générale au Collège de France* (Rome, 1869); Abel Lefranc, *Histoire du Collège de France depuis ses origines jusqu'à la fin du premier empire* (Paris, 1893). Ramus' principal attack on Aristotle was in his *Aristotelicae animadversiones* (Paris, 1543). See also Roijer Hooykaas, *Humanisme, science et reforme: Pierre de La Ramée (1515–1572)* (Leiden, 1958). Andreas Vesalius, *De humani corporis fabrica* (Basel, 1543). See also, Charles D. O'Malley, *Andreas Vesalius of Brussels: 1514–1564* (Los Angeles and Berkeley, 1964).

3. Nicolaus Copernicus, *De revolutionibus orbium coelestium libri vi* (Nuremberg, 1543). See also Thomas Kuhn, *The Copernican Revolution: Planetary Astronomy in the Development of Western Thought* (Cambridge, 1957), and Edward Rosen, *Copernicus and the Scientific Revolution* (Malabar, 1984). Ramus' position was enunciated in his *Proaemium mathematicus* (Paris, 1567).

4. Galileo Galilei, *Sidereus Nuncius* (Venice, 1610), *Tres epistolae de maculis solaribus* (Augsburg, 1612), and *Il Saggiatore* (Rome, 1623), as well as *Discov-*

eries and Opinions of Galileo, ed. Stillman Drake (Garden City, 1957). Galileo's *Dialogo sopra i due massimi sistemi del mondo, Tolemaico e Copernicano* (Florence, 1632) was the source of his troubles with the Inquisition. See also Giorgio de Santillana, *The Crime of Galileo* (Chicago, 1955); Alexandre Koyré, *Etudes galiléennes* (Paris, 1966); and Stillman Drake, *Galileo Studies: Personality, Tradition, and Revolution* (Ann Arbor, 1970). Johann Kepler, *Astronomia nova* (Prague, 1609). See also Max Caspar, *Johannes Kepler* (Stuttgart, 1948), English translation by C. Doris Hellman (New York, 1959).

5. Peiresc published nothing, but his extensive correspondence may be consulted in *Lettres de Peiresc,* ed. P. Tamizey de Larroque (Paris, 1888–98), 7 vols. Collection des documents inédits sur l'histoire de France, ser. 5, vol. 9. Pierre Humdert, *Un amateur: Peiresc* (Paris, 1933); Bernard Rochot, *Les Travaux de Gassendi sur Epicure et sur l'atomisme: 1619–1658* (Paris, 1944); *Pierre Gassendi (1592–1655): sa vie et son oeuvre,* Centre International de Synthèse (Paris, 1955); Marin Mersenne, *Quaestiones celeberrimae in Genesim* (Paris, 1623), and *Correspondence,* ed. C. de Waard, R. Pintard, and B. Rochot (Paris, 1932–); Robert Lenoble, *Mersenne ou la naissance du mécanisme* (Paris, 1943); Rio Howard, "Guy de La Brasse: botanique et chimie au début de la révolution scientifique," *Revue d'histoire des sciences* XXXI, 4 (October, 1978), 301–26; Marguerite Duval, *The King's Garden* (Charlottesville, 1982); Howard M. Solomon, *Public Welfare, Science, and Propaganda in Seventeenth Century France: The Innovations of Théophraste Renaudot* (Princeton, 1972). See also Robert Mandrou, *Des humanistes aux hommes de science* (Paris, 1973), English edition, *From Humanism to Science* (Hassocks, 1979); and Maurice Caullery, *French Science and Its Principal Discoveries since the Seventeenth Century* (New York, 1934).

6. René Descartes, *Discours de la méthode* (Paris, 1637) and *Principia philosophiae* (Amsterdam, 1644); Etienne Gilson, *Etudes sur le rôle de la pensée médiévale dans la formation du système cartésien* (Paris, 1930); Edwin Arthur Burtt, *The Metaphysical Foundations of Modern Science* (Garden City, 1955); E. J. Aiton, *The Vortex Theory of Planetary Motions* (New York, 1972). Harvey's discovery appeared in his *Exercitatio anatomica de motu cordis et sanguinis in animalibus* (Frankfurt on the Main, 1628). For the opposition to his theory, see Francis R. Packard, *Guy Patin and the Medical Profession in Paris in the XVIIth Century* (New York, 1970).

7. Antonin Fabre, *Etudes littéraires sur le XVIIe siècle: Chapelain et nos deux premières académies* (Paris, 1890); Martha Ornstein [Bronfenbrenner], *The Role of Scientific Societies in the Seventeenth Century* (New York, 1913); Harcourt Brown, *Scientific Organizations in Seventeenth-Century France: 1620–1680* (Baltimore, 1934); E. Stewart Saunders, "Politics and Scholarship in Seventeenth-Century France: The Library of Nicolas Fouquet and the Collège Royal," *Journal of Library History, Philosophy, and Comparative Librarianship* XX, 1 (Winter 1985), 1–24.

8. W. E. Knowles Middleton, *The Experimenters: A Study of the Accademia del Cimento* (Baltimore, 1971); Charles Richard Weld, *A History of the Royal Society with the Mémoires of Its Presidents* (London, 1848), 2 vols.; Dorothy Stimson, *Scientists and Amateurs: A History of the Royal Society* (New York, 1948); Christiaan Huygens, *Horologium* (The Hague, 1658); David A. Kronick, *History of Scientific Periodicals* (New York, 1962); Betty T. Morgan, *Histoire du Journal des Scavans depuis 1665 jusqu'en 1701* (Paris, 1928); Trevor

192 / SEYMOUR L. CHAPIN

McClaughlin, "Une Lettre de Melchisédich Thévenot," *Revue d'histoire des sciences* XXVII, 2 (April 1974), 123–6.

9. René Taton, *Les Origines des l'Académie Royale des Sciences* (Paris, 1966); Roger Hahn, *The Anatomy of a Scientific Institution: The Paris Academy of Sciences: 1666–1803* (Berkeley and Los Angeles, 1971); H. L. Brugmans, *Le Séjour de Christian Huygens à Paris et ses rélations avec les milieux scientifiques français* (Paris, 1935); *Huygens et la France*, Tables Rondes du Centre National de la Recherche Scientifique, 27–29 mars 1979 (Paris, 1982); Charles J. E. Wolf, *Histoire de l'Observatoire de Paris de sa fondation à 1793* (Paris, 1902).

10. Jean Picard, *Mesure de la terre* (Paris, 1671); *Jean Picard et les débuts de l'astronomie de précision au XVIIe siècle*, ed Guy Picolet (Paris, 1987); Guillaume Bigourdan, *Histoire de l'astronomie d'observation et des observatoires en France. Première partie: De l'origine à la fondation de l'Observatoire de Paris* (Paris, 1918); Lloyd A. Brown, *Jean Dominique Cassini and His World Map of 1696* (Ann Arbor, 1941), and *The Story of Maps* (Boston, 1949); John W. Olmsted, "The 'Application' of Telescopes to Astronomical Instruments: A Study in Historical Method," *Isis* XL (1949), 213–25, "The Scientific Expedition of Jean Richer to Cayenne," *Isis* XXXIV (1942), 117–28, "The Voyage of Jean Richer to Acadia in 1670: A Study in the Relations of Science and Navigation under Colbert," *Proceedings of the American Philosophical Society* CIV (1960), 112–34, and "Recherches sur la biographie d'un astronome et géodésien méconnu: Jean Picard (1620–1682)," *Revue d'histoire des sciences* XXIX (1979), 213–22; *Roemer et la vitesse de la lumière*, Tables Rondes, 16–17 juin 1976 (Paris, 1978).

11. *Mémoires pour servir à l'histoire naturelle des animaux* (Paris, 1671); *Mémoires pour servir à l'histoire des plantes* (Paris, 1676); Claude Perrault, *Essais de physique, ou recueil de plusieurs traités touchant les choses naturelles* (Paris, 1680–88), 4 vols.; J. P. Tournefort, *Elémens de botanique ou méthode pour connoître les plantes* (Paris, 1694), 3 vols.; Francis Cole, *A History of Comparative Anatomy* (London, 1944); Jacques Roger, *Les Sciences de la vie dans la pensée française du XVIIIe siècle* (Paris, 1963); Yves Laissus, "Les Voyageurs naturalistes du Jardin du roi et du Museum d'histoire naturelle: éssai de portrait-robot," *Revue d'histoire des sciences* XXXIV (1981), 259–317.

12. Edmé Mariotte, *Oeuvres* (Leiden, 1717), 2 vols. in 1.

13. Jacques Rohault, *Traité de physique* (Paris, 1671); Jean Baptiste Molière, *Les Femmes savantes* (Paris, 1672); Nicolas Malebranche, *De la Recherche de la vérité* (Paris, 1674–5), 2 vols.; Jean Prestet, *Elémens des mathématiques* (Paris, 1675); Paul Mouy, *Le Developpement de la physique cartésienne* (Paris, 1934); Martial Gueroult, *Malebranche* (Paris, 1955–9), 3 vols.; André Robinet, *Malebranche, de l'Académie des Sciences* (Paris, 1970).

14. Henry Guerlac, "Vauban: The Impact of Science on War," in *Makers of Modern Strategy*, ed. Edward Meade Earle (Princeton, 1943); Jacques Guttin, *Vauban et le corps des ingénieurs militaires* (Paris, 1957). Compare Hahn, cited in note 9, above, with E. Stewart Saunders, "The Decline and Reform of the Académie des Sciences à Paris: 1676–1699," Ph.D. dissertation, Ohio State University (1980), and "Louis XIV: Patron of Science and Technology," in *The Sun King: Louis XIV and the New World*, ed. Steven G. Reinhardt (New Orleans, 1984), 155–67.

15. *Recit de la grande opération faite au roi Louis XIV*, ed. J. A. Le Roi (Paris, 1852), and *Journal de la santé du roi Louis XIV de l'année 1647 à l'année 1711* (Paris, 1862); Charles D. O'Malley, "The Medical History of Louis XIV: Intimations

of Mortality," in *Louis XIV and the Craft of Kingship*, ed. John C. Rule (Columbus, 1969), 132–54; Bernard de Fontenelle, *Entretiens sur la pluralité des mondes* (Paris, 1686); Leonard M. Marsak, *Bernard de Fontenelle: The Idea of Science in the French Enlightenment* (Philadelphia, 1959). Transactions of the American Philosophical Society, n.s., vol. XLIX, 1–64.

16. See note 14, above, as well as John C. Rule, "Jérôme Phélypeaux, Comte de Pontchartrain, and the Establishment of Louisiana: 1696–1715," in *Frenchmen and French Ways in the Mississippi Valley*, ed. John F. McDermott (Urbana, 1969), 179–97.

17. Edmé Mariotte, *De la Nature des couleurs* (Paris, 1681); Isaac Newton, *Philosophiae Naturalis Principia Mathematica* (London, 1687); Alexandre Koyré, *Newtonian Studies* (Chicago, 1965); André Robinet, "Le groupe malebranchiste introducteur du calcul infinitésimal en France," *Revue d'histoire des sciences* XIII (1960), 287–308, and *Malebranche de l'Académie des Sciences* (Paris, 1970); Guillaume-François de L'Hospital, *Analyse des infiniment petits pour l'intélligence des lignes courbes* (Paris, 1969); Pierre Costabel, *Pierre Varignon (1654–1722) et la diffusion en France du calcul différentiel et intégral* (Paris, 1966).

18. Louis Maury, *L'Ancienne Académie des Sciences* (Paris, 1864); Joseph Bertrand, *L'Académie des Sciences et les académiciens de 1666 à 1793* (Paris, 1869); Ernest Maindron, *L'Académie des Sciences* (Paris, 1888); *L'Institut de France: lois, statuts et règlements concernant les anciennes académies et l'Institut de 1635 à 1889*, ed. Léon Aucoc (Paris, 1889).

19. Isaac Newton, *Optiks: or A Treatise of the Reflections, Refractions, Inflections and Colours of Light* (London, 1704). Leibnitz issued his challenge in an anonymous review, universally attributed to him, that appeared in the *Acta eruditorum* of October 1713, 444–8. Jean Théophile Desaguliers, *Course in Experimental Philosophy* (London, 1730–4), 2 vols.; Jean Torlais, *Un Rochelois grand-maître de la Franc-Maçonnerie et physicien au XVIIIe siècle: le Révérend J. T. Desaguliers* (La Rochelle, 1937); Henry Guerlac, *Newton on the Continent* (Ithaca, 1981); Bernard de Fontenelle, *Eloge de Newton*, in *Oeuvres diverses* (Paris, 1790), I, 279. Jacques-Eugène de Louville, "Construction et théorie des tables du soleil," *Mémoires de l'Académie Royale des Sciences . . . 1720* (Paris, 1722), 35–84. Thomas L. Hankins, "The Reception of Newton's Second Law of Motion in the Eighteenth Century," *Archives internationales d'histoire des sciences* XX (1967), 43–65, and *Jean d'Alembert: Science and the Enlightenment* (Oxford, 1970); A. Rupert Hall, "Newton in France: A New View," *History of Science* XIII (1975), 233–50; Jacques Cassini, "De la grandeur et figure de la terre," *Suite des Mémoires de l'Academie Royale des Sciences . . . 1718* (Paris, 1720); Pierre de Maupertuis, *La Figure de la terre* (Paris, 1738); Pierre Brunet, *Maupertuis* (Paris, 1929), 2 vols.; Seymour Chapin, *The Size and Shape of the World* (Los Angeles, 1957), UCLA Library Occasional Papers, No. 6; John L. Greenberg, "Mathematical Physics in Eighteenth-Century France," *Isis* LXXVI (1986), 59–78.

20. Voltaire, *Lettres écrites de Londres sur les Anglois et autres sujets* (Basel and London, 1734), and *Eléments de la philosophie de Newton* (London, 1738); Etienne de Condillac, *Traité des sensations* (Paris, 1754); Gabrielle du Châtelet, *Principes mathématiques de la philosophie naturelle* (Paris, 1759); Pierre Brunet, *L'Introduction des théories de Newton en France au XVIIIe siècle*, I: *Avant 1738* (Paris, 1931); Gerd Buchdahl, *The Image of Newton and Locke in the Age of Reason* (New York, 1961); Isabel F. Knight, *The Geometric Spirit: The Abbé de*

Condillac and the French Enlightenment (New Haven, 1968).

21. James E. McClellan III, *Science Reorganized: Scientific Societies in the Eighteenth Century* (New York, 1985); Daniel Roche, *Le Siècle des lumières in province: académies et académiciens provinciaux: 1680–1789* (Paris, 1978), 2 vols.; *Enseignement et diffusion des sciences en France au XVIIIe siècle* (Paris, 1964); *Descriptions des arts et métiers faites ou approuvées par MM. de l'Académie Royale des Sciences*, Académie Royale des Sciences (Paris, 1761–88), 27 vols.; Arthur H. Cole and George B. Watts, *The Handicrafts of France as Recorded in the Descriptions des arts et métiers: 1761–1788* (Boston, 1952); Roger Hahn, "The Application of Science to Society: The Societies of Arts," *Studies on Voltaire and the Eighteenth Century* XXV (1963), 829–36; Seymour L. Chapin, "The Academy of Sciences during the Eighteenth Century: An Astronomical Appraisal," *French Historical Studies* V (1968), 371–404; J. L. Heilbron, *Electricity in the 17th and 18th Centuries: A Study of Early Modern Physics* (Berkeley and Los Angeles, 1979); Joseph Fayet, *La Révolution française et la science: 1789–1795* (Paris, 1960).

TWELVE

The Intellectual History of the Reign

PAUL SONNINO

Every civilization likes to think back to a golden age when life was simpler, slower, and more virtuous. The French of the early seventeenth century, however, could come up with at least three. There was the auroral piety of the Hebrew patriarchs, basking in the glow of God's creation. There was the classical splendor of Greece and Rome, mounting to the pinnacle of pagan wisdom, and there was the innocence of the early church, invincibly overpowering the city of man. For Catholics, there was also the chivalric pageant of the Crusades, in rhythm with which, moreover, human reason and divine revelation had achieved a harmonious synthesis under the aegis of the one true faith. One period, however, no one considered golden and that was the sixteenth century, when inflation, social climbing, and religious revolution had played havoc with the order of society. True, there had been ample artistry, printed books, and a widening of horizons, but what to make of those geographical discoveries unknown to the ancients, of the religious schism that had proved impossible to heal, or of the claims of Copernicus so disturbing to Aristotelian physics? A precious element had vanished from life in the sixteenth century, a sense of certainty, a sense that God had created a comprehensible world, to be replaced by the kinds of speculations advanced by Bodin—climatic determinism, numerology, sovereignty of the state.[1] Little wonder that the bemused Montaigne retired to his study and adopted the motto "What do I know?", while maintaining a passive acceptance of his Catholic religion. But to the educated French of the early seventeenth century, such genial skepticism was as abhorrent as the recollection of anarchy.

Their own time, however, offered some hopeful signs of returning to an orderly society, a unified faith, and a comprehensible world. Henry IV, Louis XIII, and Cardinal Richelieu were striving to produce the first; Pierre Bérulle, François de Sales, and Vincent de Paul were aiming at the second; while Galileo, Kepler, and Harvey were pointing the way to the third. The cultivated elite of the early seventeenth century were receptive to any intellectual movements that fitted in with these goals. This was a society that turned its back on hedonistic poetry and in which a private literary club, officially chartered by Richelieu as the Académie Française, was entrusted with enforcing Aristotle's three unities upon Pierre Corneille's offending *Cid*. This was a society that scoffed at Bodin's climatic determinism and believed that a few carefully verified documents combined with a few inspiring *mémoires* furnished all the evidence necessary to illuminate the moral lessons of history and the mysterious purposes of God. This was a society in which the leading political theorist, Cardin Le Bret, though he accepted the newfangled notions of a social contract, touted the kings's direct right and excluded revolution under any pretext whatsoever. A Minim friar, Marin Mersenne, campaigned indefatigably against Montaigne's skepticism, insisting that the recent scientific discoveries held the key to intellectual salvation. The illustrious La Mothe-Le Vayer, who had the effrontery to defend skepticism and to suggest that the ancient pagans possessed virtue, was part of a dying breed.[2]

Descartes voiced the complaint of his generation. He had gone to school in search of "clear and assured knowledge" only to be "assailed by doubts". He also proposed to his contemporaries an audacious program of intellectual reconstruction, while disavowing the remotest threat to the mysteries of religion. His program began with doubt, but it was a purely methodological doubt, which in one step conducted to certainty, certainty about his own existence, certainty about the separation of soul and body, certainty about the existence of a beneficent God. Not that the system was entirely foolproof. After so impressively postulating the two substances of thought and extension, Descartes was hard put to explain how his mind could activate his arm. (It was done, he deduced, through the pineal gland.) After maintaining that God would create only a mathematically perfect world complete with automated animals, Descartes could not confirm that this external world actually existed. (A beneficent God, he hoped, would not fool us.) But apparently He did, for after declaring man's will to be supremely free, Descartes pointed out that it was constantly being misled by the sensations. (This was, he explained, due to our sinful nature.) Nor had Descartes entirely emancipated himself from the presuppositions of Aristotelian scholasticism. His metaphysics was still based on the notion of substance. He identified the mind with the soul. He admitted that nature abhorred a vacuum, which forced him to suppose that the planets were riding on invisible cushions of subtle matter (*tourbillons*). Guardians of orthodoxy, like the Dutch Protestant Gisbert Voët, nevertheless espied a subversive; but a puritanical French Catholic like Antoine Arnauld was an early admirer, and the Flemish Catholic (later Protestant) Arnold Geulincx began to explore the hypothesis of God's direct intervention behind all apparent causes (occasionalism).[3]

It took some wandering in the desert in order to reach the promised land. The minor Louis XIV had to overcome the Fronde; the French Jansenists, led by Antoine Arnauld, reopened the dangerous debate over predestination; and not everyone was willing to embrace Cartesianism. There is no question, however, that by midcentury, the society was getting more settled and the intellectual fashion more tame. The ever popular Corneille, while sticking to his irrepressible tragic heroes, never again violated the three unities, and whether one was a Du Cange, painfully collating the manuscripts of Villeharduin, or a Mézeray, creatively embellishing the reputations of past kings, history remained a handmaiden to the prevailing moral norms. France at midcentury also produced Blaise Pascal, a rare genius with the scientific credentials to restore the harmony of reason and revelation. Alas, he had too much integrity to do so. All he could suggest to an age seeking certainty was that they bet on Jesus, and even that he kept to himself until his *Pensées* were published after his death. But the personal reign of Louis XIV, which began in 1661, exuded all the odor of milk and honey. He considered himself a hardheaded hero installed by Heaven to "restore all things to their natural order". Along with the subservience of society, the classical literary movement fitted in perfectly with his purposes. Molière's comedies ridiculed people who did not know their place. Boileau's criticisms satirized authors who would not follow the rules, and Racine's tragedies domesticated the heretical theology of Jansensism into a prescription for catharsis. The king himself presided over past and future. He wrote *Mémoires* for his son the dauphin in order to "correct history if it should go astray", and Louis' ministers were avid collectors of old documents. He established the Académie des Sciences in 1666, although a little suspicious about those "thorny and obscure recesses of the sciences where the mind strives with difficulty to rise beyond itself". He ended up by entrusting the education of the dauphin to an eloquent guardian of orthodoxy, Bénigne Bossuet, the Bishop of Condom.[4]

Unfortunately, when it came to topping off the edifice of wisdom, the field was dominated by a pair of godless foreigners. One was Thomas Hobbes, the ambulatory English recluse whose physical timidity was surpassed only by his ideological spunk. He was fed up with the use of religion to justify revolution, and he resolved to employ the most up-to-date scientific ideas to prove his point. Like Galileo (though not

Descartes) speculating on the behavior of matter in a vacuum, Hobbes in *De Cive* theorizes on the condition of mankind in a state of nature. He finds it, as is well known, to be a state of war, from which the elementary dictates of reason compel us to escape, but the most striking feature of his theory is his identification of these primitive human reactions with the Divine Law, making man's reason, for all practical purposes, superior to revelation. And since the social contract gives the sovereign absolute power, whatever religion it may choose to establish thereby becomes lawful. Hobbes is even more explicit in the *Leviathan*, where he sandwiches his political theory between a baldly materialistic philosophy and a scathing critique of the biblical canon, asserting, among other things, that Moses was not the author of the Pentateuch. This last theme was happily picked up by Benedict Spinoza, an emancipated Jew of Portuguese origins, and a semi-Cartesian, breathing the free air of the Dutch Republic. His *Tractatus Theologico-Politicus* is another rationalistic critique of scriptural politics. The prophets, he maintains, interpreted God's will according to their own preconceptions and those of their barbarous times. Example follows example to demonstrate that the canon of the Old Testament was sloppily compiled after the Babylonian captivity, most likely by Ezra. Whatever moral principles can be extracted from the Bible may also be found more conveniently in our hearts. For politics by revelation Spinoza substituted a very Hobbesean state of nature, social contract, and omnipotent state, which should, however, be popular, like the Dutch Republic, and thrive on religious toleration. Having thus redefined religion as a matter of universal morality and having considerably secularized the state, he proceeded in his *Ethics* to embarrass both scholastic and Cartesian philosophy with the most infuriating question of all: Why should an infinitely perfect God wish to create anything? Wouldn't it be more logical to assume that there was only one eternal substance, of which man was a modification? This sublime pantheism, along with Hobbes' and Spinoza's cavalier treatment of revelation, kept haunting an age that insisted on keeping its faith and reasoning it too.[5]

As long, however, as order prevailed at home and their king was engaging in his early wars of magnificence, the intellectual elite of France considered that time was on their side. And indeed, there soon emerged from their own midst a more respectable volunteer for the prestigious role of synthesizer. This was the ascetic Nicolas Malebranche, a pious priest of the Oratory, who found in the philosophy of Descartes the fullest confirmation yet for the mysteries of Christianity. Malebranche, in his *Recherche de la vérité*, exults in the Cartesian identification of our sinful nature with the unreliability of our senses, and goes

Descartes one better by claiming that "we see all our ideas in God". In other words, God enters into our mind just as he moves our body in response to our free will and other occasional causes. Such assertions enthusiastically announced as new discoveries were not universally applauded. In the course of the 1670s the teaching of Cartesianism was banned in many French schools, including Malebranche's own Oratory, and the publication of Spinoza's *Ethics* in 1677 made too much intimacy with God a risky business. But Malebranche insisted on pushing his philosophy right into the jaws of revelation. In his *Traité de la nature et de la grâce* he presumed to explain why God had not created a more satisfactory world. It seems that being too wise to act capriciously, He could create only worlds that function by simple laws. For example, though He would like everyone to be saved, He could not bring Himself to cheapen salvation. There was something disturbingly impersonal about this muscle-bound God, which put Arnauld, who proceeded to write against Malebranche, and Bossuet on the alert.[6]

If society had not yet settled on its ideal theologian, there were plenty of ideal historians to take up the slack. On the one hand Mabillon and his fellow Benedictines of Saint-Maur devoted themselves to the methods of authenticating manuscripts. His research was both respected and safe, since it often confirmed the legality of the existing order, but his philosophy of history, by his own admission, was not much different from that of Saint-Réal, who extracted the human spirit from a few curious *mémoires* and emerged with the best-selling *Conjuration des Espagnols contre Venise*. Louis XIV's own approach to history fitted neatly with such practices. He composed *Mémoires* on his war against the Dutch, describing exploits that "posterity will find hard to believe", for the information of his official historians, Boileau and Racine. They were so appreciative of their authoritative source that they reproduced it almost verbatim in their *Eloge historique de Louis XIV*. Even historians, however, occasionally stepped out of line, as when Richard Simon, another learned priest of the Oratory, decided to discredit Spinoza's biblical criticism by a most disconcerting tactic. Simon agreed in his *Histoire critique du Vieux Testament* that Moses could not have composed the Pentateuch. The Catholic, in fact, outdid the Jew in demonstrating the ineptitude of the biblical text. But to Simon, this merely confirmed the necessity, denied by the Protestants, of relying on ecclesiastical tradition. The book was too much for Bossuet to swallow. He managed to prevent its publication in France, with the result that it came out in the Dutch Republic, which, in spite of all the historians, had not been subjugated.[7]

Not surprisingly, the most respectable attempt at official synthesis in the whole reign may be found in Bossuet's triptych of writings for the education of the dauphin. Never before had so much purified wisdom been squandered on a bigger dolt, but then, Bossuet was also laboring for the world at large. The first of his essays, *De la Connaissance de Dieu et de soi-même*, was a young person's guide to scholastic philosophy. The dauphin was not to be chagrined by any Cartesian dilemmas, and the only concession to modern science was the circulation of the blood. All philosophers, in any event, were dwarfed by Moses. It was, however, in his second essay, the *Discours sur l'histoire universelle*, sweeping from the creation to the fall of Rome, that Bossuet unfolded his full dramatic talent. The model here was Saint Augustine, with his mysterious hand of God deftly manipulating the unsuspecting cities of man, and here the possible mischief came not from Cartesianism, but from the new biblical criticism, which Bossuet dismissed with extraordinary dudgeon. But also, preponderant France was not declining Rome. There is in the comfortable Bossuet little of Augustine's revulsion for the city of man. Nor would it do to have a dauphin who shunned earthly glory. Certainly empires rise and fall, but "in this bloody game the most capable of adapting to circumstances have gained the advantage". The Romans were a case in point, as was the present king of France, who, "being equal in valor to the most famous ancients, surpasses them in piety, wisdom, and justice". The proper organization for this city of man was the topic of the third essay, *Politique tirée de l'Ecriture Sainte*. It was the most eclectic in inspiration. Arguments from Aristotle, Hobbes, and Spinoza combined with hard-pressed testimony from Scripture to prove that hereditary monarchy was the most natural, sacred, and inviolable form of government. The absolute power of princes should be restrained only by the fear of God and by their own reason. Religion, and especially the true one, aids them in controlling the passions of their subjects. The revolts of David, the Maccabees, and the Carolingians embarrass Bossuet, but then, they were God's doing. The rough and tumble of the Hebrew chroniclers is made to foreshadow the sophisticated policies of Louis XIV—militarism, mercantilism, and persecution. Such was Bossuet's ideal prescription for the king's son and heir— reason soaked in revelation, seasoned with censorship to taste, served up by a company of dragoons.[8]

Bossuet represented a large intellectual constituency that proved unflagging in its adulation of Louis and staunchly supported his persecution of the Huguenots. After all, had not the Protestants begun as rebels against royal authority? And had it not been necessary, in Jesus' parable of the recalcitrant guests, to "compel them to enter"? The revocation of the Edict of Nantes in 1685 was thus the crowning glory of a brilliant reign; the only issue left to settle was just how brilliant it had been. On January 27, 1687, Charles Perrault got up in the Académie Française to provide his answer. The age of Louis XIV, Perrault affirmed in rolling Alexandrine couplets, was so brilliant that it surpassed the ancients. Everybody knew that the scientific ideas of Plato and Aristotle were passé, and in the arts, the rustic Homer had been surpassed by Molière and Corneille, the garden of Alcinous by the fountains of Versailles. It was Perrault's contention that knowledge accumulates and nature retains its vigor. Present at this performance were the great Boileau and the great Racine. In the middle of it Boileau got up and walked out. Racine was more hypocritical. At the end, he congratulated Perrault on his "joke". But whose fault was it that self-satisfaction had risen to such heights? Had not Boileau and Racine themselves recorded that the exploits of Louis XIV would strike posterity with wonder? And had not Bossuet, that other adversary of innovation, divinely sanctioned the superiority of the reign? The poem had been artfully devised. Its emphasis was on the age of Louis XIV's having surpassed the ancients, not on future ages' surpassing that of Louis XIV. Perrault could hardly be pilloried until he abjured Corneille.[9]

Even as Perrault was reciting, his middle-aged king, who had disciplined his nobility without suppressing it, imposed religious uniformity without obtaining religious agreement, and humiliated most of Europe without subjugating a single enemy, was about to stumble into new wars that would seriously jeopardize his preeminence. His court too was losing its sparkle. Molière and Corneille were gone. Racine was past his prime. But other holdovers continued to maintain their positions. In 1688 Bossuet published the most scholarly work of his career, the *Histoire des variations des églises protestantes*. It was a doleful expose of the reformers' vagaries, which drew its most novel evidence from their agonizing struggles within themselves and their divisive struggles against each other. Could anything be more damning in an age that strove for certainty? This archconservative had now invented intellectual history, but he could not allow this heretical phenomenon to contaminate his own church. He thus encouraged the young Abbé de Fénelon to try his hand at writing against the innovating Malebranche. This work for some reason remained unpublished. Perhaps Bossuet was not entirely satisfied with the result. If so, he was becoming more rigid in his orthodoxy at a time when imposing it on others was getting increasingly difficult.[10]

For, by his persecution of the Huguenots, Louis XIV had created an angry expatriate intelligentsia completely beyond his reach. The center of their activity was the Dutch Republic, where Pierre Jurieu, pastor of the Walloon Church in Rotterdam, assumed the functions of a Protestant Bossuet. If, Jurieu reasoned, the Hebrew prophets could call the wrath of Jehovah upon Israel, why could he not anticipate a coming millennium? He did and it arrived in the form of William of Orange, who staged his "Glorious" Revolution in England and united Europe against France. The Protestants, pressed to it, were rediscovering their revolutionary heritage. Meanwhile, a more subtle attack upon the prevailing intellectual style was being carried out by Jurieu's protégé, the inimitable Pierre Bayle. Himself the product of a clerical family, he combined a rigorous sense of right and wrong with a revulsion against the habitual inclinations of mankind. A seeker after truth, he was also attracted to Cartesianism, but the more he examined it, the more he was impressed by its skeptical side. One of his first writings was the *Pensées sur la comète*, occasioned by the comet of 1680. On the banal pretext of dispelling the superstitions surrounding comets, he deftly disserted, expanding widely on La Mothe-Le Vayer, on the thesis that morality and religion were not necessarily related. Bayle went still further in his *Commentaire sur ces paroles*: *contrains-les d'entrer*, holding that Jesus could not possibly have been advocating something patently immoral—namely, compelling men's consciences. Between 1684 and 1687 Bayle served as editor of the *Nouvelles de la République des Lettres*, a monthly review of books in which he managed to explore the most scandalous ideas with the abandon of a high-minded innocent. Was he putting everyone on? His patron Jurieu thought so and broke with him. But perhaps the best entrée into Bayle's complex mind lies in examining his famous *Dictionnaire*. The article "Bunel", praising a life devoted to learning, also voiced the theory, so contrary to the grain of his age, that skepticism provided the best foundation for the dogmas of religion. "David" seemed to attack both Bossuet's and Jurieu's justifications for revolution. God could not possibly have condoned David's immoral acts as, by implication, He could not have condoned William of Orange's. Could it be so? Could Bayle at the same time have been confident of his moral sense, skeptical of his reason, ready to base his salvation on blind faith, and opposed to revolution? He claimed he was, but most of his readers felt compelled to fidget with his recipe.[11]

The intellectual opposition was not limited to heretical refugees. It sprang up spontaneously within France itself and at the very court of the king, where it took the form of an aristocratic religious revival, not easy to impugn. The Abbé de Fénelon joined it, sustained by the Quietism of his friend Mme. Guyon. In 1689 the highly regarded abbot was entrusted with the education of the dauphin's son, the Duke de Bourgogne. Almost as dense as his father, but considerably more self-righteous, the little duke was an ideal candidate for indoctrination. And it is very clear what kind of indoctrination he received. In 1693, while France was beset by famine and war, Fénelon composed an omnisciently sanctimonious letter to Louis XIV, upbraiding him as if he were an intemperate schoolboy. Here were his deficiencies. He had let himself be corrupted by evil ministers into overthrowing "all the old maxims of the state". He had engaged for his own vanity in unjust wars, impoverishing his subjects and turning all Europe against him. He was a religious hypocrite, worshiping God with his lips but not with his heart. Never before had anyone written to the king in such a manner, nor would anyone ever do so. The letter was suppressed by Mme. de Maintenon, and Fénelon did not object. In 1695, moreover, he accepted from the tyrant the Archbishopric of Cambrai. But the lessons abandoned on Louis were not lost on the Duke de Bourgogne. They are muted yet unmistakable in the most famous work that Fénelon wrote for the duke's education, *Les Aventures de Télémaque*. It was a supplement to the *Odyssey*, recounting the search of Telemachus for his father, accompanied by the wise old Mentor. Everywhere they went there was a new lesson to be learned: in Egypt that "kings who think only of making themselves feared are the scourge of humanity"; at Tyre that "commerce is like certain springs, if you endeavor to divert their course, you dry them up"; in Salentium that kings should rely on their nobility. No friend of the moderns, Fénelon had exhumed the yearning for a bygone age. His support of Quietism involved him in a quarrel with Bossuet, condemnation by Rome, and retirement to Cambrai, but the subversive epic was published in 1699 to universal acclaim.[12]

Even before Perrault, Bayle, or Fénelon, however, a young literary fop was initiating the reading public to a new and better way of feeling superior. He was the charming, witty, and erudite Bernard de Fontenelle, who began his career as a panegyrist of Louis XIV and ended it as a patron of the "Enlightenment". Fontenelle was eminently suited to exploit the shifting intellectual currents of his time. He was cheerfully attuned to the absurdity of life, the vanity of human strivings, and the limitations of human knowledge. He possessed an uncanny ability to express the most irreverent ideas under the banner of perfect orthodoxy. He knew how to entertain and yet instruct. In 1683 appeared his *Dialogues des morts*, a succession of spectral conversations between ancients and moderns in which such apparently divergent types as the third false Dimitri and René Descartes discover that they have much in common. (Both expected to be believed while claiming that all their precursors had been impostors.) In this work, Fontenelle did not take sides, but his position emerged more clearly in his three famous writings of 1686. The first, *Histoire des oracles*, explodes the claims of the early Christians that the pagan oracles were inspired by demons. Underlying the logic, however, was the implicit commentary on the trickery of all priests, the gullibility of all masses, and the fallibility of the ancients. His second writing, *Entretiens sur la pluralité des mondes*, provides an alternative to such superstitions. A philosopher extols to a marquise the advantages of a mechanistic Cartesian scientific view of the universe, which, he promises, will eventually bring mankind into contact with the inhabitants of other worlds. But Fontenelle was not a Cartesian without qualification. In his *Doutes sur le système physique des causes occasionelles*, he retorts to Malebranche that the simplicity of the parts is no excuse for a machine to function badly and that, in any case, there is nothing simple about a God who has to inaugurate every single movement in the universe. What was Fontenelle doing? He was divorcing social criticism from social conformity, science from dogma, the idea of progress from the reign of Louis XIV. The measure of his success was his subsequent election to the Académie Française and as perpetual secretary to the Académie des Sciences.[13]

While the French intellectuals were extending the parameters of their own synthesis, two English thinkers were pointing the way to its complete reversal. One was John Locke, the asthmatic physician, philosopher, and secretary to Anthony Ashley Cooper, the later Earl of Shaftesbury. Contemptuous of the quest for metaphysical certainty and proud of the scientific achievements of the moderns, Locke stoutly supported the proposition that all our knowledge comes from the senses, envisaging the mind as an instrument for the calculation of experiences, sufficient by themselves to disclose the laws of nature and to verify the existence of a beneficent God, though insufficient to penetrate into the substance of things. As to his political thought, it was more Hobbesean than his adulators like to admit, at least until his patron led him into political opposition in England and later exile in the Dutch Republic. Locke's ideas might have relegated him to a dilettantish obscurity had it not been for several turns of fortune, beginning with the publication of Newton's *Principia* in 1687. At first glance, the presence of universal gravity working its wonders through empty space and calculated with the aid of infinitesimal numbers might seem like the worst possible recommendation for a commonsense philosophy. But Newton, in the introduction of this work, had praised the inductive method, and it was he who had humbled the ancients, not the Cartesians, with their pineal glands, *tourbillons*, and occasional causes. If, moreover, Locke's claim that human reason unencumbered by dogmas or metaphysics could discover the laws of nature was vindicated by Newton, the

"Glorious" Revolution provided Locke with evidence that man's reason was able to control his passions, even in the absence of a Leviathan state. Thus a new vision of the state of nature, radically different from Hobbes', Bossuet's, or even Bayle's, where men were rational enough to identify their natural rights and moral enough, willy-nilly, to respect those of others. Thus a social contract entered into solely for the more efficient enforcement of these rights and revocable if they were violated. Thus a morality that, like Bayle's, did not depend on the succor of dogma and a secular government that not only had no interest, like Spinoza's, in coercing the consciences of its citizens, but also had no business in doing so. Hobbes and Spinoza haunted the haughty French synthesis. Locke and Newton confronted it in the full light of day.[14]

Not that the contributors to this synthesis hadn't asked for it. They had feared for the dissolution of society while it was becoming more solidified. They had admitted the utility of reason while trying to maintain a balance between it and revelation. They had made a fetish out of certainty while searching for it on the fringes of metaphysical space. They had sanctified the authority of the state while expecting optimistically that it would always do their bidding. They had praised their king to the skies while recalling at funerals that all glory was fleeting. Now they were about to suffer the consequences of their presumption: a cohesive aristocracy more wary of royal abuses than of popular discontent, a triumphant rationalism abandoning theology for science, moral certainty exchanging airy metaphysics for empirical terra firma, secular authorities contemplating the tangible costs of persecution. Following in the traces of Fénelon, Saint-Simon and Boulainvillier began to formulate the first and, as it turned out, the most durable, reinterpretation of the reign. They advanced the thesis, as exaggerated as it may have been, that Louis XIV was a tyrant who had enervated the nobility and subverted the liberties of France, this while Bossuet's quibbles with Fénelon and the king's attack on a reviving Jansenism covered his intolerance with ridicule.[15]

Still, in spite of its murky beginning, the eighteenth century was one of renewed expansion, with the social groups that had entrenched themselves under Louis XIV discovering fresh opportunities in the periodic embarrassments of the monarchy. So too the philosophes of the "Enlightenment" turned Bossuet inside out, always putting reason above authority and encouraging the impression that good intentions could move mountains. The early Montesquieu made the French laugh at their own bizarre customs, along with those of the Persians. Only his imaginary Troglodytes attested to the common substratum of all humanity. The young Voltaire made the French consider a thoroughgoing revision of their social principles: belief in dogmas does not make men moral, but decency and simplicity do; an established church does not ensure political order, but toleration does; a privileged clergy tends to meddle in affairs about which it knows nothing and accuses anyone who disagrees with it of heresy. In England, where the role of the church was limited and the king combined with the commons to hold the aristocracy in check, commerce, art, and science flourished. The *tourbillons* of Descartes and the "sublime illusions" of Malebranche gave way to the philosophy of Locke and the discoveries of Newton.[16]

Although the *philosophes* continued to refer to an arcadian past, they would have only traded their own time for the future. Not satisfied with his gentle ribbing of contemporary customs, Montesquieu proceeded to account for their variety and to examine what mankind could do about them. He restored the physical, à la Bodin, as an explanation for historical movement. It was the soil, the topography, the climate that determined the peculiarities of the Persians as well as of the French, and the unfortunate Persians were condemned by their enervating surroundings to an eternity of sensual submission. Not so the French or the English. In the more fertile temperate climes, governments tend to be more moderate and men have a chance to be free . . . if they will only apply the principle of separation of powers that Montesquieu claims to have discovered. The English had come closest to practicing it, and the French could achieve it by restoring their abused aristocracy to its natural role. Voltaire, too, looks back only to find more arguments for reform. He provided his age with a philosophy of history that ignored the inscrutable intentions of God and made progress dependent on the volitions of mankind. When it opted for superstition and persecution, as in the Middle Ages, it stagnated. When it promoted the arts and sciences, as in classical times, or in the age of Lorenzo de Medici, or in the age of Louis XIV, it progressed.[17]

The *philosophes* had hardly devised the perfect solutions to the mystery of human existence. Montesquieu and Voltaire did not see eye to eye. Nor did it take long for the "Enlightenment" to produce such independent-minded offspring as La Mettrie, Hume, or Rousseau.[18] And yet its clear secular touch has managed to strike a familiar chord with posterity, which is far from the case with the mid-seventeenth century. It is easy to forget that its intellectuals too were aiming at something durable, and for a brief moment, they thought they had attained it.

NOTES

1. Jean Bodin, *Methodus ad facilem historiarum cognitionem* (Paris, 1566), *Les Six livres de la République* (Paris, 1576). See also Adalbert Klempt, *Die Säkularisierung der universalhistorischen Auffassung* (Göttingen, 1960).
2. Jean Chapelain, *Les Sentimens de l'Académie Françoise sur la tragi-comédie du Cid* (Paris, 1638); Marin LeRoy de Gomberville, *Discours des vertues et des vices de l'histoire* (Paris, 1620); Cardin Le Bret, *De la Souveraineté du Roy* (Paris, 1632); Marin Mersenne, *La Vérité des sciences contre les sceptiques ou Pyrrhoniens* (Paris, 1625); François de La Mothe-Le Vayer, *De la Vertu des payens* (Paris, 1641). See also Richard H. Popkin, *The History of Scepticism from Erasmus to Descartes* (Assen, 1960).
3. René Descartes, *Discours de la Méthode* (Paris, 1637), especially the *première partie*, *Meditationes de prima philosophia* (Paris, 1641), which includes Antoine Arnauld's objections and Descartes' responses, and *Principia Philosophiae* (Amsterdam, 1644); Gisbert Voët, *Theologiae in Acad. Ultrajectina Professoris, Selectarum Disputationum Theologicarum* (Utrecht, 1648); Arnout Geulincx, *Metaphysica vera et ad mentem peripateticam* (Amsterdam, 1691), ΓΝΩΘΙ ΣΑΥΤΟΝ, *sive Ethica* (Amsterdam, 1696). See also Francisque Boullier, *Histoire de la philosophie cartésienne* (Paris, 1868), 2 vols.
4. Charles Du Cange, *Histoire de l'empire de Constantinople sous les empereurs Français* (Paris, 1647); François de Mézeray, *Histoire de France* (Paris, 1643–51), 3 vols.; Orest Ranum, *Artisans of Glory* (Chapel Hill, 1980); Blaise Pascal, *Pensées de M. de Pascal sur la religion et sur quelques autres sujets* (Paris, 1669); Fortunat Strowski, *Pascal et son temps* (Paris, 1907), 3 vols; *Oeuvres de Louis XIV*, ed. Ph. A. Grouvelle (Paris, 1806), I, 5, 21. See also Albert Guérard, *The Life and Death of an Ideal: France in the Classical Age* (New York, 1928).
5. Thomas Hobbes, *Elementorum Philosophiae, sectio tertia, de Cive* (1642). The French could also read the translations by Samuel Sorbière, *Eléments philosophiques du citoyen* (Amsterdam, 1649), and by Du Verdus, *Les Eléments de la politique de M. Hobbes* (Paris, 1660). See also Hobbes' *Leviathan* (London, 1651). Most French readers had to use the Latin translation, *Opera philosophica quae latine scripsit omnia* (Amsterdam, 1668), vol. 3. Benedict Spinoza, *Tractatus theologico-politicus* (Hamburg, 1670). The *Ethics* was first published in his *Opera posthuma* (1677). See also Paul Vernière, *Spinoza et la pensée française avant la Révolution* (Paris, 1954).
6. Nicolas Malebranche, *De la Recherche de la vérité* (Paris, 1674–5), 2 vols., especially bk. 3, pt. 2, ch. 6, *Traité de la nature et de la grâce* (Amsterdam, 1680); Antoine Arnauld, *Des vrayes et des fausses idées contre ce qu'enseigne l'auteur de la Recherche de la vérité* (Cologne, 1683). See also Henri Gouhier, *La Philosophie de Malebranche et son expérience religieuse* (Paris, 1926).
7. Jean Mabillon, *De re diplomatica* (Paris, 1681); César de Saint-Réal, *De l'Usage de l'histoire* (Paris, 1671); *Conjuration des Espagnols contre la République de Venise en l'année 1618* (Paris, 1674). See the favorable comments on Saint-Réal in Mabillon's *Traité des études monastiques* (Paris, 1691), 232. Emmanuel de Broglie, *Mabillon et la société de l'abbaye de Saint-Germain-des-Prés à la fin du dix-septième siècle: 1664–1707* (Paris, 1888), 2 vols. Compare Louis' *mémoire* published in Camille Rousset, *Histoire de Louvois et de son administration politique et militaire* (Paris, 1861–3), I, 515–40, with Dominique Bouhours, *Pensées ingénieuses des anciens et des modernes* (Paris, 1689), 142, and Jean

208 / PAUL SONNINO

Racine and Nicolas Boileau, *Eloge historique du roi Louis XIV sur ses conquêtes depuis l'année 1672 jusqu'en 1678* (Amsterdam, 1784). Please also see my "Jean Racine and the *Eloge historique de Louis XIV*," *Canadian Journal of History* VIII, 3 (1973), 185–94. Richard Simon, *Histoire critique du Vieux Testament* (Paris, 1678), (Amsterdam, 1680). See also Auguste Bernus, *Richard Simon et son Histoire critique du Vieux Testament* (Lausanne, 1869).

8. Bénigne Bossuet, *Introduction à la Philosophie ou de la Connaissance de Dieu et de soi-même* (Paris, 1722), *Discours sur l'histoire universelle* (Paris, 1681), especially pt. II, chs. 2 and 8, *Politique tirée des propres paroles de l'Ecriture Sainte* (Paris, 1709). I dissent from Amable Floquet, *Bossuet: précepteur du Dauphin* (Paris, 1864) and from Thérèse Goyet, *L'Humanisme de Bossuet* (Paris, 1965), 2 vols.

9. See Louis Maimbourg, *Histoire du luthéranisme* (Paris, 1680), *Histoire du calvinisme* (Paris, 1682), and *Histoire de La Ligue* (Paris, 1684); Antoine Varillas, *Histoire des révolutions arrivées dans l'Europe en matière de religion* (Paris, 1686–9) 6 vols. On "compel them to enter", see Augustine's *Letter to Boniface on the correction of the Donatists*, 5:24, and Philippe Gorbaud-Dubois, *Conformité de l'Eglise de France pour ramener les Protestans: avec celle de l'Eglise d'Affrique, pour ramener les Donatistes à l'Eglise Catholique* (Paris, 1685). See also Elizabeth Israels Perry, *From Theology to History: French Religious Controversy and the Revocation of the Edict of Nantes* (The Hague, 1973). Charles Perrault, *Le Siècle de Louis le Grand* (Paris, 1687); and Hippolite Rigault, *Histoire de la querelle des anciens et des modernes* (Paris, 1856), especially pp. 146–8.

10. Bénigne Bossuet, *Histoire des variations des églises protestantes* (Paris, 1868), 2 vols.; Alfred Rébelliau, *Bossuet: historien du protestantisme* (Paris, 1891); François de La Mothe-Fénelon, *Refutation du système du père Malebranche sur la nature et la grâce* (Paris, 1820).

11. Pierre Jurieu, *L'Accomplissement des prophéties, ou la délivrance prochaine de l'Eglise* (Rotterdam, 1686), 2 vols.; Pierre Bayle, *Pensées diverses écrites à un docteur de Sorbonne à l'occasion de la comète qui parut au mois de décembre 1680* (Rotterdam, 1683), *Commentaire sur ces paroles: contrains-les d'entrer* (Canterbury, 1686), *Nouvelles de la République des Lettres* (Rotterdam, 1684–7), *Dictionnaire historique et critique* (Rotterdam, 1697). On the breach, see Pierre Jurieu, *Apologie du Sr. Jurieu* (The Hague, 1691), *Courte revue des maximes de morale et principes de religion de l'auteur des Pensées diverses sur les comètes & de la critique générale sur l'Histoire du calvinisme du Maimbourg* (n.d.o.p.), and *Le Philosophe de Rotterdam accusé, atteint et convaincu* (Amsterdam, 1706). See also *Pierre Bayle, le philosophe de Rotterdam*, ed. Paul Dibon (Amsterdam and Paris, 1959).

12. The letter to Louis XIV was first published by Jean d'Alembert in his *Histoire des membres de l'Académie Française depuis 1700 jusqu'en 1771* (Paris, 1787), III, 351–70. See also François de la Mothe-Fénelon, *Les Aventures de Télémaque* (Paris, 1699), 5 vols., especially bks. 2 and 3. See also Ely Carcassonne, *Fénelon, l'homme et l'oeuvre* (Paris, 1946).

13. Bernard de Fontenelle, "La Gloire des armes et des lettres sous Louis XIV" (1675), in *Oeuvres* (Paris, 1825), V, 202–5, *Dialogues des morts* (Paris, 1683), *Histoire des oracles* (Paris, 1686), *Entretiens sur la pluralité des mondes* (Paris, 1686), and *Doutes sur le système physique des causes occasionelles* (Rotterdam, 1686). See also Leonard Marsak, *Bernard de Fontenelle: The Idea of Science in the*

French Enlightenment (Philadelphia, 1959). Transactions of the American Philosophical Society, n.s., vol. XLIX, 1–64.

14. Isaac Newton, *Philosophiae Naturalis Principia Mathematica* (London, 1687). John Locke, *Epistola de tolerantia* (Gouda, 1689), English edition (London, 1690), *An Essay Concerning Human Understanding* (London, 1690), and *Two Treatises of Government* (London, 1690). See also Paul Hazard, *La Crise de la conscience européene* (Paris, 1935), 3 vols. English edition, *The European Mind: 1680–1715* (London, 1953).

15. Louis de Saint-Simon, *Mémoires* (London, 1788–9), 6 vols. Henri de Boulainvillier, *Lettre sur les anciens parlemens de France que l'on nomme Etats-Généraux* (London, 1753), 3 vols.

16. Charles de Montesquieu, *Lettres persanes* (Amsterdam, 1721), 2 vols.; and F. de Voltaire, *Lettres écrites de Londres sur les Anglois et autres sujets* (Basel and London, 1734), especially letter 13.

17. Charles de Montesquieu, *De l'Esprit des loix* (Geneva, 1748), 2 vols.; and F. de Voltaire, *Le Siècle de Louis XIV* (Berlin, 1751).

18. Carl Becker, *The Heavenly City of the Eighteenth Century Philosophers* (New Haven, 1932); and Norman Hampson, *The Enlightenment* (Penguin, 1968).

THIRTEEN

The Art History of the Reign

ANN FRIEDMAN

The influence of the past was strong on French art of the seventeenth century, but it was dominated by no single art style. The Late Mannerist School, developed by artists of the Second School of Fontainebleau, perpetuated the forms of the recent, Italianate past, with acid colors describing elongated figures in "unnatural" space. The more regular Classicism of Poussin was no less linked to the past, for the style and subject matter alike were indebted to Roman art, and especially to its bas-reliefs. The Baroque style of Simon Vouet exhibited greater drama and freedom of technique, but looked to Caravaggio, Pietro da Cortuna, and Rubens for inspiration. The painters of northern France, the Le Nains, Philippe de Champaigne and Frans Vandermeulen, were also influenced by the realistic painters of the north and duplicated the style of their sober, austere works.[1]

After the middle of the century, and at a brisker pace after the commencement of Louis XIV's personal reign, the crown attempted to marshal and direct the efforts of France's artists. In 1648 several prominent ones had established the Académie Royale de Peinture et de Sculpture, but it was fully reorganized to serve the interests of the king in 1663 by Jean-Baptiste Colbert, who placed it under the jurisdiction of the *bâtiments du Roi*. Colbert, aside from his financial and other duties, was also Superintendant of Buildings and Vice-Protector of the Academy (protector after 1672). Charles Le Brun, a founding member, was rector and held the official position of *premier peintre du Roi* in the *bâtiments*. All painters, sculptors, and engravers who worked for the king were required to be members. Now that Louis had firmly established himself in power, he used the academy extensively to advertise his greatness.[2]

The academy, like its Italian forerunners, functioned as both a professional organization for artists and a training institution for art students. Drawing was considered the basis for all arts—painting, sculpture, and architecture—and was the most important part of painting, even more so than color, because it presumably appealed to the rational.[3] Drawing after the Antique was supposed to be the best way to fix in the artist's mind those proportions of antique sculpture considered the most perfect.[4] Emphasis was placed on discovering rules for the production of art, based on the distillation of the best in Nature and the Antique, and the best modern synthesizers, Raphael and Poussin. It was a tenet of academic training in France, as in Italy, that perfect art *could* be produced by following such rules, and that they could be learned by reason. Less emphasis was placed on personal experimentation and development. This training ensured a minimum level of quality in the art produced for the king and, equally important in large decorative schemes like the king's apartments at Versailles, a certain homogeneity of style.

The theoretical side of academic training was provided by the *conférences* given each month by the member artists.[5] The early lectures, delivered between 1667 and 1670, discussed individual paintings by Raphael, Titian, Veronese, and, above all, Poussin. Those given in the 1670s were both more general and more practical: on the study of the Antique; on the making of bas-reliefs; and six lectures by Sébastien Bourdon and Henri Testelin on the principal aspects of painting (light, chiaroscuro, color, expression, outline) and of drawing (proportions and composition).

It is easiest to discuss these principles by illustration: Charles de Lafosse's *Jason Landing at Colchis,* part of the ceiling of the Salon of Diana, Versailles, painted between 1671 and 1681.[6] Lafosse, one of the principal painters working under Le Brun, has produced a work that adheres to academic teaching. A few large figures are located at the front of the picture plane and make a progressive frieze that carries the eye to the right, where two large figures from the island of Colchis turn the composition back again. Jason is off-center, providing asymmetry; his aggressive stride and the swirl of his cloak mark him as the most active, important figure. The facial expressions are lively, and the hand gestures make clear that it is a friendly encounter. The meeting of hands is set against a clearing in the background so that it is clearly visible. The costume is appropriate: the Greeks wear armor that had been well researched from surviving monuments, and the Colchis men wear more exotic dress, given an Eastern flavor by the turban. Some adjustment has been made in the proportions of the figures and the angle of the *Argo* to allow for the fact that the work is to be seen from below. The colors are mainly reds and oranges. The boy in the foreground is dressed in a blue-green that echoes the color of the sky and waves;

Lafosse is careful to allow only a small part of it to touch the highly contrasting red of the cloak next to it. The secondary figures of the oarsman and the Argonauts blend more with the pale gold of the ship; as a group they express varying degrees of curiosity and direct the viewer's eyes toward the main group. Only the bare essentials of the landscape are given: no trees or grass or plants distract the eye from the human story being told here.

The art promoted by the academy meant that there was now an "official" style of painting in France, approved by the king and applauded by the aristocracy. The sober Classicism of Poussin was held up as the ideal; Lafosse's painting follows this in its relieflike arrangement of the figures, the mythological source of its subject matter, and the noble emotions—courage and friendship—that the figure of Jason is meant to convey. Academic painting—with its emphasis on an art that is clear and easily readable, using natural proportions and coloring; setting figures and objects in a well-defined space—is firmly anti-Mannerist. Le Brun and his contemporaries pay the sixteenth-century Italian painting and decoration at Fontainebleau a backhanded compliment in their lectures by recognizing their attractiveness and warning against them. The style of the Le Nains and Champaigne, on the other hand, appealed mainly to a middle-class clientele, although Vandermeulen was much in demand through the 1670s for battle scenes and views of royal palaces for the king.

Not all artists and critics agreed with the teachings of the academy, and two important controversies developed around their objections. The first was the Quarrel of the Ancients and Moderns, in which the writer Charles Perrault argued against too much adulation of the artists of antiquity because modern painting had developed so far beyond them, able to draw on new styles and devices like perspective.[7] The other controversy was the debate over whether drawing or color was predominant: the academy held drawing to be the most important part of painting, while the critic Roger de Piles, in *Dialogue sur le Coloris* (1673), favored color, because painting is meant to appeal to the eye and this is the chief element of painting that does so.[8] De Piles also promoted the art of Rubens, virtually ignored by the French since he had painted the Marie de Medici series in the Luxembourg Palace in the 1620s, over that of Poussin, the idol of the academy. These quarrels—Ancients versus Moderns, drawing versus color, Rubenistes versus Poussinistes—established the parameters of French painting style until the era of the Impressionists.

Since the academy was part of the larger institution of the *bâtiments du Roi*,[9] all aspects of art and architecture produced for the king were brought within it, from the coordination of raw materials and manual labor for the vast building programs at royal palaces, to the Academies of Painting and Sculpture and Architecture, to the Gobelins factory, which produced tapestries and furniture for the king. This brought the arts into line with the growing bureaucracies in other parts of government and with Colbert's policy of "mercantilism". For example, one function of the Versailles Hall of Mirrors: 1678–1684, was to display the products of the new French mirror industry.

In work produced for the king, very little was left to the initiative of the individual artists. During the tenure of Le Brun (1661–1690), most painting and sculptural programs were designed by him after consultation with the *petite académie,* a group of scholars culled from the literary academy in 1663 to serve as advisors to the *bâtiments du Roi,* on iconographic matters, and who designed many of the medals of Louis XIV. Once they had approved the content, the design was shown to the king for his approval. Sometimes the entire program would be fully worked out only to be rejected by Louis, as in the case of the Hall of Mirrors. If the design was approved, it was then turned over to the painter or sculptor who would execute it. First, however, he would make an oil sketch or plaster model, which would incorporate any changes he wished to make from Le Brun's design. When Le Brun had approved this, the painting or sculpture was carried out. While this process did not place a high value on the initiative of the artist, it by no means entirely restricted innovation on his part. Martin Desjardins transformed Le Brun's static drawing for *Evening,* or *Diana,* one of the garden sculptures at Versailles, into a figure that strides forward, her drapery spiraling about her as if whipped by the wind, her hound leaping beside her.[10]

Because art for the king was so much a group product, the kind of artist who flourished best under this system was the "team player" who could adapt to Louis' changes of mind and who was willing to create along lines set for him by others. Artists who worked for the *bâtiments* were expected to conform to the standards of the academy and to remember that, when dealing with Louis XIV, there was only one ego that mattered. Much of Le Brun's continued success in his post was due to his adaptability in this respect.

One artist who refused to fit the mold was the sculptor Pierre Puget.[11] His art explores the powerful painful emotions, as in *Milo of Crotona,* the Greek hero devoured by a lion as he was trapped with his hand caught fast in the cleft of a tree. Puget's talent and genius were appreciated by the king and his ministers, yet they failed in their attempts to fit him within the established structures of the *bâtiments.* He spent his career in his native Marseilles and Toulon, far from the centers of Paris and Versailles. Put in charge of a workshop for the important job of making sculptural decoration for warships, he proved a failure at designing for and supervising others. Commissioned in 1672 to make a relief for Versailles, he chose the subject of *Alexander and Diogenes*, completing and sending it in 1692, twenty years after the now middle-aged and pious Louis had ceased to be identified with the boyish pagan hero. Granted one of the many commissions for equestrian statues of the king after the revocation of the Edict of Nantes, he complained that the town square granted him was not large enough, yet seemed indignant when the commission was immediately withdrawn. Puget is temperamentally very much of a nineteenth-century artist well ahead of his time.

Setting this vast machinery in motion was the person of Louis XIV, both the leading patron of the arts and their principal subject. In a discussion of his artistic taste and patronage, as in so much else, it is difficult to separate the public and private person: so much of his preference in art or architecture or garden design was governed by the exigencies of monarchies. Only occasional glimpses of private taste come through, as when the painter Pierre Mignard writes in 1686 to the Italian sculptor Domenico Guidi that the king had found the latter's *Fame Writing the History of Louis XIV* "a little rich in drapery", explaining that the figure of *Diana*, which Louis saw every day, had given him a taste for sculptures less well clothed.[12] His particular pride in Versailles, for which he wrote the *Manière de montrer les jardins,* is well known.[13] His delight in water works caused his gardens to be decorated with a profusion of fountains, even though vast quantities of water were not readily available at Versailles. His desire for novelty caused frequent additions and changes to be made in the bosquets and fountains; at Marly one bosquet featured a cast of sculptures that changed every few weeks, so that he should see something new being installed whenever he strolled by.[14]

The king's support of the fine arts was not merely an aesthetic response; he was fully cognizant of the usefulness of art as propaganda. Sometimes the art he sponsored—decorations for his palaces, civic works, city gates, statues, triumphal arches, equestrian monuments—simply overwhelms by sheer dazzle. At other times, the art conveys an outright message. Indeed, as his reign progressed, he demostrated increasing impatience with the allegorical language of painting and sculpture habitually used to express the qualities of one's patron. Early in his personal reign, Louis was compared with Alexander or Jason or Apollo; indeed, Apollo remained the most frequent iconographic alter-ego of the Sun King.[15] Just as Apollo in Girardon and Regnaudin's *Apollo*

Jason Landing at Colchis, by Charles de Lafosse

Apollo Served by the Nymphs, by François Girardon and Thomas Regnaudin

Served by the Nymphs: 1666–1672 from the Grotto of Thetis in the gardens of Versailles, rests in the sea after driving the chariot of the sun through the heavens, so Louis rests at Versailles after the labors of government.[16] At the same time, however, he commissioned the *Histoire du Roy* tapestries, which recorded in a documentary manner the significant events of the reign, particularly those in which France triumphed in battle (*The Siege of Douai*) or was recognized as preeminent by foreign ambassadors (*The Apology of Count Fuentes*).[17] One set of these was made for the royal palaces, another as a gift for the pope. In the Ambassadors' Staircase: 1674–1680, the allegorical and documentary modes were placed side by side; in the Hall of Mirrors: 1678–1684, they were combined. A Hercules program that had been first worked out for the vault was rejected by the king. He demanded in its place a program in which he personally appeared, rather than a mythic substitute, and that dealt directly with the accomplishments of his personal reign and the triumphs of the recent Dutch War. When the Marquis de Louvois, the new superintandant of buildings: 1683–1691, proposed Latin captions for the scenes, Louis turned them down and insisted on French ones, which every viewer could understand. Further, the Hall of Mirrors, like many parts of Versailles, was the subject of an official handbook explaining its allegorical and political significance in full detail.[18] The actual content of these scenes is a mixture of history and allegory: in *The Crossing of the Rhine in the Presence of the Enemy*, the king, clad in Roman armor and a seventeenth-century perruque, holding a thunderbolt of Jupiter, drives his chariot over the personifications of cities already conquered, while the river god of the Rhine falls back in alarm and amazement. Hercules, Victories, and Bellona accompany him. Such a "mixed mode" had not been seen in France since Rubens' Marie de Medici paintings of the 1620s; Le Brun's adoption of the solution presented by the Flemish artist demonstrates that even those painters and theorists most Poussiniste evidenced a new appreciation of Rubens in the 1670s and 1680s.

The allegorial mode continued to be used in a number of works at Versailles, such as Coysevox's stucco *Crossing of the Rhine* in the Salon of War, Guidi's *Fame Writing the History of Louis XIV*, Tuby's *France Triumphant*, and the bronzes of the rivers of France. The mixed mode of the Hall of Mirrors continued to be used in at least some of the official paintings for Louis XV, such as François Lemoine's *Louis XV Bestowing Peace on Europe* in the Salon of Peace, Versailles; but the spirit of art in the first half of the eighteenth century is that of the *fête galante*, the lighter pastime rather than the official message.

The academy continued to be the dominant force in the French art

The Crossing of the Rhine in the Presence of the Enemy, by Charles Le Brun

world in the eighteenth century, until it was abolished during the Revolution. The Rubeniste/color/Modern camp won at first, with the predominance of the Rococo style through the 1770s. The Neoclassical movement, which began in the 1750s, saw a renewed appreciation of Poussin and Antiquity, however, that continued into the 1780s, under masters such as Greuze, David, and Ingres. It was Ingres and his school who first applied the term "Classique" to the art of seventeenth-century France.[19]

It is interesting to note, too, the shifts in attitude toward the art of Louis XIV during the reigns of his successors. In the official seventeenth-century guidebooks to Versailles, such as Rainssant's 1687 explication of the Hall of Mirrors, the political message of the art is emphasized. In the essay of 1725 that accompanies the engravings of the Ambassadors' Staircase, the author's boredom with the glory of Louis XIV is evident, and he emphasizes instead the way in which allegory is used in conjunction with historical scenes so that the viewer's eye, moving back and forth between the two, blends them in his mind, associating the virtues of the one with the person of the other.[20] Yet when the Hall of Mirrors was engraved in 1752, in the middle of Louis XV's less-than-glorious reign, the explanations of the scenes were condensed from Rainssant, and the accomplishments of Louis XIV again boasted about, to remind the rest of Europe of the preeminence of France.[21]

Louis' true heir—in art as in power and in the ambition he held for himself and for France—was Napoleon. The art made for the emperor partook of the political ideals of the Revolution as well as the cult of the person of the ruler, and impressed upon the nation and the world the new victories and *gloire* of France.

NOTES

1. The standard survey of the art of the reign is Anthony Blunt, *Art and Architecture in France: 1500–1700* (Harmondsworth, 1982).
2. The essential primary source for the academy is *Procès-Verbaux de l'Académie Royale de Peinture et de Sculpture*, ed. A. Montaiglon (Paris, 1874–96), 8 vols. The best modern studies are contained in several articles by Carl Goldstein, especially "Theory and Practice in the French Academy: Louis Licherie's *Abigail and David*," *Burlington Magazine* CXI (1969), 346–51, and "Towards a Definition of Academic Art," *Art Bulletin* LVII (1975), 102–9.
3. Carl Goldstein, "Drawing in the Academy," *Art International* XXI, No. 3 (1977), 42–7.
4. Sébastien Bourdon, "L'Etude de l'antique," *Conférence* read July 5, 1670, in *Conférences de l'Académie Royale de Peinture et de Sculpture*, ed. Henri Jouin (Paris, 1883).

5. Ibid. See also *Conférences inédites de l'Académie Royale de Peinture et de Sculpture*, ed. André Fontaine (Paris, 1903).
6. This work, illustrated here in black and white, is reproduced in color in Gerald Van der Kemp, *Versailles* (Paris, 1977, and New York, 1978), 47.
7. Charles Perrault, *Parallèle des anciens et des modernes, en ce qui regarde les arts et les sciences* (Paris, 1688).
8. The most succinct summary of the color-drawing debates is contained in Carl Goldstein, review of Teyssedre, *Roger de Piles et les débats sur le coloris*, *Art Bulletin* XLIX, (1967), 264–8. The debate over color *vesus* drawing was a long-standing one that had its origins in early sixteenth-century Italy.
9. Roger Guillemet, *Essai sur la Surintendance des Bâtiments du Roi: 1662–1715*, (Paris, 1912).
10. Jennifer Montagu, "Charles Le Brun and His Sculptors," *Burlington Magazine* CXVIII (1976), 88–94, discusses the shared creative process in several works for private patrons.
11. Klaus Herding, *Pierre Puget: das bildnerische Werk* (Berlin, 1980).
12. Letter of September 27, 1686, published in Louis Hautecoeur, "'La Renommée écrivant l'Histoire du Roi' par Domenico Guidi," *Gazette des Beaux-Arts* ser. 4, VII (1912), 46–50.
13. Louis XIV et al., "La Manière de montrer les jardins de Versailles, ed. Christopher Thacker," *Garden History* I, No. 1 (September 1972), 49–69.
14. Betsy Rosasco, "The Sculpture of the Château of Marly during the Reign of Louis XIV," Ph.D. dissertation, New York University (1980).
15. Louis Hautecoeur, *Louis XIV, Roi-Soleil* (Paris, 1952). Ann Freidman, "The 'Grande Commande' for the Sculpture of the Parterre d'eau at Versailles: 1672–1683," Ph.D. dissertation, Bryn Mawr (1983), 66–136.
16. André Félibien, *Description de la grotte de Versailles* (Paris, 1679).
17. Daniel Mayer, *L'Histoire de Roy* (Paris, 1980).
18. Pierre Rainssant, *Explication des tableaux de la galérie de Versailles, et de ses deux salons* (Versailles, 1687).
19. François-Georges Pariset, *L'Art classique* (Paris, 1961), contains an important discussion of the terms "Classique" and "Baroque", their shifting meanings, and their emotional values in art-historical literature.
20. Charles Le Brun, *Grand escalier du Château de Versailles, dit escalier des ambassadeurs*, introduction by C. Le Fèvre (Paris, 1725).
21. Jean-Baptiste Masse, *La Grande galérie de Versailles, et les deux salons qui l'accompagnent* (Paris, 1752).

FOURTEEN

Music in the Reign of Louis XIV

PETER PIERSON

Music filled the life and world of Louis XIV. Much of it came from the sounds of the streets, the ringing of church bells, the crying of hawkers, the dirges of funerals, and pipes playing for weddings, and the melodies were often traditional, such as the familiar tune Louis' court composer Jean-Baptiste Lully used for his *March of the Turenne Regiment* and two centuries later Georges Bizet employed in his incidental music for *L'Arlésienne*.

Louis XIV heard the music of the people all of his life, but his own musical education focused on music that was formally composed, and it was formally composed music in which he took keen personal interest. The place of music in education carries a long history, and because of music's mathematically definable harmonies and affective power, had been treated by Plato, Aristotle, and the fathers of the church, and continued to be a topic of lively interest in the seventeenth century.[1] Music stood among the seven liberal arts and was part of the medieval and "Renaissance" quadrivium, the science curriculum. Such cannot be said for painting and sculpture, which struggled to rise from the level of crafts by the development of a theory. In dealing with the education of the courtier, Castiglione recommended an ability to draw and paint as well as skill in singing and playing musical instruments, but the recommendation, made in the text by Count Lodovico, appears bold and needed justification, whereas none was needed for music: the count claimed that in ancient times painting had been included among the liberal arts.

Louis was, however, more than the nobleman envisioned by Castiglione, destined to serve at court: from the age of five he was King of France. His education ideally had to prepare him to rule, and for thinkers concerned with education from Plato to Castiglione's contemporary Erasmus, the education of princes had come to blend the study of statecraft with the broader program of study in the liberal arts as developed in the "Renaissance" courts of Italy to produce perfect gentlemen and ladies. Charles V, the recipient of a treatise by Erasmus, himself supervised the education of his son Philip II of Spain, which was based on the courtly ideals of Castiglione and on the theories of the Erasmian humanist Luis Vives.

Largely because of the excitement and upheavals of the Fronde, which began when Louis XIV was not yet ten years old, his formal education could not match the ideal program prepared by Charles V, well known as it was to Anne of Austria. The Palais-Royal, where Anne, the young king, and his brother resided, seemed at times like a prison and had to be abandoned on several occasions. By the time internal order was restored, the king was fourteen and had been declared of age. His education henceforth would be largely in statecraft under the tutelage of Cardinal Mazarin.

In the ceremonies surrounding his coming of age, the young king danced his first ballet in public. His education in music and dance had obviously not been entirely neglected during the troubles. Music was and had long been a part of the public and private life of the French court; Louis XIII had composed music. Mazarin, like Richelieu before him, appreciated music and dance, and used musical spectacles to entertain and flatter his sovereign and impress the court.

The tradition known by Richelieu was that of the *ballet de cour*, the vast spectacles of music and dance accompanied by sung texts for solo voice and chorus, and embellished by the spectacular use of stage machinery, dating back to the *Circé, ou le ballet comique de la Reyne Louise,* arranged in 1581 by Catherine de Medici for the court of Henry III. In 1641 Richelieu staged for Louis XIII an elaborate *Ballet de la prospérité* in the theater of the then Palais-Cardinal, which appears in a much reproduced engraving by M. van Lochom showing an entertainment for Louis XIII, Anne, and the little dauphin.[2]

With his Roman origins, Mazarin was familiar with the new form of musical spectacle that was taking Italy by storm, the opera. In 1645 Mazarin staged for seven-year-old Louis XIV the first Italian opera performed for the French court, a musical comedy, *La finta Pazza,* whose chief success derived from the stage machinery of the renowned Giacomo Torelli, which bedazzled the boy-king. If the court expected to be entertained with spectacles, Mazarin would provide them, from his own love of entertainment and, one has no doubt, in order to curtail any murmuring on that account, since there was so much murmuring against his other doings. The use of public entertainment as a means of winning support and isolating enemies is no novelty in history and is no more peculiar to Mazarin than it would be to his pupil, the king.

La finta Pazza was followed by Francesco Cavelli's opera *Egisto* and Luigi Rossi's *Orfeo*, which Mazarin commissioned for the court. For everybody, Torelli's elaborate stage machinery again proved a major attraction, and the king and queen-mother were thoroughly entertained. However, Mazarin's critics attacked its extravagance, and it became an issue in the outbreak of the Fronde.

But musical plays enhanced by spectacular machine-produced effects grew in popularity, luring even the talents of Pierre Corneille, whose *Andromède* included music by Charles d'Assoucy, used, however, as much to conceal the rumble of the machinery as to advance the dramatic argument.

So long as Mazarin lived, the role of the king in making policy, whether state or artistic, was limited. He seems to have trusted Mazarin. Much in Mazarin's statecraft and artistic tastes Louis clearly admired and strove during his life and personal reign to emulate, though when it came to martial swagger and the strenuous life, the king thought the cardinal wanting.

When Mazarin died, in March 1661, Louis XIV took personal charge of the government, filled with a youthful determination to be master in his kingdom. He added his royal will and energy to the growing tendency of government to take cognizance of every aspect of the lives of his subjects (though it lacked the personnel and means), as part of the crown's divinely ordained mission. The musical life of France, with all of its twenty million inhabitants, centered on the court and the capital city. The situation of Italy, the birthplace of so many of the cultural tendencies of the "Renaissance" and of the seventeenth century, was very different. The thirteen or so million Italians of the time looked to eleven princely, republican, or viceregal capitals, three of which—Rome, Venice, and Florence—in no way needed to defer to Paris.[3] Louis, of course, believed they should and strove with considerable success to make France surpass the artistic achievements of Italy and become the cultural leader of Christendom.

The musical establishment of the court, which Louis knew well and controlled from the moment of Mazarin's death, was the most obvious instrument for the achievement of his goal. To ensure that the court's musicians were the finest in the kingdom, competitions were held, which the king attended, for vacant posts. In 1683 thirty-five musicians competed for posts of *sous-maîtres* of the royal chapel.[4] Because the court offered prestige and security, it could attract the finest musicians; and together, the court and Paris formed the magnet that drew into their craw the best and most ambitious musicians of the realm. This is not to say that the provinces enjoyed no formal musical life: their capitals and cathedrals did, but little of the known music of the *grand siècle* has come from them, unless through the court and Paris. One such piece, performed still today, is the *Messe des Morts* of Jean Gilles, a Provençal who directed the choir school of Saint-Etienne in Toulouse; its survival, however, is owed to its "discovery" by the eighteenth-century musical circle, the Concerts Spirituels. The provincial capitals saw and heard mainly performances of works that had been hits in the capital. Mme. de Sévigné mentions a performance of Lully's opera *Atys* in Rennes in 1689; it had been first performed at court and in Paris in 1676.

The musical organization of Louis XIV's court[5] dates from the reign of Francis I, who was dazzled by "Renaissance" Italy and determined that France should excel in the arts. Francis established the music of the Chapelle Royale, the Chambre, and the Grande Ecurie, whose members were referred to as the *musiciens du roi* or simply as *officiers de la maison du roi*. At the time of Louis XIV the members of the three establishments numbered over two hundred instrumentalists and singers, who collaborated for great occasions. In addition to these, the guards regiments attending the king had their own music of trumpets, fifes, and drums, and these could join with the rest.

The Royal Chapel tended to be musically conservative, hewing to the hoary traditions of church music. Of more than a hundred musicians, some ninety were singers. The organists included such significant composers and players of the instrument as Nicolas Gigault and François Couperin.

The more than forty musicians of the Grande Ecurie played trumpets, sackbuts, oboes and other wind instruments, and drums, for cavalcades, promenades, hunts, and other outdoor activities; they also provided the brass, woodwinds, and percussion of the orchestras for the concerts, ballets, *divertissements*, and operas that graced the life of the court and form an integral part of our image of Versailles in all its splendor.

The chief element in these imposing orchestras, the strings, came from the Musique de la Chambre. Its backbone, established to entertain the king indoors, were the Vingt-Quatre Violons du Roi, or Grande Bande. They were often augmented by the twelve Grands Hautbois of the Ecurie. Sometime around 1648 the Petits Violons du Roi appeared, established by the king—prompted by Anne or Mazarin?—because of dissatisfaction with the strings players of the Grande Bande. How typical of the old regime to add new *officiers* without eliminating the old!

Louis' own knowledge of music was good. In his education he had learned, as Castiglione would have wished, both drawing and music. He played the lute, not an easy instrument, and the guitar, which was simpler to play, and which he favored. The contemporary music historian Jacques Bonnet claims the guitar was the king's "favorite instrument".[6]

Louis' musical tastes changed somewhat with the years. As a young man the king enjoyed the majestic music that accompanied court ceremonies, carousels and *divertissements*, the spectacular ballets and the emerging opera, as well as the more intimate music provided for his *appartements*, those glamorous evenings of entertainment for the court nobility, with banqueting, dancing, and gambling. From the late 1680s onward, however, the king began avoiding when he could grander occasions with their musical spectacles, and heard the new operas chiefly through selections performed in the *appartements* of Mme. de Maintenon, his second wife, who also provided him with frequent chamber concerts. Regarding the Mass, which he usually heard daily, he preferred throughout his reign Low Masses to High. The sequence of the High Mass was fixed, and the music largely traditional; the Low Mass allowed the introduction of motets, a form he favored and that therefore flourished during his reign.[7]

Paris, where the court resided during Louis' youth—save when in flight or on royal progress—had its own musical life, dominated by the well-entrenched guild, first chartered in 1321 by the provost, called the Confrérie de Saint-Julien des Ménéstriers, and more modernly, the Corporation des maîtres de danse et joueurs d'instruments. The guild had its own church, hospital, and concert hall. Its head was styled the *roi des ménéstriers* and, later, the *roi des violons*, and its members included all who were licensed to play and teach the playing of musical instruments and all who taught dance in the city.

Louis XIV, as he used the musical establishment of the court to exalt the music of France, encroached on the musical independence of Paris and attacked the privileges of the confrérie, with only mixed results.[8] The power of the guild waned more as a result of the artistic triumphs of the court than of the legal efforts of the crown, which were endlessly bogged down in lawsuits. Louis XIV's absolute monarchy, with its legalistic, if sometimes heavy-handed, proceedings, should not be mindlessly compared with a twentieth-century totalitarian dictatorship such as Hitler's or Stalin's, in the arts or any other area, any more than should Louis' tastes. For Stalin, good music was something he could whistle.

Louis' assault on the privileges of the confrérie seems not to have begun by royal design, but rather as a result of the dance masters' effort to establish their own guild, independent of the musicians. The king's own dance master begged Louis to back them. When the king issued *lettres patentes* for the formation of the Académie Royale de Danse, on March 31, 1661, Mazarin's body was hardly cold in its grave. Had the king and Mazarin been looking for an opportunity to establish a royal academy? The name of Colbert, Mazarin's former secretary, is linked with the formation of this and other academies of the arts and sciences under Louis XIV, although the concept of royal academies had a long pedigree. The term "academy" smacks of "Renaissance" Platonism, and Louis XIII and Richelieu had employed it for the literary circle chartered in 1635 as the Académie Française, while the Académie de Poésie et Musique, founded by Jean-Antoine de Baïf, had flourished in Paris under the last Valois.

The head of the confrérie, Guillaume Dumanoir—called Guillaume I by his foes[9]—responded to the new Académie Royale de Danse with petitions to the king, protests in the *parlement* of Paris, and public polemics, to no avail. A few years later Dumanoir and the confrérie faced a new and more deadly threat with the establishment of the Académie Royale de Musique and subsequent royal efforts to extend its privileges at further cost to the confrérie, which feared for its very existence. These new royal efforts also fell short in the long run, and the result was a compromise solution reached in 1691, by which the confrérie's place and privileges were clarified.

The establishment of the Académie Royale de Musique, like the establishment of the academy of dance, resulted from the seizure of an opportunity rather than from a careful design, although it fit well with the determination of young Louis XIV to exalt France as he saw best in every way, including music. A royal academy, amenable to the royal hand, appeared the obvious means to Louis and Colbert, who both placed much confidence in academies established under the aegis of the crown.

The Académie Royale de Musique began with the establishment in 1669 of "Académies d'Opéra, ou représentations en musique en langue française sur le pied de celles d'Italie." The coming of Italian opera to Paris had excited literary and musical circles, and argument broke out over opera's merits and whether or not the French public would take to the new form that combined music and drama. The French were devoted to the spectacle-ballet, exemplified in the *ballets de cour*, for musical entertainment, and took seriously their spoken drama, with its stately Alexandrines and exalted declamation. Could music and theater, and possibly dance, be combined, or should they? Many held that the French language itself was unsuited to operatic singing, with its increasingly coloratura vocalism that obscured increasingly inane texts. Opera, they insisted, was best suited to the Italian tongue and Italian taste. The quarrel between supporters of French or Italian taste joined the quarrel between ancients and moderns in the birth of modern literary, artistic, and musical criticism, and affected the reports of musical events in the *Gazette*, the *Mercure Galant*, and the *Journal des Savants*.[10]

Among those who argued for a French operatic style and attempted to stage operas in French was the ambitious poet and speculator Pierre Perrin (he had married a rich, elderly widow). In 1659 he produced a pastoral opera in French, *Le Pastoral d'Issy*, with music composed by Robert Cambert. Crowds flocked to see it, and he took it to Vincennes by royal invitation for a performance before Louis, Anne, and Mazarin.

Mazarin, so often accused of partiality for things Italian, astutely agreed to back Perrin in producing a second pastoral opera. He died before it was completed, and Perrin was imprisoned for debt. After being freed, Perrin resumed in 1666 his efforts to produce opera in French and appealed to the king and Colbert for backing, which he received four years later. The *lettres patentes* for Académies d'Opéra, signed by the king and Colbert, in effect granted Perrin and Robert Cambert, who became his partner, a monopoly for producing operas in Paris and elsewhere in the kingdom. With debate over the relative merits of French or Italian taste raging all around them, Louis and Colbert seized the chance to establish a French opera.

All Perrin now needed was money. Backing was promised by the Marquis de Sourdeac, who enjoyed designing stage machinery, and his associate, the Sieur de Champeron. The new academy's first production, *Pomone*, opened in June 1671 and proved a great popular success. A contemporary critic, Charles Marguetel de Saint-Denis, Sieur de Saint-Evremond, wrote that it was "the first French opera to appear on stage. The poetry in it is very bad, the music is beautiful. Monsieur de Sourdeac built the machines; this is enough to give you some idea of their beauty; one observed the machines with surprise, the dances with pleasure; one listened to the songs with delight, to the words with disgust".[11]

Despite popular success, the academy was soon in financial straits, supposedly because of Sourdeac's mismanagement, while Perrin landed again in jail for debts. What followed cannot be entirely untangled from the pertinent documents, letters, and memoirs, but what clearly resulted was the acquisition of the academy by the royal Superintendant of the Musique de Chambre, Jean-Baptiste Lully.[12]

Jean-Baptiste Lully has proved one of the more intriguing personalities of the reign of Louis XIV, and one of the most significant figures in the history of French music.[13] Born in Florence in 1632, the son of a miller, he was brought to France at the age of fourteen by the cousin of

Mlle. de Montpensier, to serve in her household and speak Italian with her. His recommendation was probably his musical talent, but who in Florence recommended him is not known.

In the household of Mlle. de Montpensier he became an accomplished dancer and musician under the tutelage of the composer Michel Lambert, whose daughter he eventually married. In 1652 Lully danced in a ballet for the young king and soon after received appointment to the recently vacated court post of *compositeur de la musique instrumentale.* Since Mazarin and Anne were making the decisions for Louis, Lully must have been their choice, most likely for reasons no more sinister than recognition of his talents and in response to Lambert's urgings. Appointing an Italian—though with chiefly French training—at a time Italian music was in vogue also makes some sense, as does appointing one not deeply enmeshed in the intrigues of the royal or Parisian musicians.

Once in the royal service, Lully rose rapidly. By 1656 the Petits Violons were under his control, and in May 1661, two months after Mazarin's death, he received appointment as superintendant and composer of the Musique de Chambre, which became the foundation of his musical empire. The next summer he married Madeleine Lambert, who brought a fat dowry, and was guaranteed succession to Lambert's offices. The king, who attended the wedding, united Lully's offices under that of *surintendant,* valued at thirty thousand *livres* with hereditary rights.[14] Now a naturalized Frenchman, Lully added the noble particle *de* to his name, for which he had to receive royal recognition.[15] However politely the nobility may have addressed Lully in public, among themselves, if Mme. de Sévigné can be used as an example, they referred to him as "Baptiste".

Among his duties for the king Lully supervised the musical aspects of the extravagant *grands divertissements*, which extended over several days and dazzled all Europe. In 1664 a *divertissement* entitled *Les Plaisirs de l'île enchantée,* based on Ariosto's *Orlando Furioso*, was produced at Versailles, ostensibly to honor the queen and the queen-mother. Gorgeously costumed and feathered, Louis XIV and his nobles rode magnificently caparisoned horses in carousels and strutted and danced in elegant ballets—with the accomplished Lully fussing about the nobles' lack of skill. The poet Isaac de Benserade, known for his ballet scripts, included the queen's claims to the Spanish throne in his verses. Molière contributed the play *La Princesse d'Elide* to the *divertissement,* which concluded with the spectacular destruction of Alcine's palace in a *Götterdämmerung*-like finale of fireworks and explosions. Similar grand or near-grand *divertissements* were produced in 1668, 1671, 1674, and 1685, all with music by Lully and several immortalized in engravings by François Chaveau and Israel Silvestre.

In the year of *L'Ile enchantée*, Lully began his fruitful collaboration with Molière, writing music and ballets to accompany Molière's comedies in what were called *comédies-ballets*. Their collaboration culminated in 1671 with *Le Bourgeois Gentilhomme; Psyché*, a *tragédie-ballet*, with text by Molière and song lyrics by Philippe Quinault, was their last work together. The next year Lully acquired control of the Académies d'Opéra.

The Académies d'Opéra, despite financial problems, had opened, in January 1672, with the pastoral opera *Les Peines et plaisirs de l'amour* to great public acclaim. Robert Cambert composed the music, which served well a fine text by Gabriel Gilbert. If we accept Saint-Evremond's adverse judgment of Perrin's poetry, it was perhaps fortunate for French opera that Cambert's partner and previous librettist Perrin was languishing in the *concièrgerie* for debt. Lully was finally convinced that opera in French was worthwhile.

Lully offered early in 1672 to buy Perrin out, with encouragement from Colbert, who was upset no doubt at the shortcomings of the academy he had urged the king to establish to promote French opera. With support of the king and Colbert, and in spite of furious opposition from some of Perrin's associates, Lully succeeded. The charges they subsequently raised in court against him have provided much ammunition for Lully's many detractors. The question they raised remains: Was, as they argued, Lully simply ambitious, unscrupulous, and greedy, or were the king and Colbert behind the matter, determined to promote French opera and convinced that Lully was the obvious person to achieve what they wanted? Lully himself suggested that the whole idea was Colbert's.[16] Since the academy had been losing money although drawing large audiences, it would seem unlikely that Lully was greedy, unless he saw a way to turn the academy's fortunes around. Given the general suspicions of Sourdeac's management, perhaps he did. Whatever the case, Lully had the academy and was faced by costly litigation.

The *lettres patentes* issued in March 1672 to Lully (on the eve of the Dutch War) expressed the king's confidence in him and permitted him to establish in Paris what was now called the Académie Royale de Musique, with a monopoly of the production of operas in French and foreign languages throughout the kingdom. The theater of Perrin's associates was forced to close. Lully was not permitted to employ royal musicians, which must have gratified the musicians of the city, until he began to obtain regulations limiting the number of musicians other Parisian theaters could employ, in order to protect his monopoly of the French musical stage.

For his own productions, Lully made a contract with the stage machine designer Carlo Vigarini, famous for his spectacular special effects for royal *divertissements*. He appealed to the king, who had joined his army for the invasion of Holland, for use of the Louvre's theater; the king thought it "inappropriate". Lully therefore hired a theater, the Jeu de Paume de Bel Air, on the Rue Vaurigard near the Luxembourg Palace. Complaining that the difficulties he encountered in establishing the academy hindered composition, he staged a musical spectacle, *Les Fêtes de l'amour et de Bacchus*, based on earlier works, with a libretto pieced together by Philippe Quinault from texts by himself, Molière, and others. It opened in November 1672 and celebrated the king's early triumphs in the Dutch War.

Lully's first *tragédie lyrique*, *Cadmus et Hermione*, was presented the following April before king and court at Saint-Germain-en-Laye, then opened in Paris, becoming a resounding success. With a libretto by Quinault, who admired the dramatic technique of Pierre Corneille and Jean Racine, and interspersed when appropriate with ballet and spectacle, *Cadmus* initiated a series of brilliantly orchestrated and precisely sung operas that determined the main direction of French operatic style for the following two hundred years. Carefully heeding the high declamatory style of the French theater, Lully and Quinault forged in the *tragédies lyriques* operas in which the music scrupulously respected the literary text, which had been the initial ideal of the Florentine camarata from which Italian opera had strayed, so its critics charged, in pursuit of musical and melodic pyrotechnics.

To achieve what he wanted from his musicians and singers, Lully insisted upon disciplined subservience to his will and, with royal support, broke the confrérie's hold on them. He moved his productions in the summer of 1673 into the theater of the Palais-Royal, displacing the troupe of his erstwhile collaborator Molière, who had died that February. His productions at the Palais-Royal, which held up to two thousand people in a long but relative narrow auditorium,[17] almost always sold out. He grew extremely rich, and his employees were well paid.[18]

Lully's critics were many and included Molière's players, who were steadily stripped of their musicians, singers, and attendance. The beleaguered troupe banded with other threatened companies to form the Comédie Française and, forced to eliminate the musical and balletic parts of their productions, developed the style of performance known to this day.

Satires of Lully's operas abounded in spite of sporadic royal efforts to check them.[19] The chief culprits were the Italian comedians who played at the Hôtel de Bourgogne. In 1697 they were expelled from the kingdom for a satire, *La Fausse prude*, aimed at Mme. de Maintenon, but their mock operas were continued by the vaudeville entertainments of Parisian Fair Theatres,[20] whose players circumvented the academy's monopoly on singing actors by presenting placards carrying the text to the audience, who sang the songs.

Moralists protested to the king that indecencies were rife in the galleries among operagoers excited by Lully's sensuous music. After the death of Lully, whose morals the king did not question, the king issued a code of conduct for the members of the company, about whose behavior he had received complaints.[21]

The Jansenists, whose opposition to theater was properly Augustinian, extended their disapproval to opera and ballet. They accused the Jesuits, who had long staged religious plays with their pupils as actors and had added opera and ballet to their repertory, of risking the corruption of their pupils' morals.[22]

The king regarded Lully's operas to be morally sound because he personally had discussed them in every detail during their composition with Lully and his librettists. Lully wrote all but two of his *tragédies lyriques* in collaboration with Quinault. The other two he composed to texts written by Thomas Corneille, Pierre Corneille's nephew, and the precocious Bernard de Fontenelle. The first ten were based on Greek and Roman myths, and the last three on chivalric romances, which the king felt represented French heroics.[23] Each dramatized on epic scale the timeless quest for love and glory, while containing topical allusions to contemporary events and extolling the majesty of the king.

The premieres of most were produced for the king and court, including six at Saint-Germain-en-Laye and two of the last four at Versailles. The king also attended Lully's operas at the theater of the Palais-Royal, where five had their premieres. An idea of the grandeur of the royal performances is provided in the oft-reproduced etching of the July 4, 1674, performance of *Alceste* in the Cour de Marbre at Versailles.

Several of Lully's operas have been recorded for the phonograph; to most modern listeners the instrumental and choral music still carries a certain appeal, while the recitatives and airs soon acquire a stately monotony. The modern critic Joseph Kerman describes Lully's recitative as "bloodless, its vigor carefully paced, its passion channeled, its nobility stereotyped and labored".[24]

Opera, however, should ideally be a total experience, and to understand Lully's full appeal to his audience, his works must be seen as well as heard. The visual and spectacular aspects played no small part in packing Lully's theater. In *Phaéton* (1683), Proteus rose from the sea and turned into a lion, a tree, a sea monster, a fountain, and flames.[25] Ballet dancers were gorgeously costumed as "Egyptians, Indians, and Ethiopians". Parisians flocked in such numbers to see and hear *Phaéton* that it was called the "people's opera".

Modern performances of Lully have been rare, though both the earlier operas of Monteverdi and growing numbers of the late Baroque operas of Handel have been mounted recently. Kerman, who treats Baroque opera from Lully through Handel in a chapter titled "The Dark Ages", admits that the period deserves careful scholarly and critical reexamination, which indeed it is receiving. A 1980 performance of *Alceste* at Hesse-Darmstadt was called a "triumph", leading the critic to quote Mme. de Sévigné's description of it as "prodigiously beautiful".[26]

Because Lully was so close to the king, and seemed to share Louis' imperious manner, his works seem synonymous with the *grand siècle*. The critics of his works were also most often critics of the king, and their ranks grew through Louis' fifty-four-year personal reign. Lully's death, in 1687, came in the middle of a difficult decade of the reign, when Louis seemed to lose sight of the ends he sought as he and Louvois bullied subjects and foreign powers alike.[27]

Yet if much of the criticism of Lully was also criticism of the king, it appears sustained by modern criticism as well as modern taste. In recordings and performance two French-born composers of the *grand siècle*, Marc-Antoine Charpentier and François Couperin, far exceed him; and others also, less well known, match or surpass him.

Charpentier, two to four years younger than Lully, never held a proper court office, though the king was aware of his worth. Lully, according to his critics, was jealous of Charpentier, yet Charpentier served as music teacher to the grand dauphin, for whose chapel he wrote several masses, and to Philippe d'Orléans, the later regent, and as *maître de musique* to the Duchess de Guise. It would thus seem that Lully was willing to accommodate Charpentier, though hardly willing— and why should he have been?—to share his advantages with him.

In 1684 Charpentier became music master at the Jesuit church of Saint-Louis and in 1698 at the Sainte-Chapelle. His musical training began in Rome, where he studied under Giacomo Carissimi, most famous for his oratorios, a form at which Charpentier later excelled. Charpentier's critics, of the circle of Lully and his heirs, claimed his music was too Italian.

Soon after his return from Italy, Charpentier collaborated with Molière, who had broken with Lully. He provided new incidental music for a revival of *Le Mariage forcé* (not without some difficulty with Lully, who had written the original score), and the music for *Le Malade imaginaire*, Molière's last work. In 1688 a Charpentier opera was performed at the Jesuit college of Louis-le-Grand, and in 1693 his *Médée* was staged at the Académie de Musique, to mixed response, despite the king's praises. The guardian of the cult of Lully, Lecerf de La Vieville, dubbed it the *méchante opéra de Médée*,[28] while Sébastien de Brossard acclaimed it and blamed its closing after ten performances on a "cabal of the envious and ignorant".[29]

Charpentier's last major work, the oratorio *Historia Judicium Salomonis*, was performed in 1702 for the "Messe Rouge" that celebrated the opening of *parlement*. Given the traditional view that Louis reduced *parlement's* powers, a modern author sees the subject as "mischievous".[30] Lately, however, it has been argued that Louis simply restricted *parlement's* political activities, with the result that its judicial authority was secured.[31] Perhaps "apt" better describes the subject.

François Couperin was of the new generation who would provide the music of France during the last years of the Sun King's reign and for the period of the regency. He was born in 1668, at the time Lully had come to rule the musical roost of the court and was about to rule that of the capital. Of a musical family, Couperin became organist of the church of Saint-Gervais at seventeen, and in 1693, *organiste du roi* in the Royal Chapel. He admired the music of Arcangelo Corelli and brought sweetness and melody into his compositions. A superb player of the *clavecin* (harpsichord), as well as organ, he wrote and performed keyboard and chamber music to entertain the aging king.

Louis, at war with most of Europe after 1688, sorted through his policies and their goals, and after the death of Louvois, in 1691, reorganized his government. His personal life had become settled earlier with his attachment to Mme. de Maintenon, who became his morganatic wife sometime following the death in 1683 of the queen. Mme. de Maintenon did not enjoy grand *divertissements*, operas, and ceremonial, which she considered frivolous and wasteful. The king's involvement with music shifted from the active support of Lullian musical extravaganzas to the simple enjoyment of the intimacies of chamber music, written and played by Couperin and other composers of his generation, such as Michel-Richard Delalande, who succeeded Lully as *surintendant de musique*, and Louis-Nicolas Clérambault. Rather than hear long, elaborately staged operas, the king heard selected scenes, such as the tempest scene from *Alcyone* (1706), by Marin Marais (best known for his compositions for viol), which was performed in 1711 at Marly.[32]

The new court composers when required responded brilliantly to the demand for ceremonial splendor, as they did for the festivities that surrounded the proclamation in 1700 of Philippe, Duke d'Anjou, as King Philip V of Spain. These, which proved the last great festivities of the reign, commenced in the royal chapel of Versailles with a motet by Delalande, which brought tears of "joy and sadness" to the king's eyes,[33] and continued with the grandiose ceremonies at each stage of the progress to Spain of Philip V, accompanied to the frontier by his brothers, the Dukes de Bourgogne and Berry. Louis XIV supervised all arrangements from their departure to the return of the two dukes to Versailles.

Not content with occasional spectacles, but seeking a steady diet of such entertainments, the bright young courtiers of the new generation flocked to Paris in the 1690s, leaving behind Versailles, which, as was said, had become like a convent. They also made their own *châteaux* new centers of musical activity. Led by the king's grandsons, the Dukes de Bourgogne and Berry, his nephew, Philippe d'Orléans, his natural sons, the Duke de Maine and the Count de Toulouse, the Duchess de Maine, and the Prince de Conti and his circle, they continued to patronize the Académie de Musique, where Lully's sons and his artistic heirs, Pascal Colasse and Henri Desmarets churned out inferior operas and ballets; and sought new lights, such as André Campra, whose opera-ballet *L'Europe galante* was the hit of the season of 1697, the year of the Peace of Ryswick. Campra, who held the post of organist at Notre-Dame, would prove the leading composer of opera during Louis XIV's last years and the regency. Campra's style was light and tuneful, and suited musically the world that Watteau would soon portray in painting. With *livret* by Antoine Houdar de La Motte, the theme of *L'Europe galante* was how the French, Spaniards, Italians, and Turks make love. Its lighthearted combination of comedy, song, and ballet made it in some ways the precursor of the lavish revues staged in Paris to this day. Its success was followed by similar works, *Les Fêtes galantes* by Desmarets (1698), Campra's *Le Carnaval de Venise* (1699), and his most famous, *Les Fêtes vénitiennes* (1710).

Another form that flourished during these years was the secular cantata, or *cantate françoise*,[34] at first using the poetry of Jean-Baptiste Rousseau. Superb cantatas to texts from the Old Testament were composed by Elisabeth Jacquet de La Guerre, an accomplished harpsichordist and protégée of Mmes. de Montespan and Maintenon. She also contributed to the Paris season of 1694 a *tragédie-lyrique*, *Céphile et Procris*, which extolled Louis' cause in the Nine Years' War.

The old king, withdrawn to a somber Versailles to win for his grandson the crown of Spain, through diplomacy following the Peace of

Ryswick, and after 1702 through war, largely left the musical life of France to the new generation, who gave themselves, when they could, to the pursuit of pleasure. The rich mélange of lyric theater that blossomed in Paris, the *fête* operas, the enduring grand operas of the Académie de Musique, the vaudeville of the Fair Theatres, with the Opéra Comique almost in sight, gave the French capital the effulgent and effervescent musical life that would henceforth characterize the "City of Light".

The fresh cultural and intellectual climate of the regency, so stimulatingly treated by Arnold Hauser in his *Social History of Art*, in a chapter entitled "The Dissolution of Courtly Art", had emerged in the last years of the Sun King's reign. Full of hope and energy, Louis XIV had pursued during the first two dozen years of his personal reign perhaps too many elusive goals for the exaltation of himself and France. He and his ministers tried to impose their ideas of order on twenty million subjects in an extensive kingdom. They stressed grandeur and duty, and the king and court talked of love and glory. All these themes the king wished his music to stress. By the late 1680s, his energy was flagging, but, even as he saw his queen and early ministers die and his mistresses grow old, he stubbornly persevered, with the devoted support of a new team of ministers and of Mme. de Maintenon. Wisely, he came to understand the art of the possible and settled for what he could get. Louis XIV ceased trying to dominate French music, whose course he had done much to determine. Yet through the concerts in the apartments of Mme. de Maintenon, he remained in touch with the musical life of his realm until the time of his death. During his reign and with his active encouragement, French music had found its particular character and would henceforth stand alongside the Italian and other national traditions of Europe as one of the great schools of Western music.[35]

NOTES

1. Robert M. Isherwood, *Music in the Service of the King* (Ithaca, 1973), has a particularly good discussion of this topic. Isherwood commendably places music, of which his knowledge is sure, in the context of the reign, for which he has unfortunately depended too much on outdated sources.
2. The figure in the engraving leaning toward the king is usually described as Cardinal Richelieu, who is gallantly dressed and looks rather healthy. It appears in Isherwood, among others, who (see p. 108) identifies the figure as Richelieu, who died in 1642, with the date 1643.
3. In addition to Rome, Venice, and Florence were the princely capitals of Savoy (Turin), Parma, Mantua, and Modena, republican Genoa, and viceregal Naples, Palermo, and Milan.
4. James R. Anthony, *French Baroque Music from Beaujoyeulx to Rameau* (New York, 1978), 10.

5. Anthony, ch. 1.
6. Quoted in Anthony, 242.
7. See Anthony, ch. 13. For a superb example of this musical form, hear the recording *Motets à voix seule et à deux voix* by Marc Antoine Charpentier, Harmonia Mundi France (1984), compact disc *HMC 901149* (also on *LP*).
8. Isherwood, 153–6; Anthony, 16–20.
9. Anthony, 18.
10. See Georgia Cowart, *The Origins of Modern Musical Criticism: French and Italian Music: 1600–1750* (Ann Arbor, [1980] 1981). Isherwood and Anthony make considerable use of the *Mercure Galant*.
11. Quoted in Anthony, 65.
12. Compare Isherwood, 170–83; Newman, 46–51; Anthony, 20–3.
13. Newman, ch. 2.
14. Newman, 44.
15. André Danican, known as Philidor *l'aîné*, Louis XIV's music librarian, when he copied the musical score of *Le Bourgeois Gentilhomme*, referred to Lully as "Monsieur de Lully, Surintendant de la Musique du Roi" and to Molière simply as "Sieur Molière". Quoted by Joseph Braunstein on album notes to a recording of the music, Vox Productions, New York, DL 1070.
16. Newman, 48–50; Isherwood, 180–1.
17. Anthony, 21.
18. Isherwood, 238–9.
19. Isherwood, 238–47.
20. For these, see Anthony, 154–5.
21. Isherwood, 317–20. Lully's own morals were subject to many scurrilous attacks, examples of which Isherwood uncovered in his painstaking archival research (see pp. 241–3). Lully, a husband and father, supposedly had an affair with a page named Brunet and the Duchess de la Ferte at the same time.
22. Isherwood, 320–32.
23. Lully's *tragédies lyriques*, with libretti by Quinault save as noted, are as follows: *Cadmus et Hermione* (1673); *Alceste* (1674); *Thésée* (1675); *Atys* (1676); *Isis* (1677); *Psyché*, with Th. Corneille and Fontenelle (1678); *Bellérophon*, with Corneille and Fontenelle (1679); *Proserpine* (1680); *Persée* (1682); *Phaéton* (1683); *Amadis* (1684); *Roland* (1685); *Armide* (1686).
24. Joseph Kerman, *Opera as Drama* (New York, 1956), 54.
25. *Simon and Schuster Book of the Opera* (New York, 1978), 22.
26. Horst Koegler, review printed in *Opera* XXXII, No. 2 (February 1981), 179–80. A well-received recording of *Alceste* is available, with Jean-Claude Malgoire leading a group aptly named the Grande Ecurie et Chambre du Roy, 3-CBS M3-34580.
27. Andrew Lossky, "The General European Crisis of the 1680s," *European Studies Review* X (1980), 193–4; and "The Intellectual Development of Louis XIV," in *Louis XIV and the Craft of Kingship*, ed. John C. Rule (Columbus, 1969), 332–6, reprinted with modified text in *Louis XIV and Absolutism*, ed. Ragnhild Hatton (London and Columbus, 1976), 101–29.
28. Anthony, 119.
29. Susan Theimann Sommer, review of a recording of *Médee*, Opus I, No. 5 (August 1985). Sommer praised both the work and the recording, Harmonia Mundi France LP, HMC 90.1139/21 (also on compact disc), by a group

named "Les Arts Florrisants", directed by William Christie.
30. H. Wiley Hitchcock, quoted in Isherwood, 300.
31. Andrew Lossky, "The Absolutism of Louis XIV: Reality or Myth?" *Canadian Journal of History* XIX (1984), 12.
32. Isherwood, 312.
33. Isherwood, 314.
34. Anthony, ch. 23.
35. Much music from Louis' reign can be heard on recordings, often played on instruments from and in the style of the period. Joseph Kerman, *Contemplating Music: Challenges to Musicology* (Cambridge, 1985), deals not only with the problems of musicology, but also with the "historical performance movement".
Schwann Record and Tape Guide (Boston, 1985), lists the following composers of the period, to whose names I have added the number of titles (or groupings) of compositions listed:

Jean-Henri d'Anglebert (1635–91)	2
André Campra (1660–1744)	1
Jacques Champion Chambonières (1602–72)	1
Marc-Antoine Charpentier (c. 1634–1704)	19
Louis-Nicholas Clérambault (1676–1749)	6
François Couperin (1668–1733)	20
Jean-François Dandrieu (1682–1738)	2
Michel-Richard Delalande (1657–1728)	4
Philibert Delavigne (d. 1700)	1
André-Cardinal Destouches (1672–1749)	1
Henri DuMont (1610–84)	2
Nicholas Gigault (1627–1707)	1
Jean Gilles (1668–1705)	1
Elisabeth Jaquet de La Guerre (1659–1707)	2
Michel Lambert (1610–96)	1
Louis XIII (1601–43)	1
Jean-Baptiste Lully (1632–87)	7
Marin Marais (1656–1728)	13
Louis Marchand (1669–1732)	3
Michel de Monteclair (1667–1737)	3
Jean-Joseph Mouret (1682–1738)	2
Jean Ferry Rebel (1666–1747)	2
Sainte-Columbe, Sieur de (seventeenth century)	1

FIFTEEN

The Essays:
An Overview

HERBERT H. ROWEN

About half a century ago, our impression of Louis XIV and of his age was, for the most part, a masterpiece of anachronistic incomprehension. True, the Sun King was described as the very model of an absolute monarch, but although this judgment has held form to the present day, the meaning of the term "absolute monarch" has undergone immense change. Then "absolutism" was equated to the dictatorships of Europe, first to the pale terror of Mussolini and then to the garish juggernaut of Hitler. Now historians have come to see that the pattern of governance practiced by Louis XIV was not unbounded terror, but embodied the rule of law under the conditions of sovereignty—all legitimate power—concentrated in the hands of a single person. Furthermore, prodded by the frightening experience of power limited only by the armed resistance of those it threatened, historians have learned to look away from the verbal claims of total power made on behalf of the early modern monarchy to the reality of its limitations, moral no less than technical. The king has at last received his due as a man in John B. Wolf's masterly biography. The present work has a different aim. It sets out to provide a broad sketch of Louis XIV's reign that reflects the modern state of our knowledge. It has been assembled with the aim of providing a survey which will be of service to students.

The book starts without ceremony, plunging immediately into Bill Roosen's essay "The Demographic History of the Reign". Demography, the *longue durée* of Braudel's *Annaliste* typology, has become in recent decades the most fundamental and deep-lying element studied by historians. There is first of all the simple necessity to get the numbers right, then to observe the trends, and finally to explain them. Roosen confirms for us the great population explosion of the sixteenth century. He notes that, as the level of population stabilized, France retained its status as the most populous state in Europe in the period of Louis XIV.

We see that the new population explosion of the eighteenth century did not bring for France the immense expansion of numbers that it did for other countries. However, as so often happens in historical studies, greater precision of knowledge also calls commonsensical explanations into question. Benefiting from a sojourn at the Institut National d'Etudes Démographiques, Roosen reflects upon this burgeoning field of historical investigation. Particularly significant is his submission of the "late marriage theory" to rigorous criticism, as well as his picture of the limited control by the population over its fertility. He takes due note of the depredations of the Four Horsemen of the Apocalypse, but adds the important observation that we have little knowledge of why some catastrophic diseases, particularly the plague, passed off the scene. As to that other effect of the dread quartet—war—upon population numbers, he places emphasis upon the physical damage wrought by armies in their passage across the land, rather than on the indirect effect of massive taxation. If his conclusions are tentative, this is merely a forthright testament to the state of the art.

His study leads quite naturally to the question of the importance of economic activity in shaping events. This is the topic of Tom Schaeper's imaginative "Economic History of the Reign". It too stresses Braudel's *longue durée* and finds, if anything, even less fundamental growth than in population numbers. Schaeper clearly works on the neo-Malthusian assumption that, as population growth forces the utilization of less-productive land, this leads sooner or later to demographic fallback, but he is more concerned with assessing the role of Louis XIV's great controller-general of the finances, Jean-Baptiste Colbert, whom nineteenth-century historians like Clément represented as indefatigably laying the foundations for the modern protectionist state. Schaeper develops a more complex view of the matter. He sees Colbert and his immediate successors as neither complete failures nor complete successes. Both he and the king, Schaeper holds, sought to enrich the royal treasury by enriching the people. Colbert was able to pursue this double goal up to the Dutch War in 1672; thereafter the needs of the treasury took precedence. Schaeper also concludes that the impact of Colbertian protectionism was limited to luxury trades and therefore had a relatively minimal impact on the vast majority of the population. Colbert, in other words, faced not a single "nation", but a variety of particular groups, some of which supported and others of which opposed his policies. All in all, he is shown to have had little impact upon the economic life of the country. Both Roosen and Schaeper introduce us to a world in which individuals, even great kings and ministers, contend with forces beyond human control.

With Betsy Perry's "Popular History of the Reign", we enter the world of *mentalité*. Here is proof that the editors are in no way unresponsive to the "new" history. Perry's picture of the poor, the deviant, and the criminal is so vivid as to place us, almost uncomfortably, into their midst. Evoking the methodology made fashionable by Natalie Davis, Perry actually provides us with the *changing* history of the Paris rabble, deftly tracing the *varying* impact of their ideology on the more respectable elements of society. She is the first scholar, as far as I know, to advance a theory on the relationship between popular culture and the monarchy in seventeenth-century France, arguing that if Louis XIV failed to suppress the congenitally antisocial elements in his state, at least he deprived them of much of the spell that they had previously exerted over his more conventional subjects. It's a profound insight, and worth testing.

One thing should be noted. Though appropriately conscious of the *longue durée* and avowedly humble about the capacity of human beings to control their destinies, these essays do not set out to dehumanize history. This is clearly manifested in Charlie Steen's implacable pursuit of "The Social History of the Reign". It begins à la Mousnier by describing a social order built upon the possession of status, yet strained by the recurring discrepancies between status and wealth. In part this was a reflection of the way in which new wealth came into being, not as the patient accumulation of rent from the land, but from trade, which was viewed as degrading, and from the perilous but rewarding business of catering to the credit needs of the state. Social ascent under this system operated through the medium of venal office and produced, by the beginning of the seventeenth century, a distinction between the old nobility of the "sword" and the parvenu nobility of the "robe". Steen also gives us a traditional account of the taming of the aristocracy by Louis XIV. But this essay is neither a prosopographical soporific, in which a given number of "sword" families intermarry with their upwardly mobile rivals, nor a *son et lumière* spectacle of empty-headed courtiers skipping in rhythm with the *gaillarde*. Steen infuses his study of this society with a decidedly bitter flavor. It was a society that coexisted with the dingiest view of human nature. It was a society that cultivated boredom and elevated it to a virtue. It was a society in which anyone who wished to escape from his origins had to end up by consistently denying himself. Seldom has a more scathing condemnation of seventeenth-century France appeared in print, but then, seldom has the social and the literary evidence been juxtaposed so unmercifully.

The interplay, on the other hand, between personal quarrels, the role of society as a mediator, and the ultimate intervention of the king is the subject of Duane Anderson's essay "The Legal History of the Reign". Here we have a work that takes full cognizance of the fact that, in every "civilization", most quarrels, crimes, and vendettas remain unreported. But still, the legal system of France in the reign of Louis XIV, as described by Anderson, represents an observable point of contact between the stubbornness of society and the obtrusiveness of the state. The mediators were hundreds of hereditary notables, who derived their *raison d'être* from the administration of the law, and who endowed it with their own particular ethic. It was through their hands that the tendency of seventeenth-century civil jurisprudence toward enhancing paterfamilial power both foreshadowed and overshadowed the similar tendencies of the king's government. Anderson, in keeping with the observations of Robert Mandrou, likewise suggests that the decline in the prosecution of witchcraft, if not the decline in the use of torture, emerged from the experience of the judges themselves. Anderson makes it clear that the entire high judiciary became quite comfortable with and entrenched itself during the zenith of Louis XIV's "absolutism". One of Anderson's particular contributions in this essay is to put the king's much ballyhooed judicial reforms in a historical perspective. They represented an extremely ambitious effort, championed by Colbert, which might have severely restricted the autonomy of the judiciary, had the effort not floundered, like the economic reforms, upon the shoals of the Dutch War. It should hardly be surprising that, by the end of the reign, we can observe very little tension between Louis XIV and his judicial officials, while legal procedure, if a little more humane, had certainly become more cumbersome.

Unlike the story of the development of France's legal system during Louis XIV's reign, John Rule considers the "Administrative History of the Reign" strictly from above. He gives us a king in the tradition of his great-great-grandfather Philip II of Spain, a king who is a master of the machinery of his government, who creates new instruments of power and uses the old ones effectively to serve his purposes. The new administrative system heightened immensely the power of the "absolute" king in France, but in a paradox of great significance, as Rule hints, the administration through which the king governed became a largely autonomous force, the embodiment of the "abstract state" of modern political theory. The ability of Louis XIV to make and carry through policies was confined almost exclusively to the most exalted realms of decision making. Below the higher ranges of administration, where he was able to impose personally upon a large proportion of the office-holders, the expanding bureaucracy became not so much his empire as that of the ministers and of their subordinates.

Of all the institutions in their state, it was the army, as Ron Martin exclaims, that occupied first place in the hearts of French kings, and Louis XIV, who was no exception, brought it to a level of operation that, even in the most difficult years of his reign, permitted him to withstand the great alliances that opposed him. It was the nineteenth-century historian Rousset who attempted to do for Louvois what Clément was simultaneously attempting to do for Colbert—documenting the labors of an indefatigable minister who laid still another foundation for the modern French state. Martin is more skeptical. He insists on asking the hard questions and comes up with an extremely hardheaded description of the king's army in the mid-seventeenth century: its physical appearance, its weaponry, its organization, its fortresses, its battle formations. He does not discount Louis' and Louvois' strenuous efforts to fashion a more effective military machine based on drill, inspections, uniforms, limitation of casualties, the defense and attack of strongholds. But Martin points out that these practices simply implemented prevailing ideas and scarcely revolutionized warfare. The generals may have been less independent, the soldiers less riotous, but regiments and companies were still bought and sold, and the more strained the resources of the monarchy became, the greater was the tendency of the army to revert to its traditional patterns of indiscipline. What is more capable of giving us pause is if we compare the demographic statistics of Roosen with the military statistics of Martin. In a period when the population of France kept hovering at the same level with hardly any noticeable upswing, the king managed to increase the size of his army from fifty thousand to four hundred thousand and adorn his frontiers with a ring of forbidding fortifications. How could he accomplish this? Certainly not, we can be assured by Schaeper, with the help of any economic boom. Certainly not, we can deduce from Perry, thanks to the predecessors of the *sans culottes*. But if we keep these limitations in mind, this helps us to appreciate Steen's message all the more fully. The contempt for the underprivileged, the acceptance of the social order, the lack of apparent alternatives to "absolute" monarchy, would seem to have been sufficient to produce four hundred thousand men until such time as Voltaire and Rousseau could come along to inspire a *levée en masse*.

If the army was part and parcel of the fabric of the monarchy, the navy, as Geoffrey Symcox demonstrates, was undeniably an ornament. But, by the same token, it is one of the few settings where we can see what the great Colbert could accomplish when he was given but half a chance. The result is striking! Who can deny that, with considerably less to work with, he was infinitely more imaginative than Louvois? Colbert's warships quickly became the best in Europe, his bases sprang up out of nowhere, his support industries complemented the economy, his seamen were conscripted systematically, and his officers selected by merit—all this producing an armada that survived him to defeat the combined forces of England and the Dutch Republic! Even so, of course, as with Colbert's other great projects, the expensive fleet had to be sacrificed to the imperative demands of Louis XIV's land wars. Symcox accuses both Colbert and his successors of never defining the navy's mission. After every indecisive major sortie the critics immediately began to question the value of the *guerre d'escadre* and clamor for a shift to privateering. And yet, Symcox ingeniously argues, the dispersal of the great ships merely redirected France's maritime energies. The sailors who boarded the armadas also manned the privateers that wreaked havoc upon English and Dutch commerce. This essay not only describes the creation of a great new tradition for the French nation, but also, in conjunction with the previous essays, leaves us to wonder what a Colbert who was left to his own devices might have accomplished for the French economy and the French legal system, notwithstanding the lethargy of the *longue durée*.

The army and the navy were Louis XIV's most terrifying instruments of persuasion. His more ingratiating side is the object of Jack O'Connor's essay "The Diplomatic History of the Reign". The nineteenth-century historians, exploiting the newly opened archives and imbued with the spirit of nationalism, tended to center their attention on the negotiations of a single ambassador, on the equilibrium between states, and on territorial acquisitions, but O'Connor, inspired by more modern approaches, is equally interested in the functioning of the system. He also owes a great deal to John B. Wolf, particularly in emphasizing Mazarin's influence on the young king. But, with a subtlety of understatement that no reader should disregard, O'Connor clearly implies that Mazarin's conception of glory was different from Louis' and that, following Mazarin's death, the king pushed ministers like Lionne much farther than they would otherwise have gone. O'Connor finds the policy that led to the Dutch War full of contradictions and amply confirms the suspicion that the king sacrificed a promising program of domestic reforms to the more spectacular temptations of war and diplomacy. With each military victory he seemed to lose another ally. While he was conquering cities his enemies were overrunning kingdoms. To put his grandson on the throne of Spain was Louis XIV's supreme achievement. Yet he did not distinguish clearly between the interests of his family and the interests of his state.

When we get to John Grever's "Religious History of the Reign", we meet the first and perhaps the only "grass-roots" movement in seventeenth-century French society. Unlike the economic trends of the *longue durée*, or the embarrassed shuffling for social position, the great Catholic revival is conscious, conspiratorial, and goal-oriented. Like its sister trends, it antedates, transcends, and sometimes even subverts the intentions of the monarchy. Grever follows very closely the maneuvers of French Catholicism in its determined counterattack upon the Huguenots: the new energy of bishops in individual dioceses, the establishment of seminaries by religious orders, the powerful missionary movement both in France and abroad. Not surprisingly these efforts produced their share of disagreements within the church itself: the recurring tussles between regular and secular clergy, the bitter conflict between Jesuits and Jansenists, the embarrassing commotion over Quietism. Thus the personal reign of Louis XIV, in this as in so many other areas, merely confirmed the existing trends. As Grever shows, the king's struggles with the Holy See kept interfering with his efforts to get rid of the Jansenists, and he ended up by pleading for the support of the pope. But Grever also describes Louis XIV's patient solution to the problem of religious dissent—the steady appointment of reputable bishops—as slowly having its effect. These men may not have been saints. They may have served Caesar with at least as much enthusiasm as they served Christ, but they never exemplified the kind of licentiousness upon which the early Protestants had thrived. It is interesting to note that, of all the idealistic intentions of the king's youth, the only one he carried to a successful conclusion was the suppression of the Huguenots. French Protestantism, the *bête noire* of the Catholic revival, could not withstand its onslaughts, but its own brainchild, Jansenism, he could never eliminate. It was there to haunt him until his dying day.

Seymour Chapin's "Science in the Reign of Louis XIV" introduces us to a movement that is conscious, widespread, but hardly, "grass roots". It was made up of dedicated intellectuals like Cesi who employed the patronage of princes in order to achieve a program of scientific regeneration. But Chapin uses a method of exposition not always common to histories of science. He does not talk down to the reader. Along with the achievements of the scientists, Chapin considers their dilemmas, as when he explains how Cartesianism, for all its mathematical pretensions, removed from calculation precisely those phenomena that Galileo had been struggling to quantify. Once again Louis XIV emerges as a man who captured the spirit of his age without entirely mastering it. Ever suspicious of Cartesianism, he created the Académie des Sciences, whose members were Cartesians and which became the last great bastion of Cartesianism. Each of his ministers put his own particular imprint on the academy, yet by the end of his reign the leadership in European science had passed to England.

So frequently the intellectual history of the seventeenth century has simply been considered as a transition between the "Reformation" and the "Enlightenment". When, moreover, the explanation has focused on France, the emphasis has been placed on the exclusively aesthetic movement of French "Classicism". Paul Sonnino, in "The Intellectual History of the Reign", seeks to improve on both of the prevailing interpretations. He relies on a very basic, yet not very frequently recognized, theme in the intellectual history of Western civilization—namely, the relationship between the place of revelation and the place of reason. He attempts, moreover, to view the ideas of the French intellectuals in terms of their own goals and purposes, very much in the spirit of Guérard's *Life and Death of an Ideal: France in the Classical Age*, but Sonnino goes further in attempting to tie this search not merely to the field of aesthetics, but also to the realms of philosophy, historiography, and science. What emerges is an interpretation of the intellectual history of the reign as an effort, growingly self-confident, to reconstruct the medieval scholastic synthesis upon newer philosophical foundations. It was a balancing act that neither Louis XIV's divines nor his dragoons had the dexterity to sustain for long.

The art history of the reign, with its roots in the Italian "Renaissance", is a bit reminiscent of the history of science, though the self-centered, self-satisfied Louis XIV depicted by Ann Friedman is in somewhat tighter control. There is almost no place in this art for high individualism. It is an art with an explicit message—the glory of the king—that hardly requires the symbolization that, as Friedman points out, is increasingly downplayed. Potentially the greatest miscalculation of the reign, the Dutch War, emerges on the ceiling of the Hall of Mirrors with nary a touch of embarrassment. Yet what we see with our eyes, if not with our minds, is strangely pale, as if Louis XIV objected to intensity of feeling in anyone but himself. It is not an endearing art, monumental even in its miniatures, and there are not many of these. Friedman notes ironically that the true heir of this art proved to be Napoleon, the revolutionary usurper.

Music in the reign of Louis XIV, so wittily analyzed by Peter Pierson, follows the analogous pattern of being adopted from the Italians and appropriated by Louis XIV. As Pierson indicates, musical life was dominated by a single composer, the Gallicized Italian Lully. Indeed, Pierson's account of Lully's encounter with French society—his legal privileges, his artistic collaborators, his conflicts with his detractors—recalls us to many of the themes that we have encountered in the previous essays. His greatest gift, we might well say, was that he knew how to manipulate the king as no other musician of his time was able to do, and in the process Lully Gallicized and popularized the two spectacular art forms of the opera and the ballet. Louis XIV never established such an intimate connection with any other composer, but then, he had other things to worry about in the heyday of Charpentier and Couperin.

These essays tend to resolve the question of the *longue durée* versus human intervention in favor of the former rather than the latter. The authors seem overwhelmingly of the opinion that the movement of society during the reign was more than a match for the expanding bureaucracy. They see Louis XIV living for glory, shaping only the surface of France, not its deeper life. But these essays, by the same token, do not presume to equate the character of the king with a fatalistic interpretation of his reign. Without him, they imply, the France of his day could conceivably have been different, perhaps worse, but possibly better.

Contributors

WILLIAM ROOSEN is Regents' Professor of History at Northern Arizona University. He is the author of *The Age of Louis XIV: The Rise of Modern Diplomacy* (1976) and former editor of the *Proceedings of the Western Society for French History*.

THOMAS J. SCHAEPER is Associate Professor of History at Saint Bonaventure University. He is the author of *The Economy of France in the Second Half of the Reign of Louis XIV* (1980), *The French Council of Commerce: 1700–1715* (1983), and is book review editor of *The Eighteenth Century: A Critical Bibliography*.

MARY ELIZABETH PERRY is Research Assistant at the Center for Medieval and Renaissance Studies at the University of California at Los Angeles. She is the author of *Crime and Society in Early Modern Seville* (1980) and is currently working on a book on women and disorder in Counter-Reformation Spain.

CHARLIE R. STEEN is Associate Professor of History at the University of New Mexico. He is the author of *A Chronicle of Conflict: Tournai: 1559–1567* (1984) and is currently working on a biography of Margaret of Parma.

DUANE ANDERSON serves on the staff of the University of California at Santa Barbara library. He is currently completing a dissertation entitled "The Early Career of Colbert de Croissy".

JOHN C. RULE is Professor of History at Ohio State University. He is the editor of *Louis XIV and the Craft of Kingship* (1969) and is currently completing a biography of Colbert de Torcy.

RONALD MARTIN is Instructor in History at Rancho Santiago College. He has published numerous articles on French military history in the early modern period and is currently completing a biography of the Marquis de Chamlay.

GEOFFREY W. SYMCOX is Professor of History at the University of California at Los Angeles. He is the author of *The Crisis of French Sea Power: 1688–1697: From the Guerre d'Escadre to the Guerre de Course* (1974) and *Victor Amadeus (1983)*.

JOHN T. O'CONNOR is Professor of History at the University of New Orleans. A specialist in international relations, he is the author of *Negotiator out of Season: The Career of Wilhelm von Fürstenberg: 1629–1704* (Athens, 1978). He is currently engaged in a comparative study of treason in early modern Europe.

JOHN H. GREVER is Professor of History at Loyola Marymount University. He has a broad interest in the institutional history of the seventeenth century and has published numerous articles on relations between France and the Dutch Republic during that period.

SEYMOUR L. CHAPIN is Professor Emeritus of History at California State University at Los Angeles. He has authored or coauthored over sixty articles, monographs, and books of the history of science, specializing in eighteenth-century French astronomy. He is currently completing a book on the history of pressurized flight.

PAUL SONNINO is Professor of History at the University of California at Santa Barbara. He is the author of *Louis XIV's View of the Papacy: 1661–1667* (1966), editor of *Louis XIV: Mémoires for the Instruction of the Dauphin* (1970), and author of *Louis XIV and the Origins of the Dutch War* (1988).

ANN FRIEDMAN is a member of the education department of the J. Paul Getty Museum in Malibu, California. She is the author of numerous articles on the art history of the reign of Louis XIV.

PETER PIERSON is Professor of History at the University of Santa Clara. He is the author of *Philip II of Spain* (1975) and has just finished a manuscript titled "Commander of the Armada: A Life of the Seventh Duke of Medina Sidonia".

HERBERT H. ROWEN is Professor of History at Rutgers University. He has written widely on early modern European history, his most notable works including *John de Witt* (1978), *The King's State* (1980), and *The Princes of Orange* (1988).

Index

Abbeville, 32
absolutism, 64, 68, 239, 242–3
Académie de Poésie et Musique, 226
Académie Française, 67, 181, 182,
196, 201, 204; its *Dictionary*, 67
Académie Royale de Danse, 226
Académie Royale de Musique, 226,
229–30, 231, 233, 234, 235
Académie Royale de Peinture et de
Sculpture, 211–4, 217–8
Académie Royale des Sciences,
184–5, 186–7, 188–90, 197, 204,
247–8; its *Description des arts et
métiers*, 190; its *Mémoires*, 187,
188; its *Mémoires pour servir à
l'histoire naturelle des animaux*, 185
Académies d'Opéra, 226–7, 229
Acadia, 36, 184
Accademia dei Lincei, 180
Accademia del Cimento, 182
Acta eruditorum, 189
Ad sacram, 163
Africa and African, 36–7, 38, 40,
139, 155
Agen, Bishop of, *see* Joly
Aix-en-Provence, 104; *parlement* of,
102, 180
Aix-La-Chapelle, Treaty of, 148
Albion, *see* England
Albizzi, Francesco, 162–3
Alcine, 228
Alcinous, 201
Alençon, 34
Alexander, 215
Alexander VII, Pope, 163, 167;
nuncio of, 166
Alexander VIII, Pope, 169
Alexandria, 185
Alps, 111, 133
Alsace, 143, 150, 153, 156
Ambassadors' Staircase, 217, 219

America and Americans, 38, 39;
North, 36–7, 40; revolutionaries
in, 156; South, 140; Spanish, 30,
155. *See also* New World
Amiens, 34
Amsterdam, 133
Ancients and Moderns, Quarrel of,
64, 201, 203, 213, 219, 227. *See
also* progress
Angers, Bishop of, *see* Arnauld,
Henri
Anjou, 47
Annat, Father, 162
Antilles, 36
Apollo, 215
appel comme d'abus, 75, 86
Argo and Argonauts, 212–3
Ariès, Philippe, 17, 18
Ariosto, his *Orlando Furioso*,
228
Aristotle and Aristotelianism,
179–80, 181, 195–6, 200–1,
221; anti-, 179
Arnauld, Antoine, 162, 163, 197,
199
Arnauld de Pomponne, 123, 130
Arnauld, Henri, Bishop of Angers,
166
Ashley Cooper, Anthony, later Earl
of Shaftesbury, 204
Asia, 37, 38, 40, 167; East, 36, 167;
South, 36; Southeast, 161
asiento, 155
Assemblée Générale du Clergé, 84,
163, 165, 168, 169
Assoucy, Charles d', 223
Ath, 118
Atlantic, 36, 38, 40, 132, 138, 139
Audience of the Seal, 95, 100
audiencier, grand, and *audienciers*, 98,
99

251